TRIBAL RIGHTS in
INDIA

TRIBAL RIGHTS in INDIA

Dr Shambhu Prasad Chakrabarty

PARTRIDGE

Library of Congress Control Number: 2018959827
ISBN: Softcover   978-1-5437-4796-6
               eBook   978-1-5437-4795-9

Print information available on the last page.

To order additional copies of this book, contact
Toll Free 800 101 2657 (Singapore)
Toll Free 1 800 81 7340 (Malaysia)
orders.singapore@partridgepublishing.com

www.partridgepublishing.com/singapore

*For
my mom and dad,
whose blessings are omnipotent,
for my wife and children,
whose love is omnipresent*

FOREWORD

Cultural homogeneity is more of a misnomer than an identifier at present. This is because in the past cultural homogeneity was accompanied by a common mode of living – now it is achieved by the commonality of aspiration. Ubiquitous internet and satellite television with targeted programming have ensured that people, by and large, aspire to similar things, are encouraged to have similar "me-too" mindsets and their opinions are formed, unless they are eternally vigilant, by peer groups and social networking sites regardless of whether they stay in hovels where such expectations are not likely to be fulfilled or whether they are actually living that life.

In such a world, "tribes" as analyzed by Dr. Chakrabarty, a personal junior friend and fellow traveler in the journey towards knowledge, may seem an archaic construct which does not really exist. Even the author admits that the meaning of the word has undergone a sea-change to the extent that in India it is more of a euphemism than a description. Most Indians know "tribes" as an extension of the word "Scheduled Tribes" with its history of oppression, affirmative action, reservation and the baggage of ideas and counter-ideas including discrimination in reverse which barely three decades back set the nation and its youth on fire – literally.

However, as the Author has demonstrated in his well-researched, analytical and informative tome, "tribes" in India nonetheless have a distinct and atavistic existence, however muted by civilization it has become. He has taken us through the criteria which for him distinguishes a tribe from, let us say, a group of residents in a cooperative housing society or students in a hostel. He has shown us their ethnicity and place in history, society and the law, their general way of life and their faith, their beliefs and what has sustained them and the problems they faced and still face and the ameliorative measures which the State, the society at large and people individually have taken for their upliftment. He has also illuminated the darkest deeds against members of the tribe and how exploitation of the weak, where strength comes from money or possession of resources and the ability to defend them, continues from day to day. Strangely, perhaps for reasons of space or for tact, while the Author has dwelt upon the causes and effect of the Bastar uprising of 1911 and the struggle for retention of their ancestral forest lands, I have not found much information about a more recent attempt to render them homeless and bereft of even legal help which occurred in 2016, at about roughly the same time as the demonetization.

I am usually economical with my words of praise, but this is one book which has taught me more about the subject and its history, and the issues involved at some detail, which is hard to find elsewhere, particularly written such simply but comprehensively and which is as easily accessible to the serious scholar as the browsing dilettante. I pray and wish that the Author continues to write so engagingly about such matters which would otherwise have been dry and boring to the point of dehydration.

Protik Prakash Banerjee,
Judge, High Court at Calcutta.

September, 2018

ABSTRACT

The world is falling apart. People are forgetting their basic values that life teaches us all. Morality and law has parted ways, since some time now. But it was not long enough to remember when humanity reigned supreme. Let us not forget those moments, that moment of sacrifice, moments of help and chivalry that provides an unparallel sense of happiness within us. Let us realize that third world is not a world apart and the members of these countries are also humans. Let us come out of our comfort zones and realize the truth. Let us ignore it, no more.

Some religious fanatics led by super speciality weapons, once decided to promote it. On wherever they landed and explored because of their power became their property. Power was what corrupted them. And such absolute corruption led to the birth of certain philosophy the world would never forget nor forgive. The concept of civilization started and the process of de-humanization followed. Corporations developed and with it consumerism. Suddenly the world break up to create a concept known as the third world, which are meant to serve the whims and comfort of the first world with their everything, including their life.

Darkness was so bright that sun never showed its face for centuries. World has indeed fallen apart by then.

The world decided to change and the change came at a price. The irretrievable socio economic conditions of the original and aboriginal people of the planet, which grew with the planet itself, had to pay the ultimate price. The systematic annihilation of the third world countries and their resources by the first world has left them only to die the death that follows hunger and starvation. They have been waiting for death. But their spirit and courage and their motivation to survive has led to come out of debris to generate and build great international movements which forced the world to accept the fact that they are the deprived lot and the subjects of violation. World today has a different light to show, the light which leads the way to the new world. The modern civilization and the new world need these people to be part of the whole and not someone different in the struggle to survive the ordeal the future has stored for the human civilization.

International movements of indigenous communities ultimately led its voice heard to the world through the United Nations Organization (UNO) and its various wings. The world today hear it from the voice of those who suffered and the time has come for all of us, to learn and provide the remedy they deserve for centuries.

This work critically examines the exploitation of tribes more specifically in this third world country which is also the biggest democracy of the world. The history of tribal existence, the butchery of barbaric colonial laws followed by the post independent era of colonial legal regime and the continuing oppression that which has been led by both State and non-state agencies leading to deprivation and destruction of the survival base of the tribals. In the name of development, the unethical deprivation and annihilation of the tribals from their land and forest for centuries has led to various socio-economic and legal conflicts between the tribes on one hand and the non-tribals and the state administration on the other.

This work apart from the woes of the conflicts that shed blood of the innocent people, would also make a positive analysis as to why the term indigenous has been left out and the term tribe been accepted in the Indian legal system another interesting analysis between castes and tribes has been made in the book. The veil has been removed from the political intent to protect the tribals in India. It must be understood that ILO 169 and 107 are based on completely different set of philosophies and India must adhere to ILO 169 instead of 107. All the efforts that is been taken for the tribals today is based on ILO 107 and hence would be infructuous in the years to come. The sooner it is the better for India to accept ILO 169. India must stand by the promises it makes before the tribal and indigenous and tribal and her tribal and indigenous communities. Time has come to work for these people and that to in the term.

Apart from the conflicts, the book surveys and refers to the relevant laws in the form of legislations in this regard and also proposes a host of legal reforms, both substantive and procedural in nature, to protect the tribals from losing their identity and to prevent gross violation of human rights and ultimately their indigenous existence.

The various judicial determinations outside the ambit of colonial precedents shall also be an interesting aspect to research upon. How the judiciary in the garb of judicial activism is upholding the principles of human rights will be dealt with accordingly. Various international conventions and declarations shall be analyzed as they are the creators of modern indigenous rights movement and would also be the future of these people.

The study should be a part of the critical legal studies and would also try to be a part of post modern jurisprudence. However bleak the situation may be for the tribals and indigenous peoples of the world, there is ample scope for their survival and true development in the era of human rights where human life and dignity reigns supreme.

PREFACE

At the very outset, I would like to thank Professor (Dr.) Rathin Bandyopadhyay, Head, Department of Law and former Head, Department of Management, University of North Bengal for being a friend, philosopher and guide.

I would also take this opportunity to thank everyone from the Department of Law, University of North Bengal for their help. Special credit must go to Dr. Rajendra Dhar Dubey, Dr. Kaushik Ghosh of the Department of Political Science, Bankura University and Dr. Rudranil Chatterjee, for accompanying me in my empirical research at Bankura and Totopara respectively.

I would also like to convey my sincere regards to Dr. Michael Sandel of Harvard University, Professor Robert Miller, Sandra Day O'Connor College of Law, Arizona State University, Late Dr. Clarence J. Dias, Former President of the International Centre for Law in Development, New York and IFS Mr Subhas Mukherjee. I must convey my sincere regards to Mr. Martyn Brown, David Roe from Melbourne, Australia and Dr. Debal Deb, (known as the Seed Man of India) an eminent researcher on indigenous plant varieties, showing me the true picture of tribals and indigenous peoples in Australia and India respectively.

The little knowledge I have been able to acquire in this life so far is all because of my father, Mr. Debi Prasad Chakrabarti, FCA who has been my motivation all throughout and my mother Mrs. Shefali Chakrabarti whose efforts made me what I am today. It was them who stood by my side to overcome all odds of life. Without their blessings this day would never have come. Thanks to my Father-in-Law, Late Buddhadeb Guha Roy for his inspiration.

This book would not have been complete unless my beloved wife Nabaneeta would have taken all the burden and responsibility of our two children Aanandee and Aarya on her shoulders singlehandedly and pursuaded me in every possible way to complete this work with perfection and peace of mind. I also acknowledge the co-operation and help on the part of my in-laws and all near and dear relatives including my sister Mrs Gargi Mukherjee and sister-in-law Ms Kamalika Guha Roy. Special credit must also go to Advocate Tanusree Nag for her contribution. I must convey my regards to Professor Tilak Nath Roy and Late Professor Debotosh Haldar of Surendranath Law College, Kolkata, Prof (Dr) Dhrubyajyoti Chattopadhyay, Hon'ble Vice Chancellor Amity University Kolkata, Prof (Dr) Manik Chakraborty, Advisor, Amity Law School, Prof (Dr) Sachi Chakraborty, Head, Department of Law, Calcutta University and Prof (Dr) Nirmal Kanti Chakraborty, Director, KIIT Law School, for their invaluable contribution in my life.

Date: October 2018   Dr. Shambhu Prasad Chakrabarty

CONTENTS

Foreword..vii

Abstract..ix

Preface xi

Table Of Cases...xvii

Table Of Statutes...xxi

Abbreviations xxiii

Introduction...xxvii

CHAPTER 1. RIGHTS OF TRIBAL PEOPLES: A CONCEPTUAL AND HISTORICAL PERSPECTIVE 1

An Overview...3

1.1. Tribe: A Conceptual Understanding 3

    1.1.1. Nomenclature 4

    1.1.2. Constitutional Interpretation. 6

    1.1.3. Sociological, Political and Anthropological interpretations. 6

    1.1.4. Colonial interpretation...10

    1.1.5. Features of Tribes...11

1.2. Reviewing the Tribes in India...13

    1.2.1. Problems in Nomenclature...13

    1.2.2. Reference in Epics. 20

    1.2.3. Reference in Smritis and Sutras. 20

1.3. Invasions in India and Tribal Confrontation..................................21

    1.3.1. Various Major Invasions in a Nutshell..................................21

    1.3.2. Tribal Movements 24

1.4. Colonial Period and Tribes 29

    1.4.1. Colonial Period Laws and Tribals...29

    1.4.2. Post-Colonial Period and Tribals in India 31

1.5. Caste and Tribes: Relationship..33

    1.5.1. Castes 33

    1.5.2. Classification of Castes 34

    1.5.3. Tribal-Caste Continuum..36

1.6. Tribes in India: Classification 36

    1.6.1. Traits of Indian Tribes 37

        1.6.1.1. Dravidian 37

        1.6.1.2. Protoaustraloid.. 38

1.6.1.3. Mongoloid Element 39
1.6.1.4. Caucasoid 40
1.6.2. Major Language Families in India...41
1.6.2.1. Austro Asiatic 41
1.6.2.2. Tibeto-Burman 41
1.6.2.3. Dravidian 42
1.6.2.4. Indo-Aryan 42
1.6.2.5. Andamanese 42
A Sum Up 42

CHAPTER 2. CIVIL AND ECONOMIC RIGHTS OF TRIBALS: THE INTERNATIONAL PERSPECTIVE 45

An Overview...47
2.1. The Concept of Indigenous and Tribal peoples under International Law...............49
2.2. Indigenous Communities of the World 51
2.2.1. Latin America..52
2.2.2. Africa..54
2.2.3. Australia (Oceania/Pacific) 56
2.2.4. Hawaii (Oceania/Pacific)...57
2.2.5. Bougainville (Oceania/Pacific)..58
2.2.6. Arctic 59
2.2.7. Asia 59
2.3. Categories of International Movements 61
2.4. Rights of Indigenous peoples...62
2.4.1. Land and Resources...63
2.4.2. Culture, Religion and Language...67
2.4.3. Citizenship 70
2.4.4. Self Determination 70
2.4.5. Human Rights...71
2.4.6. Consultation and Participation...72
2.4.7. Health 72
2.4.8. Economy, Education and Intellectual Property Rights.........72
A Sum Up..73

CHAPTER 3. CIVIL AND ECONOMIC RIGHTS OF TRIBALS: THE INDIAN PERSPECTIVE 77

An Overview...79
3.1 Indian Political Division...79
3.1.1 Various Political Divisions of the Country and Tribal Existence.........79
3.1.2 Ethnic Groups and Tribal Traits 80
3.1.2.1 Caste system in India and its Origin 80
3.1.2.2 Communities in India and Tribal existence 81
3.1.2.3 Traditional Occupational Groups 82
3.1.3 Marriage 82
3.1.4 Inbreeding in Indian Society and Tribal Dilution 83
3.1.5 Religious Groups and Tribal Religion in India 84

3.1.5.1 Hinduism and Tribals 84

3.1.5.2 Islam and Tribals 85

3.1.5.3 Influence of Christianity on Tribals of India 85

3.1.5.4 Buddhism and tribes in the Northeast...85

1.1.1.5 Other Religious Aspects of Tribals...86

3.1.6 Linguistic Groups in India and Tribal Languages 86

3.1.6.1 Classification of Indian Languages..87

3.1.6.2 Linguistic Regions 92

3.1.7 Languages Specified in Schedule VIII to the Constitution of India................93

3.2 Natural Regions of India and Socio Economic Position of Tribals 94

3.3. Historical Analysis and Racial Classification in India 95

3.3.1 Pre historic and Historical Analysis of India and Tribal Development............95

3.3.2 Historical analysis of India and Tribal Development......................................98

3.3.2.1 Racial Classification and the Position of tribals in India.............................99

A Sum Up 100

CHAPTER 4. ROLE OF STATE LEGISLATIVE ORGANS IN THE PROTECTION OF CIVIL AND ECONOMIC RIGHTS OF TRIBALS IN INDIA 101

An Overview...103

4.1. Constitutional Guarantees for Tribes and Tribal peoples..................................103

4.1.1. Equality and Non-Discrimination..106

4.1.2. Equality and Opportunity in Public Employment 107

4.1.3. Protection against Untouchability...107

4.1.4 Other Fundamental Rights..108

4.1.5. Directive Principles of State Policy and Rights of Tribals............................108

4.1.6. Constitutional protection as to the Administration and Control of Schedules Areas and Scheduled Tribes. 109

4.1.7. Right to Representation in the Legislative and other Bodies 112

4.1.8. Agency for monitoring safeguards...114

4.2. Major Enactments passed in India to Protect Civil and Economic Rights of Tribals....................115

4.2.1. The Schedules Caste and Scheduled Tribes (Prevention of Atrocities) Act, 1989................115

4.2.1.1. Overview 115

4.2.1.2. Backdrop and Object of the Act 116

4.2.1.3. Meaning of Atrocity 117

4.2.1.4. Rights Guaranteed under the Act 118

4.2.1.4.1. Right to Cast Vote and Access to Customary Right of Passage and Clean Water.....118

4.2.1.4.2. Right against Exploitation 119

4.2.1.4.3. Right to Property...120

4.2.1.5. Efficacy of the Rights Guaranteed under this Act.................................121

4.2.2. The Protection of Civil Rights Act, 1955 122

4.2.2.1. Overview: 122

4.2.2.2. Backdrop and Object of the Act 123

4.2.2.3. Meaning of Untouchability 124

4.2.2.4. The Protection of Civil Rights Act, 1955 124

4.2.2.4.1. Right against Religious Disabilities...124

4.2.2.4.2. Right against Social Disabilities 124

4.2.2.5. Efficacy of the Rights Guaranteed under this Act 125

4.2.3. The Provisions of the Panchayats (Extension to the Scheduled Areas) Act, 1996 (PESA)......126

 4.2.3.1. Overview 126

 4.2.3.2. Backdrop and Object 126

 4.2.3.3. Various Rights Guaranteed under the Act 126

 4.2.3.4. Efficacy of the Act 129

4.2.4. The Scheduled Tribes and Other Forest Dwellers (Recognition of Forest Rights) Act, 2006......129

 4.2.4.1. Overview 129

 4.2.4.2. Backdrop and Object of the Act 130

 4.2.4.3. The Forest Rights Act and the Rights of Tribal Peoples 130

  4.2.4.3.1. Title Rights...130

  4.2.4.3.2. Right to Use 131

  4.2.4.3.3. Management Rights 131

 4.2.4.4. Efficacy of the rights guaranteed under this Act............132

4.3. Minor Enactments and Executive functioning and Civil and Economic Rights of Tribal Peoples.......133

 4.3.1. An Overview 133

 4.3.2. Economic Rights..134

  4.3.2.1. Nodal Agency Facilitating Tribal Economic Activities 134

  4.3.2.2. Government Schemes Facilitating Tribal Economic Rights 134

  4.3.2.3. National Rural Employment Guarantee Act, 2005 135

  4.3.2.4. Distribution of Ceiling Surplus Land 135

  4.3.2.5. Legislations Protecting against Land Alienation..............135

  4.3.2.6. National Mineral Policy, 1993 and the Tribes National Mineral Policy, 1993 136

  4.3.2.7. National Policy on Resettlement and Rehabilitation, 2003........136

  4.3.2.8. Scheme for Primitive Tribal Groups, 2008 137

  4.3.2.9. The West Bengal Land Reforms Act 1955 137

 4.3.3. Civil Rights 138

  4.3.3.1. Criminal Tribes Act 138

  4.3.3.2. Health 138

  4.3.3.3. Educational Schemes for the Benefit of Scheduled Tribe Students.........139

A Sum Up 140

CHAPTER 5. ROLE OF JUDICIARY IN PROTECTING THE CIVIL AND ECONOMIC RIGHTS OF TRIBALS IN INDIA..........141

An Overview..143

5.1. The Principles of Common Law...................................146

5.2. Constitutional Guarantees and Judicial Remedies 150

 5.2.1. Pre Commencement Period 150

 5.2.2. The Constitutional Provisions....................................150

5.3. Tribal Courts and Justice System 153

5.4. The Judicial Awakening...155

5.5. The Way Ahead 168

A Sum Up 169

CHAPTER 6. CONCLUSION AND SUGGESTIONS 171

TABLE OF CASES

FOREIGN

A. AUSTRALIA
1. Gerhardy v. Brown
2. Mabo and Ors v Queensland
3. Milirrpum & Ors' v Nabalco Pry Ltd.
4. The Commonwealth of Australia v Yarmirr

B. UNITED STATES OF AMERICA
1. Bethany R. Berger, U.S. v. Lara as a Story of Native Agency
2. Brendale v. Confederated Tribes & Bands of the Yakima Indian Nations
3. Cherokee Nation v. Georgia
4. Cobell v. Norton
5. Duro v. Reina
6. In Ex Parte Crow Dog
7. In Re Snake River Basin Adjudication (Idaho)
8. In Re Warm Springs Tribe Water Negotiations (D. Ore.)
9. Inyo County v. Paiute-Shoshone Indians
10. Johnson and Graham's Lessee v. McIntosh
11. Lone Wolf v. Hitchcock
12. Maynard v. Narrangansett Indian Tribe
13. McClanahan v. Arizona State Tax Commission
14. Montana v. United States
15. Oliphant v. Schlie
16. Oliphant v. Suquamish Indian Tribe
17. Seminole Nation v. United States
18. Teague v. Bad River Band
19. U.S. v. Kagama
20. U.S. v. Sandoval
21. United States v. Holiday
22. United States v. Washington Department of Ecology (Lummi)
23. Williams v. Lee
24. Worcester v. Georgia

A. SOUTH AFRICA

1. Administration of Papua v. Dera Guba
2. Booi v. Xozwa
3. Coe v. Commonwealth
4. Daniels v. Campbell and Ors
5. Hlope v. Mahlalela
6. Madlokovu Ngidi v.Thandiwe Ngidi (Qadi Tribal Court)
7. Marshall v. Chaka
8. Mgedezi v. Bontsa & Another
9. Rayneth v. S
10. Richtersveld', South Africa, 2003
11. S v. Moodie
12. Tradax Ocean Transportation SA v. MV Silvergate
13. Yako v. Beyi

B. CANADA

1. Calder et al. v. Attorney-General for British Columbia
2. 'Delgamuukw', Canada, 1997

C. INDIA

1. A.R. Antulay v. R.S. Nayak
2. Administrator-General of Madras v. Anandachari
3. Amrendra Pratap Singh v. Tej Bahadur Prajapati
4. B. Basavalingappa v. D. Munichinnappa
5. Banwasi Seva Ashram v. The State of U.P
6. Bhaiyalal v. Harikishan Singh
7. Bipinchandra Diwan vs. State of Gujarat
8. C.M. Arumugam V. S. Rajgopal and ors
9. Chatturbhuj Vithaldas Jasani v. Moreshwar Parashram
10. Comptroller And Auditor General v. K.S. Jagannathan & Another
11. Coopoosami Chetty v. Duraisami Chetty
12. Dahanu Taluka Environment Protection Group v. Bombay Suburban Electric Supply Ltd
13. Dattu s/o Namdev Thakur v. State of Maharashtra & Ors
14. Durgaprasada Rao v. Sudarsanaswami
15. Dy. Collector vs. S. Venkataramaniah
16. Fatesang Gimba Vasava v. State of Gujrat
17. G. Michael v. S. Venkateswaran
18. Gurusami Nadar v. Irulappa Konar
19. Indra Sawhney etc v. Union Of India And Ors
20. K.P. Manu v. Chairman, Scrutiny Committee for Verification of Community Certificate
21. Kailash Sonkar v. Maya Devi
22. Kodikunnil Suresh @ J. Monian v. N.S. Saji Kumar & Ors
23. Kumari Madhuri Patel v. Addl. Commissioner, Tribal Development
24. Lingappa Pochanna v. State of Maharastra
25. M/S. Indian Wood Products Co. Ltd. v. State of U.P. and Another
26. Madan Lal & Ors v. The State of Jammu & Kashmir And Ors
27. Mahadeo and Ors v. State of Maharashtra and Ors

28. Muthusami v. Masilamani
29. N.D.Jayal vs Union of India
30. N.E. Horo v. Jahanara Jaipal Singh
31. Nandini Sundar & Ors v. State of Chattisgarh
32. Narmada Bachao Aandolan v. Union of India and Ors
33. NCERT vs State of Arunachal Pradesh
34. Olga Telis Vs Bombay Municipal Corporation
35. P. Rami Reddy Vs. The State of Andhra Pradesh
36. Perumal Nadar v. Ponnuswami
37. Prem Sankar Sukla v. Delhi Administration
38. Puneet Rai v. Dinesh Chaudhary
39. Rajagopal v. Armugam
40. Rajeshwar Baburao Bone v. The State of Maharashtra and Another (Civil Appeal)
41. Rameshbhai Dabhai Naika v. State of Gujarat & Ors
42. S P Gupta v. Union of India
43. S. Anbalagan v. B. Devarajan and ors
44. S. Swvigaradoss v. Zonal Manager, F.C.I
45. Samantha v. State of Andhra Pradesh
46. Sanjay Lodha vs State of Jharkhand and Ors
47. Shalini v. New English High School Association & Ors
48. Sheela Barse v. Secy., Children's Aid Society
49. Siddharam Satlingappa Mhetre v. State of Maharashtra
50. Sri Machegowda v. State of Karnataka
51. Srish Kumar Choudury v. State of Tripura
52. State Of Kerala & Another v. N. M. Thomas & Ors
53. State of Kerala & Another. v. Chandramohanan
54. State of M.P. and Another v. Ram Kishna Balothia and Another
55. State of Madras v. Champakam Dorairajan
56. State of Orissa v. Ram Bahadur Thapa
57. Suresh Lohia v. State of Maharastra
58. T.N. Godavarman Thirumalpad v. Union of India & Ors
59. The Principal Guntur Medical College, Guntur & Ors. v. Y. Mohan Rao
60. Tuka Ram and Another. v. State Of Maharashtra (Mathura Rape Case)
61. Union of India and Another v. Kunisetty Satyanarayana
62. Union of India and Ors v. R.P. Singh
63. Union of India v. Abdul Jalil
64. Union of India v. Raghubir Singh
65. Vishakha and Ors v. State of Rajasthan
66. Young v. Bristol Aeroplane Co. Ltd

TABLE OF STATUTES

A. INDIAN STATUTES
1. Abolition of Zamindari Act, 1950
2. Agency Tracts Interest and Land Transfer Act, 1917
3. Chhota Nagpur Tenancy Act, 1924
4. Criminal Tribes Act, 1924
5. Forest Rights Act, 2006
6. Gram Nyayalayas Act, 2008
7. Indian Forest Act, 1927
8. Indian Penal Code, 1860
9. Indian Succession Act, 1925
10. Land Acquisition Act, 1894
11. Land Acquisition (Amendment and Validation) Act, 1967
12. Prisoners Act, 1908
13. Representation of People Act, 1950
14. Santhal Parghanas Tenancy Act, 1854,
15. The Code of Civil Procedure, 1908
16. The Code of Criminal Procedure, 1973
17. The Constitution of India, 1950
18. The Constitution (Eighty-Ninth Amendment) Act, 2003
19. The Indian Easement Act, 1882
20. The Indian Evidence Act, 1872
21. The Limitation Act, 1963
22. The Orissa Gram Panchayat (Amendment) Act, 1997
23. The Panchayat (Extension to the Scheduled Areas) Act, 1996
24. The Protection of Civil Rights Act, 1955
25. The Provisions of the Panchayats (Extension to the Scheduled Areas) Act, 1996
26. The Indian Registration Act, 1908
27. The Scheduled Castes and the Scheduled Tribes (Prevention of Atrocities) Act, 1989
28. The Scheduled Castes and Scheduled Tribes (Identification) Act, 1994
29. The Scheduled Castes and Scheduled Tribes Orders (Amendment) Act, 1976
30. Untouchability (Offences) Amendment and Miscellaneous Provisions Act, 1976
31. The Scheduled Tribes and Other Traditional Forest Dwellers (Recognition of Forest Rights) Act, 2006
32. The Explosives Act, 1884
33. The West Bengal Land Reforms Act, 1955
34. Tripura Land Revenue and Land Reforms Act, 1960
35. West Bengal Premises Tenancy Act,1957

36. West Bengal Premises Tenancy Act,1997
37. The Protection of Human Rights Act, 1993
38. The Wildlife Protection Act, 1972
39. The Manipur Land Revenue & Land Reform Act, 1960
40. The Manipur (Village Authority in Hill Areas) Act, 1956
41. Representation of the People Act, 1951
42. Naga Hills Tuensangs Area Act, 1957
43. Government of India Act, 1919
44. The Scheduled Districts Act, XIV of 1874

B. FOREIGN STATUTES
1. Australian Constitution
2. Racial Discrimination Act, 1975 (Australia)
3. Constitution of the United States of America
4. Indian Reorganization Act, 1934
5. Public Law 280, 1953
6. The General Allotment Act (Dawes Act), 1887

C. INTERNATIONAL INSTRUMENTS
1. Indigenous and Tribal peoples Convention, 1989
2. Indigenous and Tribal Population Convention, 1957
3. The General Conference of the International Labour Organization:
4. The UN Declaration on the Elimination of All Forms of Racial Discrimination, 1969
5. The Universal Declaration of Human Rights.
6. UN Declaration on the Rights of Indigenous peoples.
7. International Covenant on Civil and Political Rights, 1966
8. International Covenant on Economic Social and Cultural Rights, 1966

ABBREVIATIONS

AATS	All Assam Tribal Sangha
AIR	All India Reporter
Art.	Article
BPL	Below Poverty Line
BWC	Block Welfare Committee for Schedule Castes & Schedule Tribes
CBI	Criminal Bureau of Investigation
CCD	Conservation-cum-development
CJ	Chief Justice
Cr LJ	Criminal Law Journal
Cr PC	Code of Criminal Procedure, 1973
CRI	Cultural Research Institute
CSWI	Commission on the Status of Women in India
CWN	Calcutta Weekly Notes
DLCC	District Level Co-ordination Committee for Scheduled Castes & Scheduled Tribes
DWC	District Welfare Committee for Schedule Castes & Tribes
IAS	Indian Administrative Service
Ibid	Same as above
ICCPR	International Covenant on Civil and Political Rights, 1966

ICESCR	International Covenant on Economic Social and Cultural Rights, 1966
IFC	Industrial Finance Corporation
IPACC	Indigenous peoples of African Coordination Committee
IPC	Indian Penal Code, 1860
IPS	Indian Police Service
IRDP	Integrated Rural Development Project
ITDP	Integrated Tribal Development Project
ITPA	Immoral Traffic Prevention Act
J	Judge
JJ	Judges
LAMPS	Large Sized Multipurpose Co-Operative Society
LIC	Life Insurance Corporation
MADA	Modified Area Development Approach
NGO	Non Government Organization
NREP	National Rural Employment Programme
NSCFDC	National Scheduled Caste Finance & Development Corporation
NSTFDC	National Scheduled Tribe Finance & Development Corporation
OBC	Other Backward Classes
ONGC	Oil and Natural Gas Corporation
p	Page
PIL	Public Interest Litigation
pp	Pages
PTG	Primitive Tribal Groups
PVTGs	Particularly Vulnerable Tribal Groups

RLI	River Lift Irrigation
SC	Supreme Court
SC & TW	Scheduled Castes & Tribes Welfare
SCC	Supreme Court Cases
Sec	Section
Secs	Sections
SHG	Self Help Group
SHRC	State Human Rights Commission
SITA	Suppression of Immoral Traffic in Women and Girls Act
ST	Scheduled Tribes
TAC	Tribal Advisory Council
TDD	Tribal Development Department
TSP	Tribal Sub Plan
UDHR	Universal Declaration on Human Rights, 1948
UT	Union Territory
v.	Versus
WBCS	West Bengal Civil Service
WBSCSTDFC	West Bengal Scheduled Caste & Scheduled Tribes Development and Financial Corporation
WBTDCC	West Bengal Tribal Development Co-operative Corporation

INTRODUCTION

There has been a plethora of laws made by some people of the world for the ors with little knowledge of the beneficiaries. The former thought that they are superior, rightly in the position of making laws in the form of rules and regulations. They assume rights upon themselves to decide who their subjects are, with no respect and honour for those millions. This is the story of the modern legal history of tribals and indigenous peoples across the world. Such application of laws and enactments in force has successfully left majority of these people homeless with no livelihood and sustainability. Their futile resistance turned and proved to be wrong and suppressed with much vigour and power. The modern advocates are supposed to plead these laws as true and basic for the development of modern civilization. Those would be termed terrorists or to the least as criminals, under these laws, who would try to explain the true story of hypocrisy and fraud that has been continuously played by those men in power. However, in the later part of the 20th Century, various Indigenous movements have to a great extent materialised forcing various changes and shifting of power from colonial laws to those uplifting human rights and rule of law in the true sense of the term. The contribution of the UNO and its various organs are indispensible as they have played a vital role in making a substantial change in the laws of the tribal and indigenous communities in the later years. The Supreme Court at times has also come to their rescue in many important and critical cases. The most important of the various rights that needs immediate protection by various domestic laws today are those relating to the economic and social aspects of these people. The author and this book would make an effort towards this end with the vision of uplifting the human rights of the tribals and indigenous peoples in existence in India with special reference to the state of West Bengal where an empirical study has been conducted unearthing interesting facts. Therefore, the economic and social rights of the tribal and indigenous communities must be protected in India with the incorporation of new laws which will be in tune with and also in furtherance of the human rights movements across the world.

Tribes and tribal peoples are to be found in every part of the world as well as in every state of our country. Even when their number is not dangerously decreasing, their culture and indigenous knowledge are. The causes and consequences of such decline depend upon various socio economic factors as well as the political intent of the government and their various national and international policies. It also depends upon the steps taken by the various governments with the objective of protecting these least developed sections of our society. There have been many factors, general and specific that has caused great impact and turbulence to the tribal communities of different countries including that of ours. Some of the major factors being *inter alia*, exploitation, drainage of wealth, neglect. There have been instances of mass destruction in the veil of development. It is those developmental projects, which is one of the primary reasons behind the elimination, eradication and displacement of thousands of members of indigenous communities in India.

These people for ages have been considered to be having very limited potential of contributing towards national income or towards social upliftment of the country. Even the projects and proposals for their improvement were intended to provide them some institutional care, medical support or providing financial assistance. However, these measures virtually backfired leading to greater isolation and making them even more vulnerable to the issues relating to human rights violation.

The problems in respect of tribals are aplenty. Majority of them emanates from the so called symbolization of tribals as undeveloped and uncivilised. This has to a great extent left them in the dark with neglect and ignorance surrounding them along with disrespect of their beliefs and aspirations. The very thought of accepting them as one of us has led to the mental gap that has been ever increasing between the two communities, the tribals and the non tribals. It has now become almost impossible to bridge. Time came when the efforts were made to shorten the disparity between the two. However, it was effective partially and to little effect, when states across the country took various projects sans any comprehensive rehabilitation plan to restore the tribals with land or other opportunities. This led to mass agitation amongst the tribals leading to application of police force to implement the projects killing innocent tribals. This has, unfortunately been the case in most of the countries across the globe especially with the advent of British colonization. Infliction of inhuman methods was applied indiscriminately making the tribals flee from their motherland. Such has been the stories of such human rights violation that many a times Supreme Court has stepped in to stop the states to deploy ways barbaric in nature and unrealistic in object. Mass displacement followed. Women were raped. Men killed, tortured, exploited in inhuman condition leading to the growth of unorganized labour in India.

Growth of human rights has been a boon to the tribal communities across the globe, of which Indian tribes were beneficiaries to some extent. So does the advent of electronic media which has to a great extent exposed the brutality and misleading statements of our elected bureaucrats as well as their so called measure to protect the simple people in the tribal belts of India by creating reservations. This benefited a few individuals by giving them a tenuous foothold in the Indian state structure as bureaucrats, law enforcers and politicians. However this facilitates the exploitation of the mass of the tribal peoples. It was inevitable for the tribal culture to hold out the onslaught of the dominant bourgeois culture which was sanctioned as developed and backed by the state.

The laws enacted for forests, exploitation of natural resources, land acquisition, etc, being based upon colonial principles are in direct contravention of Part II, IV and the provisions of the sixth schedule of the Constitution of India, thus giving the lie to the stated objectives of protecting tribal culture.

Although various steps have been taken to provide elementary care for the tribal peoples and various tribal communities, in various states of our country, such measures have been proved to be of little effect and short lived. Most of them died midways. In some areas however, with the effort of the government, both central and state, the tribal peoples have got some relief, like protection of land against illegal transfers, participation in various handicraft fares and creation of handloom houses etc. But, it is not to the extent the situation demands. It is thus very much visible that the government has to play the pivotal role in securing a better habitat for these people for a better and sustainable future.

Tribals, being the ancient inhabitants of this world, have been facing various challenges for time immemorial. However, the era of the British colonialism was exceptional and has caused the gravest harm to the tribals and their life, liberty, population, economy, society, culture and religion among other things. It is them who introduced the theory of drainage of wealth amongst other theories alien to community ownership. Post independence era has not been really a boon or a blessing for these people as the march of civilization and so called developmental projects like dams, bridges etc. has caused havoc in the eradication and annihilation of natural tribal life and living process. This vulnerable section of the community is often the victim of circumstances. The laws relating to this community is far and few. Moreover they seem to be more exploitative than welfare. In most of the cases they act as a regulatory machine of exploitation than protection. Some legislation were made to fulfil international and national obligations but sadly without any real intent to protect, shelter and further the interests of the tribal communities, behind them.

The problem area, *inter alia,* is the paucity of adequate legislation to protect the rights of this section of the society. The existing legislations fall short to provide the basic rights to these people and to a great extent fulfil the basic need of these people or to further their actual interest. Neither, they fulfil the Constitutional objectives in the form of equality before law and equal protection of law.

Since the protection of Human Rights of the tribal peoples is an issue that attracts global norms transcending national boundary, the present study has taken into account the development of the laws relating to the tribal peoples in the international as well as the national sphere. The study has taken into consideration the part played by the judiciary, so far as protection and upliftment of these people are concerned.

United Nations Organization has played the most dominant role in acknowledging the indigenous communities in the international forum and voiced the need to protect them against gross and mass violation of human rights. The role played by the United Nations is evident from the various resolutions passed by the General Assembly and the International Instruments passed by it in responding to various issues involving gross violation of Human rights in Africa, Australia, Asia and other parts of the world.

The UN Resolution and Convention on Human Rights have depicted the rights of human beings as to the indigenous communities, which constitute the basis for the making of national legislations., viz.,
1. The Universal Declaration of Human Rights.
2. The UN Declaration on the Elimination of All Forms of Racial Discrimination.
3. The General Conference of the International Labour Organization:
   i. Indigenous and Tribal Population Convention, 1957
   ii. Indigenous and Tribal peoples Convention, 1989
4. UN Declaration on the Rights of Indigenous peoples.
5. UN Convention on Biological Diversity, 1992
6. Convention on International Trade in Endangered Species of Wild Flora and Fauna, 1975
7. UN Resolution Concerning Indigenous and Tribal peoples.

In India, the Constitution was framed by taking into consideration the rights and duties of the people, including that of tribal communities. An attempt to incorporate those provisions shall also make the study more fruitful to portray the status of these communities. The Indian Constitution has certain specific provisions for the protection of these people. These rights may be classified under the following heads:
1. Educational and cultural rights. [Articles 15(4), 29, 46 and 350]
2. Economic rights. [Articles 244 and 275]
3. Social rights. [Articles 23 and 24]
4. Political rights. [Articles 164(1), 243, 330, 334 and 371]
5. Employment rights. [Articles 15(4), 16(4) and 16(4A)]

In addition to the aforesaid rights, the Fifth and the Sixth schedule of the Constitution of India exclusively deals with the tribal communities and tribal areas. The 89th Constitutional Amendment Act, 2003, has amended Article 338 and added a new Article 338-A, which provides for the establishment of National Commission for the Scheduled Tribes to provide specific protection to the rights of these communities. The measure taken by the Parliamentarians in furtherance to the protection of social and economic condition of the tribals also is far and few for drums and yells.

The legislations *inter alia*, in connection with the tribal peoples of India, that needs a reflection are:
1. Criminal Tribes Act, 1924
2. Indian Forest Act, 1927
3. The Protection of Civil Rights Act, 1955
4. Forest Rights Act, 2006
5. The Scheduled Tribes and Other Traditional Forest Dwellers (Recognition Of Forest Rights) Act, 2006
6. The Provisions of the Panchayats (Extension to the Scheduled Areas) Act, 1996
7. Land Acquisition Act, 1894
8. The Scheduled Castes and the Scheduled Tribes (Prevention of Atrocities) Act, 1989
9. The West Bengal Land Reforms Act, 1955
10. Gram Nyayalayas Act, 2008

The legislations, the executive orders and the provisions of the Constitution has stood as a barrier against tribal exploitation which has turned fruitless as the laws were proved inadequate and filled with major limitations. The book has also been made to understand the extent these provisions have been fruitful to the protection of the interests of tribals in India and to the extent of understanding the true situation of the position of tribal and indigenous peoples in India and summarise the various emerging issues and dimensions of tribal life and culture. It also systematically identifies the vulnerabilities the modern legal and political conditions pose for their economy, culture and human rights.

The study also tries to analyze the cause and effect relationship of the current scenario concerning tribal life and their welfare in India. In a nutshell, the following objectives of the study were made to reveal the immediate and updated position of tribal peoples in India:
1. To research into the dynamics of tribal life
2. The changing pattern of tribal life due to population explosion
3. To make a comparative study and examine the nature of the life and culture of various tribes in India.
4. To understand the true meaning of the term tribe and analyze the rational of using the term over indigenous that is mostly used in international forums.
5. To make a viable distinction of tribes and castes in India which are either used simultaneously or parallel
6. To review the various international developments in the field of indigenous rights movement and the response of India in this regard, including the Universal Periodic Review.
7. To analyze the various legislations prevailing in India on tribals and the mechanism of they intend to function.
8. To make a general study of the achievements of these legislations and executive functioning.
9. To study and identify the role of judiciary in protecting the rights of tribal peoples from the wrath of state vigor and from the atrocities of non tribals. A special note on the position of tribal courts and its implementation of justice through the principles of Primitive Law system shall also be addressed.
10. To review the role of National Human Rights Commission and the National Commission for Scheduled Tribes in protecting the rights of tribals and tribal communities in India.
11. To evaluate the concept of tribal rights in furtherance of their composite culture and their sustainable economy and to bring out ways to protect them and also to prevent them from extinction.
12. To identify the various ways they can be helpful to the Indian economy in their inherent and sustained way of life.

13. The study also aims at providing various remedial measures and suggestions to prevent the violation of rights of the tribals and their communities.
14. An analysis of the ILO 107 and ILO 169 and why the later should be adopted by India in protecting the rights of the tribal peoples in India.
15. To understand the position of India in submitting the 3rd Universal Periodic Report in January 2017.

The findings of this study will rebound to the benefit of the society considering that the tribals are just another set of people living parallel with our system. Having their (indigenous) own systematic way of life shall not hinder the way of life the other part of the society practice. It must be understood that the tribals carry with them their immense indigenous knowledge which is needed to be explored from a better system of human life on earth. The greater demand for their upliftment and preventing them from various inhuman conditions the state and the non tribals provide is an example of the acknowledgement of the world community to the need of co existence of tribal and indigenous communities.

Thus the institutions and government functionality applying the recommended approach would derive better results than what they have achieved with the existing system and would benefit from the intended results of this study. This will also act as a guiding process for further study and research in this field of study for those concerned and interested in this area of research.

The study will help the researchers and ors interested to uncover critical legal areas in the tribal economy and social life of the tribals in India, which was not explored before.

Various cases both Indian and foreign, have been studied and analyzed to have a comprehensive idea of the approach of the judiciary in furtherance of the efforts to protect these communities. The various writ petitions filed before the Supreme Court of India in respect of tribal rights have been a new dimension in the process of judicial law making in India in furtherance of the protection of human rights of the tribal peoples and tribal communities.

Further interviews were conducted to gather first hand information to further the object of this research. Electronic devices have aided in the entire process of data collection. The research took note of the views of the historians and anthropologists as well as sociologists and economists to make a positive unbiased contribution to this work.

Countries like Australia, South Africa and United States of America, in relation to tribal rights have suffered a similar fate in the hand of colonial rulers. Even when the mode of exploitation varied between countries, the method adopted for the welfare of the tribes have been found to be quite identical and in tune with the international movements for the protection of tribal and indigenous rights. In the era of globalization and industrialization the ways of protecting tribal rights is noteworthy in this research and that has been done to a considerable extent. The object to formulate a comprehensive structure for sustaining economic and social welfare of tribes and in India with special reference to West Bengal has been attempted in this research work.

A variety of case laws have been referred and analyzed in this book to uplift the rights of the tribes and various indigenous groups. The Supreme Court of India, in Pandey Orson v. Ram Chandra Sahu AIR 1992 SC 195 by striking down the verdict of the Patna High Court which took a very literary view of the term "transfer".

The Supreme Court further reiterated the need of the provision in beneficial legislation to be read for the protection of a class of citizens who are not in a position to keep their property to themselves in the absence of protection.

Again on the basis of a Writ petition being filed in the Supreme Court against the acquisition of land by NHPC, by Koel Karo Jan Sangathan in 1984, without a proper rehabilitation program, the Hon'ble SC was pleased to pass a stay on further construction unless adequate rehabilitation measures were announced.

Another interesting case law emanated in the Bihar High Court where the decision of the District Magistrate was challenged by a tribal lady Bhagini, who lives with her daughter in law in her own hut. Her son who left for Assam has never returned as they were thrown out of their habitat along with many ors. The Hon'ble High Court passed a stay order in favour of her by uplifting the rights of tribal communities.

In a landmark judgment in Banwasi Seva Ashram v. State of U.P. 1987 SCC 304, Supreme Court stated that the judiciary may become a forum for addressing and ventilating the problems of distributional equality with respect to tribals.

While discussing on the issue of distribution of government largess amongst the tribals, the Supreme Court in R.D.Shetty v. International Airport Authority 1979 SCC 489, stated that in the absence of any right or entitlements to the benefits, law requires that the government largess should not be distributed in an arbitrary and discriminatory manner.

In a momentous pronouncement in Indira Sawhney V. Union of India, 1992, the Supreme Court categorically rejected the government's attempt to identify a backward class by reference to an exclusive economic indicator.

In another effort to protect the rights of the adivasis a PIL was filed in the Supreme Court of India seeking protection and enforcement of collective right to habitat of the adivasis has against an attempt to evict them from a forest declared to be reserved. A direction made by the court upheld the rights of the adivasis refraining the Government from doing any activity that deprives the rights of the adivasis in Banwasi Seva Ashram v. State of UP AIR 1987

CJ Edward D. White, in United States vs Sandoval 231 US, 28 (1913) held that the enabling act applied generally applicable federal Indian Statutes to the Pueblo. It repudiated the earlier contention that the Pueblos were not Indians. The Statehood Act acknowledged Pueblo land as Indian Country the citizenship of Indians did not prevent Congress from enacting laws to protect and benefit tribes.

In another case worth a review, in South Dakota, the Congress specifically abrogated Treaty Rights of the Cheyenne River Sioux Tribe as to their hunting and fishing rights on reservation lands that were required for a reservoir. The court giving the judgement in favour of the interpretation of implied abrogation over express abrogation when the rule is express abrogation over implied abrogation. [South Dakota Vs Bourland, 508 US 679, 113 S CT 2309 (1993)]

In India another case has to be reflected in this review to make the contention of the Indian judiciary at par with the rights of the tribals when in the Vadanta's Case. April 2013, the British resources giant Vadanta was directed to obtain approval of tribal peoples before mining their land. SC confirmed that the tribals need to have a decisive voice in industrial projects affecting their lives.

The Hon'ble Supreme Court observed, "If the bauxite mining project, in any way, affect their right to worship their deity, known as Niyam Raja, in the hilltop of the Niyamgiri range of hills, that right has to be protected".

In a very famous case, commonly known as the Mathura Rape Case 1972, rape of minor tribal girl ultimately led to the Criminal Law (Second) Amendment Act 1983. It led to the change of the law of presumption in rape cases under the Indian Evidence Act.

If the victim says that she did not consent to the sexual intercourse, the court shall presume that she did not consent as a rebuttable presumption.

In State of Karnatake vs. Appa BabuIngale and ors AIR 1993 SC 1126, the Supreme Court dealt with the identity of a tribal in a remote village where a family belongs to a joint Hindu family. It was held that the presumption is for the incorporation within the tribe than ousting. The Supreme Court further incorporated the need of protecting the identity of these communities and help the tribals against exploitation.

Along with various cases, a number of books and articles have also been reviewed. Some of them are stated in brief.

One of the interesting works on tribal administration has been done by the researcher specifically with regard to tribal administration in Darjeeling, Dr Lalan P Gupta's Tribal Development Administration is of great relevance. Here he has made a thorough research in this field with special reference to administration of justice on tribals and the various laws and rules relating thereof.

One of the contemporary books on tribal rights is one edited by Dr Subhram Rajkhoa and Dr Manik Chakraborty published by Cambray Publication named "Indigenous peoples and Human Rights." This book is a compilation of various articles reflecting the various stories of exploitation of the tribals and the maladministration and lack of legislative intent to protect the tribes from non-tribals.

Dr Debal Deb the founder member of Vrihi, an NGO is pioneer in the field of protection of rice varieties in Eastern India. In his book "Seeds of Tradition, Seeds of Future, Folk rice Varieties of Eastern India" he has specifically acknowledged the traditional knowledge of the tribes to be more scientific and sustainable.

Stephen Pevar, in his 'The Right of Indians and Tribes', addresses the most significant legal issues facing Indian and Indian tribes today. Such issues like tribal sovereignty, social and economic exploitation and deprivasiion, reservasions, various laws etc have been discussed in details in his hard researched work.

Another write up by Stephan Corry is worth a mention. In his book, 'Tribal peoples for Tomorrows World', the author reflected a true and unbiased picture of the indigenous and tribal peoples across the world. It refutes criticism of tribal rights and answers issues relating to their life, history, their need, and their contribution to this planet.

In 'Indian Tribes, Then and Now', H.C. Upreti deals with the tribal social structure and the changes that has occurred with the passage of time. It analyses inter alia the various tribes in India and an anthropological analysis as well.

Darrell A Posey and Graham Datfield of International Development Research Centre, Canada-walks in the same direction of Dr Debal Deb as in the book "Beyond Intellectual Property: Towards Traditional Resource Rights for Indigenous peoples and Local Committees". They reflected a plethora of instances where the seeds of intellectual property germinated from tribal communities and how they were stolen by the foreign non-tribal intruders for economic political and social gains.

Some of the articles surveyed are worth reviewed:

'Tribe in India: A Problem of Identification and Integration' by K.S Mathur is a fair critique of the activities and attitude of the government towards the tribes. Reflecting his study of the unequal treatment of the tribes, he emphasized the contribution of the British Government's effort of classification of tribes in India, which was later taken up by the government of independent India. This led to the formation of the Schedule Castes and Scheduled Tribes.

Another interesting Article is Nirmal Kumar Bose's 'Integration and Secularism'. Here the author emphasizes the influence of various religions contributing towards the loss of indignity amongst tribal communities.

Mala Mukherjee in her article 'Tribal's Right to Equality' was eloquent to reflect the variety of judicial interpretations relating to the rights of tribal peoples. She also referred a number of problems the tribal faces from the non tribals. The advocate of Nagpur also emphasized the importance of collective approach of the tribes for better bargains from the government.

'Contemporary Struggles of the Tribal peoples of India' by Jaganath Pathy is yet another example of the struggle of the tribes in India against the atrocities of the non tribals over the tribals with the aid of the government. Stories of the land acquisition and the destruction of clans have been the highlights of his article.

Pradip Prabhu's 'Tribal Movements: resistance to Resurgence' is an exploration of the tribal movement during the later part of the 20th century. It reflects the struggle to possess, control over resources that the tribals used to possess for centuries. The emerging perspectives within tribal movements shift from resistance to resurgence, towards development.

David Hardman in "Healing, Medical Power and the Poor: Contests in Tribal India" refers to a workshop in Surat on access to healing and medical intervention for tribal peoples which brought academics, workers, activists reiterating the deteriorating traditional medicinal systems. The author emphasized that rather than eroticizing and romanticizing tribal communities, it is their pauperization that needs to be addressed and remedied.

Dilip D'Souza's "De-Notified Tribes: Still 'Criminal'?" the author tells the fate of tribals in the hands of British and later by the Independent Indian Government. Pinya Hari Kale was arrested, beaten up and killed in the police custody solely because he belongs to a criminal tribe even when it is now de-notified.

Mr. M K Bhasin in his famous research article 'Genetics of Cates and Tribes of India: Indian Population Milieu' has done a commendable job on the various anthropological aspects of mankind and how the human being first came up and how it reached the different parts of the globe. He highlights the importance of India in this regard as the corridor for the development of human habitat in various parts of Asia. Being an anthropologist the author made an in-depth analysis of political, natural and historical perspective of human habitat in India.

Articles written by Apoorv Kurup on tribal rights in India have made major contribution amongst the modern generation researchers on tribal peoples along side veteran thinkers like Guha and Roy. Kurup's, *Tribal law in India: How Decentralized Administration is Extinguishing Tribal Rights and why Autonomous Tribal Governments are Better*,[1] is worth a study to identify the true position of tribals in India.

---

1 Indigenous Law Journal, Vol.7, Issue.1 2008

CHAPTER 1

RIGHTS OF TRIBAL PEOPLES: A CONCEPTUAL AND HISTORICAL PERSPECTIVE

AN OVERVIEW

The term tribe has been subjected to a lot of interpretations and analysis by various jurists, anthropologists, scientists, sociologists and political thinkers for quite some time now. The term also underwent a change in its meaning in the process of time. A proper definition of the term has been the objectives of many to decipher a lot of confusion that the term carries with it.

A conceptual understanding of the term is needed to actually understand who these people are and what their actual position in the society is. In the true sense of the term, tribes and indigenous peoples are different[2], tribes and adivasis are different, tribes and castes are different. Irrespective of the fact as to their differences, there still lies a lot of confusion as these terms are confused to have been used in the society and they tend to overlap in many areas. Thus to identify the actual tribals, a proper understanding of the term is necessary along with the differences it has with other similar terminology. The absence of a specific definition by any statute including the Constitution of India has made things worse for the people belonging to these categories.

In furtherance of the objective of analyzing the term, interpretation of the term given by various researchers both national and international, must be taken in to consideration. Along with the various interpretations, the characteristics of these people must also be analyzed to understand the various dimensions these definitions and interpretations try to address.

Along with the same, a proper historical development of the term must be studied to understand who these people actually are. Hence reference to epics and other sources of law, where the term has been used, is also needed to be studied. India throughout its historical past has been the subject matter of invasions and such acts of aggression have displaced and dispossessed the aboriginals of their main land. A proper study of the same should also be done to understand the strategic positional variation of these people due to such invasions. This will provide a basic idea about the places and geographic areas of the existence of these people and who these people are before and after such invasions, in the true sense of the term.

The growth of Hindu religion has to a great extent affected the personal life of the tribals. History reveals a lot of variations in the personal life of tribals due to the assimilation of tribals with the non tribal Hindus in India. This principle may also hold well with the advent of various invasions of various rulers of various religious sects. A lot of areas where these invaders marched through have flourished their religion amongst the natives of the country.

A gross classification of the tribes in India based on various traits and language family must also be studied to achieve a conceptual understanding of the term tribe in India.

1.1. TRIBE: A CONCEPTUAL UNDERSTANDING

The term tribe generally connotes a group of primitive or barbaric clan under some recognized chiefs.[3] According to Oxford Dictionary

> *"A tribe is a group of people in a primitive or barbarous stage of development acknowledging the authority of a chief and usually regarding them as having a common ancestor."*[4]

---

2 Literally the word indigenous refers to a native that is not in existence today apart from some rare exceptions on earth.

3 John Simpson and Edmund Weiner (ed.), The Oxford English Dictionary (Oxford University Press., U.K., 1989)

4 Tribal Society, Sociology Guide, available at http://www.sociologyguide.com/tribal-society/ (visited on December 3, 2015).

The term tribe has been identified by the Romans as political divisions and the Greeks equated it with fraternities. The term indigenous peoples and tribal peoples are in many a cases been used interchangeably. Even when there is no uniform definition of tribal peoples but a set of shared and distinct characteristics may lead to one. They are considered to be living descendants of 'pre invasion'[5] inhabitants of lands and forests now dominated by ors. The attachment to the territory is a significant feature of tribal existence which has also been accepted by various United Nations Agencies inter alia in their working definition of indigenous peoples. Ors being an explicit commitment to cultural distinctiveness and a resolve to preserve both territory and culture as a means of reproducing a singular ethnic community.[6]

1.1.1. NOMENCLATURE

After studying the definition of the term tribe given by many sociologists, political thinkers and anthropologists, at various time, the researcher summed up the meaning of the term tribe with the aid of few of such definitions. However, it shold be understood that the concept of 'tribal peoples' is nowadays mostly used to refer to a type of socio political organization and that such a situation no longer exists. The reason behind this is the advent of various nation states rather than homogenous societies. The use of the word is prima facie problematic as it may invoke racial and negative connotations. It must also be noted that the international movement has further altered the relevant concept of tribal peoples and in the process of providing a meaning bereft of discrimination and racism.

Even when the term has undergone a sea change historically and anthropologically, the word tribe needs to be understood from various dimensions. The word "Tribe" is derived from the Latin word "Tribus" meaning "one third". The word originally referred to one of the three territorial groups that united together to form Rome. The Romans applied the word "tribus" to the 35 people who became a part of Rome before 241 B.C. A tribe was considered simply a territorially defined social group. They also called the conquered Gallic or Germanic populations 'tribus'. Thus, Romans primarily identified the term tribe as a 'political unit' with 'distinct name', and occupying a 'common territory' under a 'common leadership'. Apart from a tribe being a social group, which occupies a definite area, it has certain distinctive characteristics like cultural homogeneity and unifying social organization. The identity and culture of every tribe are closely linked to the land and natural resources emanating out of such land and also the environment in which they live in with their family or clan.

A tribe is generally defined as a social division of preliterate people. Again at times it can be noticed that the term tribe is defined as a series of generations, descending from the same progenitor. As a matter of practice, it is the tribals themselves who claims themselves to be the descendants of a particular mythical forefather.

Even the cultural anthropologists apply the term "tribe" to a unit of 'social organization' that is 'culturally homogeneous'. According to them, these units usually consist of multiple kinship groups, such as the family, lineage, or clan. Endogamous marriage within these groups, are usually prohibited.

There is taboo on inbreeding. Thus when it comes to marriage, Exogamy is generally endorsed. Usually tribes are politically organized within a common culture and language.

---

5 The various invasions that took place in India have been classified and discussed in details in Chapter 3 of this book.

6 Richard Falk (ed.), *Maivan Clech Lam: At the Edge of the State: Indigenous peoples and Self Determination 9* (Traditional Publishers. Inc. 2000)

A tribe is viewed by some, historically or developmentally, as a social group existing before the development of, or outside of, states. A tribe is a distinct people, dependent on their land for their livelihood, who are largely self-sufficient, and not integrated into the national society. It is perhaps the term most readily understood and used by the general public. Stephen Corry, director of Survival International, the worlds' only organisation dedicated to indigenous rights, has defined tribal peoples as

"...those which have followed ways of life for many generations that is largely self-sufficient, and is clearly different from the mainstream and dominant society".[7]

From the perspective of the terminology, a tribe is also understood as a political organization which usually refers to a group of people who share territory, language, cultural history, and usually some form of kinship. Some sociologists use the term to refer to societies organized largely on the basis of kinship[8]. Tribal groups generally do not have an official leader. Leadership is generally inherited. At times based on the factors like skills in dealing with a particular situation, temporary leaders are elected. However, these skilful men do not have an authority over anyone, but their suggestions are usually listened and adhered [9]to most of times.

The term "tribe" has arguably also been used to refer to any non-Western or indigenous society.[10] In some countries such as the United States of America and India, tribes are called indigenous peoples, and have been granted legal recognition and limited autonomy by the state.

There has been a debate as to how tribes may be characterized on the basis of the certain perceived differences. The tribes have under gone a plethora of changes in the last few centuries be it social, political or economical. Today tribes are different from pre-state tribes[11] and contemporary tribes. This development leads to the controversy between cultural evolution and colonialism. It is generally felt that tribes reflect a way of life that predates, and is more "natural", than that in modern states. Tribes also preserve primitive social ties, and there is a bond that keeps them together. Tribes are homogeneous and stable though parochial or narrow minded. It is believed that most contemporary tribes do not have their origin in pre-state tribes, but rather in pre-state bands. These tribal groups, also called "secondary" tribes, actually came about as modern products of state expansion. This was probably done when states treated tribal areas as extended administrative and economic areas, since direct political control was too costly. Moreover, states would encourage people to form clearly bounded and centralized polities, which could produce surpluses, and have a leadership which would be responsive to the needs of the neighbouring states. Examples of such state policies can be seen in the scheduled tribes of United States or British India another way in which the secondary tribes developed was through the bands forming themselves into organized groups in order to defend themselves against state expansion.

The international definition of 'indigenous peoples' is problematic. The problem emanates from the fact that the population movement and the experiences in India have been different from those of new world. Whatever the differences are whether those especially associated with a given territory are indigenous to the territory or the area they live in is a question that will always be contested. What however has come to be accepted that they have developed a special relation in question. These territories, the communities in

---

7 Elizabeth Palmer (trs.) Emilie Benveniste, *Indo-European Language and Society,* (Faber and Faber, London, 1973).

8 especially corporate descent groups

9 It depends upon the discretion of the actual leader whether such advice shall be accepted or not.

10 A lot of racism is involved in such connotation.

11 Pre state tribes may be stated to be tribes before colonisation and the formation of the state order that they belong today.

question have considered as their own as against those of other communities. They considered themselves to have prior settlement or numerical or other dominance. Following this they aspired to promote and protect the interests and the welfare of their community and confer on the member of their special rights and privileges.[12]

Tribes are primarily seen as a stage and type of society. They represent a society that lacks traits of the modern society and thus constitute a simple illiterate and backward society.[13]

The primary political objective of these communities are not to develop their own separate nation state but to have sufficient local control over the areas of their ancestors and their distinct culture. At the most they want their voice to be heard in the decision making process of the state. A typical example of this is the Latino population in the United States. Their primary concern is generally the protection of their culture through preservation of their land base.[14]

This attachment to a specific territory and insistence on the preservation of community on that territory distinguishes indigenous peoples from other ethnic minorities.[15]

One of the telling example of the attachment of indigenous peoples are the refusal of accepting an amount as huge as $400 million as compensation in lieu of the famous Black Hills of South Dakota, USA.

1.1.2. CONSTITUTIONAL INTERPRETATION.

The Indian Constitution has made important provisions for the development and welfare of the tribes. A list of tribes was adopted for this purpose. The list has been modified from time to time. In 1971, the list contained names of 527 tribes. The people who have been listed in the Constitution and mentioned in successive presidential orders are called Scheduled Tribes. This is the administrative concept of tribe.

A tribe has been defined in various ways. The Constitution, however, does not provide a definition of a tribe. The people who have been listed in the Constitution have been termed as Scheduled Tribes. The Indian Constitution does not use the term 'Adivasi' and instead refers to the STs as 'Anusuchit Jana Jati'.

1.1.3. SOCIOLOGICAL, POLITICAL AND ANTHROPOLOGICAL INTERPRETATIONS.

Many people used the term "tribal society" to refer to societies organized largely on the basis of social, especially familial, descent groups. A customary tribe in these terms is a face-to-face community, relatively bound by kinship relations, reciprocal exchange, and strong ties to place. [16]

The Hindutva forces term the tribes as 'Vanvasi'[17]. The Gandhians used the term from the culturological perspective and referred to them as 'Vanyajati'.

---

12 Virginius Xaxa, "Tribes as Indigenous peoples of India", 34, EPW 3593 (December 1999).

13 Ibid at p 3589.

14 Ibid

15 Ibid

16 James Paul, *Globalism, Nationalism, Tribalism: Bringing Theory Back In*, (Sage Publications, London)

17 This term not only conveys a sense of primitiveness but also tries to deny the territorial rights.

Academicians have been making their efforts to define tribe. The Dictionary of Sociology defines tribe as a:

"Social group, usually with a definite area, dialect, cultural homogeneity and unifying social organisation."[18]

According to the Imperial Gazetteer of India,[19]

"A tribe as we find in India, is a collection of families or groups of families, bearing a common name, which as a rule, does not denote any specific occupation generally claiming common descent from a mythical or historical ancestor and occasionally from an animal but in some parts of the country held together rather by the obligation of blood fued than by the tradition of kinship, usually speaking the same language; and occupying or claiming to occupy, a definite tract of country. A tribe is not necessarily endogamous, i.e., it is not inevitable rule that a man of a particular tribe must marry a woman of that tribe."[20]

The term tribe has been explained by Weiner in the following lines:

"Everyone in Chotonagpur can recognize a tribal. A distinctive racial type, known by physical anthropologists as belonging to the proto-Austaloid stock, they are somewhat darker than other Indians and have features that are sometimes Mongoian in appearance. They live in their own villages, many of which are wholly homogenous. Perhaps the most distinctive feature of tribal life is the very attitude towards life itself. In contrast with their Hindu neighbours, the tribals are a carefree people, hedonistic in their simple pleasures."[21]

According to Gillin and Gillin,[22]

"Any collection of preliterate local group which occupies a common general territory speaks a common language and practises a common culture, is a tribe"[23].

As Ralph Linton says,

"In its simplest form the tribe is a group of bands occupying a continuous territory and having a feeling of unity deriving from numerous similarities in culture and certain community of interests."[24]

According to Revers,[25]

"A tribe is a social group of simple kind, the members of which speaks a common dialect and act together in such common purpose as warfare"

---

18 John Scott and Gordon Marshall (ed.) A Dictionary of Sociology Oxford University Press., UK, 2009)

19 Imperial Gazetteer of India, v. 1, p 308

20 Imperial Gazetteer of India, v. 1, p.308, available at http://dsal.uchicago.edu/reference/gazetteer/pager. html?objectid=DS405.1.I34_V01_338.gif (visited on December 3, 2015).

21 Hari Mohan Mathur, "Tribal Land Issues in India: Communal Management, Rights, and Displacement", Social Change 164 (2006).

22 An American Sociologist

23 Nadgonde Gurunath, Bharatiya Adivasi, 3 Continental Publication, Pune, Third Edition, (2003).

24 Supra Note 2.

25 Ibid

According to DN Majumdar,

> *"A tribe is a collection of families, bearing a common name, members to which occupy the same territory, speak the same language and observe certain taboos regarding marriage profession or occupation and have developed a well assessed system of reciprocity and mutuality of obligation."*[26]

Further, we hardly find out any difference between minas of Rajasthan or the Bhumaj of West Bengal and their neighbours. Therefore, tribes have been considered as a stage in the social and Cultural Revolution.

For S. C Sinha the tribe is ideally defined in terms of its isolation from the networks of social relations and cultural communications of the centres of civilisation. According to Sinha

> *In their isolation the tribal societies are sustained by relatively primitive subsistence technology such as 'shifting cultivation and, hunting and gathering and maintain an egalitarian segmentary social system' guided entirely by non-literate ethnic tradition."*[27]

"Tribe" is a contested term due to its roots in colonialism. The word has no shared referent, whether in political form, kinship relations or shared culture. Some argue that it conveys a negative connotation of a timeless unchanging past.[28]

L.M Lewis believes that tribal societies are small in scale are restricted in the spatial and temporal range of their social, legal and political relations and possess a morality, a religion and world view of corresponding dimensions. Characteristically too tribal languages are unwritten and hence the extent of communication both in time and space is inevitably narrow. At the same time tribal societies exhibit a remarkable economy of design and have a compactness and self-sufficiency lacking in modern society.[29]

It must also be understood that the definition of 'Indigenous peoples' as projected by the UN Working Group for Indigenous peoples has an European bias as it states,

> *"Indigenous peoples and nations are those which, having a historical continuity with their pre-invasion and pre-colonial societies that developed on their territories, consider themselves distinct from other sectors of societies, now prevailing in those territories or parts of them. They form at present non-dominant sectors of society and are determined to preserve, develop and transmit to future generation their ancestral territories and their ethnic identity as the basis of their continuous existence as people in accordance with their own cultural patterns, social institutions and legal system."*[30]

In Hindi heartland another very popular term was 'jana' which referred the tribes in India.[31]

Anthropologists worldwide over the years have defined the term tribe in various ways. To begin with,

---

26 Ibid

27 Ibid

28 "Talking about 'Tribe' - Africa Action: Activism for Africa Since 1953", Africa Action, available at https://en.wikipedia.org/wiki/Tribe (visited on December 3, 2015)

29 Supra Note 2.

30 J J Roy Burman 2009.

31 (Ray: 1972)

F.G.Bailey[32]argues that;

> "If certain people have command over the resources and their access to the products of economy is not derived immediately through a dependent status on ors, and are a relatively large portion of the total population in the area, they are termed as tribe."

Another eminent social scientist has defined tribes

> "...as having common territory with a tradition of common descent, common linguistic background, common cultural identity and a common name."[33]

According to G. M. Lewis[34],

> "tribal societies are small in scale, people are restricted in the spatial level and political relations and possesses a morality, religion and worldview of corresponding dimensions, characteristically their languages are unwritten, but exhibit remarkable unity and coherence and they are also marked for their compactness and self sufficiency in economy, which is lacking in the modern societies".

Morgan[35] has described tribes,

> "as a completely organized society, with each tribe being individualized by a name, by a separate dialect; by a supreme government and by the possession of some territory which is of its own".

While defining the term tribe, R.C.Verma, stated

> "the autochthonous people of the land who are believed to be the earliest settlers in Indian Peninsula".[36]

As pointed out by R.C.Verma,

> "these are headed by tribal chiefs who exercise considerable influence over social, economic and religious affairs of their respective tribes".[37]

These groups are considered to be the first settlers of the land and territory they habituate and are thus nomenclated as Adivasis, meaning the first settlers. There has been a division of the tribes on various features.[38] Hierarchical discrimination was not in practice and each tribe possessed their unique nature headed by a headman usually acting as a chief. Usually the strongest and the boldest of the community used to be the chief, however, instances of intellectually higher person has also been held as chiefs of various clans and tribes in India. The community was self sustained and the function of the chief was not only to protect the community from external forces but also to regulate the internal affairs of the tribes. Usually the chief

---

32 1960: 151

33 J.J.Honingman (1964)

34 1968: 147

35 1871: 122

36 Supra Note 2.

37 Ibid

38 This was the position before the advent of the caste system in India.

was guided by the customs and rituals of the community in furtherance of protecting the homogeneity of their socio economic and cultural features. With the passage of time the population density of the tribes led to the increase of territoriality and various dynasties and kingdoms were created. Unique blend of military and administrative powers were vested upon the chief of the community who followed and developed its own system of administration. Decentralization of authority was not present in most of the smaller tribes but certain larger tribal groups founded the concept of decentralization of various authorities. This gave birth to various traditional tribal institutions. These institutions were vested with various important powers and functions including the legislative, judicial and executive powers. A unique example of the existence of such an institution can be seen amongst the Santhals in Santhal Parganas in the form the 'Manjhi' system.[39]

As discussed earlier, according to The Oxford English Dictionary the word 'tribe' is derived from the Latin term *tribus* which was applied to the three divisions of the early people of Rome. With its changing dimensions, it meant a political unit consisting of a number of clans occupying a definite geographical area. Permanent settlement for a considerable period of time usually gave a geographical identity to a tribe. For that reason the process of identifying a particular tribe relating to a specified geographic area. This practice has been seen in a number of instances all over the worlds. The aboriginals of Australia, the Maori of New Zealand, and the Bhutias of North Bengal are to name a few. India is presumably named after a tribe called "Bharata".[40]

The term 'tribe' came to denote a race of people living within a given territory.[41] Western writers in India known as Orientalists followed by anthropologists and sociologists used this term with the same connotation and argued that the tribes of India belonged to three stocks—the Negritos, the Mongoloids and the Mediterranean.[42] The Negritos are found in various remote places in Asia, mostly in the south eastern zone. They are typical ethnic groups with various unique features which may relate them to the earliest inhabitants of the Peninsula region of India. These people are mostly located at Malaysia[43], Thailand[44], Philippines[45] and India[46]. They are believed to be the earliest inhabitants of the Indian Peninsula. In India, they are scarcely found among the tribals of Andaman and Nicobar Islands, known as the Onges, the Great Andamanese, the Sentinelese and the Peniyans.

1.1.4. COLONIAL INTERPRETATION

A very important aspect of the terminology is that it has got its relevance only during the colonial exploration. However it is not true that colonization has affected all tribal populace of the world. As a matter of fact, there were some places which were too remote and dangerous to reach for the colonial rulers. The situation however changed with the growth of population and commercial exploitation of these areas. The colonial rulers were ultimately able to extend their policy in such areas as well. In recent years scientific researchers have travelled the remotest places populated with indigenous peoples. It has been accepted by

---

39 'Maniki' and 'Munda' system in Singhbhum is Another example of tribal institution.

40 States like Mizoram, Nagaland and Tripura are named after the Mizo, Naga and Tripuri tribes respectively.

41 This was primarily because of the growth of nationalism in Europe,

42 More about the traits of the tribes in India an elaborate discussion has been made in chapter 3 of this book.

43 Semang peoples

44 The Mani peoples

45 Aeta, Agta, Ati, and 30 other peoples

46 Andamanese peoples

many a scientist that the indigenous populated places has been filled with wonderful natural resources of the world that has kept these populations existent even in great odds. In a majority of cases it is perhaps for these people that these natural resources still exists on earth. A great number of constructions of hydro electric projects have also led to the exploration of remotest places. The military has also been sent to certain remote areas of the world by the government for strategic military concerns[47]. It must also be mentioned that encroachers like animal traffickers and drug peddlers[48] have also reached various parts of the world indigenous and tribal regions and has been one of the biggest dangers to these population.[49]

The Indian Constitution uses the word Scheduled Tribes and not adivasi or indigenous peoples. As Roy Burman has pointed out that the Scheduled Tribes are referred to identify the Anuschit Jana Jati.[50]

Thus from the various interpretation of the term 'tribal peoples' in the aforesaid discussion, the world has seen a sea change in the meaning of the term as what it was and has recently found a uniformity in the international forum devoid of discrimination and racism.

1.1.5. FEATURES OF TRIBES

Almost all the definitions studied, have reflected the relationship between the land and tribals to be of vital importance. The key characteristics of the relation of tribal peoples to the land may be classified into two broad categories in furtherance to the example of the Black Hill case.[51]

Firstly, while the land is important for the economic and sheltering benefits, it is crucial for the continued existence of cultures where spiritual belief is directly tied to the social and political identity of the community and is directly linked to particular sacred places.

Secondly, it reflects the tribal tendency to hold land collectively, as opposed to individually.[52]

This second feature is one of the primitive approaches towards community building. It is the jurisprudence of tribal societies. The existence of tribals as a whole and not as an individual is the benchmark of indigenous civilization. This collective ownership of property includes a combination of possessory, use and management rights.[53] Thus the land base becomes the support for and focus of the group as opposed to individual rights held by the tribe.[54] The English jurisprudence bifurcates in the upliftment in individual ownership over collective ownership. This again has been criticised for not having the requisite international standards in protection of environment, or in imparting the justice administration system in the form of distributive justice as for instance the rehabilitation of an offender in a society. The collective holding system has to a great extent helped these communities to be still in existence in whatever way they can even after so

---

47 Africa has experienced this along with many other countries.

48 The movie Blood Diamond reflects a true example of such practices in Africa and many other parts of the world.

49 Ananya S James, 'Indigenous peoples in International Law', 4 (Oxford University Press, 1996)

50 J J Roy Burman, Supra at 27

51 Jacqueline Hand, "Government Corruption and Exploitation of Indigenous peoples", vol. 3/issue2, Santa Clara Journal of International Law 2 (2005)

52 Ibid

53 Ananya, Supra note 46, at p 106

54 Ibid

much atrocities from various non tribal, governmental and nongovernmental players. They have successfully resisted various planned attack of intrusion into their culture and society through their common efforts.

Another remarkable feature of tribal communities across the world is their effort to carry on the legacy of the ancestors. Irrespective of invasion and exploration in recent past or centuries ago, these communities try to maintain their pre-invasion history, culture, thoughts and visions to their children in order to preserve their continued existence as a community. Instances of passing of tribal know how and special skills are many. Irrespective of major hindrances, various tribes still follow their indigenous culture and social behaviour.

The presence of tribals and indigenous communities across the planet is another significant example of their presence and their need of protection. Their presence in the world forms a considerable number game. The study revealed that Indigenous peoples with its various annotation and connotations are estimated to be more than 250 million people which are about 4% of the world population. They consist of approximately 5000 distinct groups living in roughly 70 nations.[55] Their participation and contribution to the world economy is minimal and largely choice specific and their attitude to the modern development is usually antagonistic as they believe to be a threat to their community and culture. There are an estimated one hundred and fifty million tribal individuals worldwide.[56]

Sustainable economy of these groups makes them unique in various ways. This distinctive feature has many contrasting approach to those of the non tribals. As a matter of fact, the term sustainable with its various dimensions became an institution by itself. However, very little has been thought about those who originated the concept and practiced it in the true sense of the term. The indigenous communities across the globe had a sustainable way of life. Whether it is their economy or attitude towards life, it is the term sustainable that perhaps suits them the best.

The most unique feature of the tribals across most of the communities in the world is their sustainable economic system. Tribals have a long history of using the resources from the land and forest for various use of their house and even transforming them for commercial use by their unique know how and skilful artistry. Business in small scale is common amongst tribal societies. Involvement of women in collection and gathering of raw materials from the forest is common and their role in the economy un-debatable. The raw materials involved in the business and the skill needed are no longer easily available and the chance to work on them to explore the skill and practice is reducing at an alarming rate. The greener pastures of the urban and semi urban developments are attracting and alluring the younger generations to a more modern life. Whether or not they are better is another question to be answered.

Tribal educational system is unique in the actual sense of the term. The most distinctive feature of tribal education does not involve any educational institute or school for tribal children. Tribal education does not depend upon schools and within books. They educate themselves through exposure in the environment under expert supervision. It provides ways of teaching and learning local knowledge relevant to protect the environment. This exposure to nature provides the tribals their much needed attachment to nature. However, the advent of colonial rulers has incorporated the western system of education and this has left the tribes to visit these educational institutes along with their cultural educational system. The practical approach of the indigenous education system targets for day to day use where as the formal education system is abstract as it is intended to pass examination.

---

55 Supra Note 4 at p 9.

56 Terminology, available at http://www.survivalinternational.org/info/terminology accessed on December 3, 2015

The formal education system has disrupted the practical everyday life aspects of indigenous knowledge and ways of learning, replacing them with abstract knowledge and academic ways of learning. Many instances of loss of mass knowledge base to live a sustainable way of life is noticed in the last century amongst the tribals and indigenous peoples. One of such example is the handicraft industry which, in most tribal areas are dying a slow death as most of the current generation are not keen to carry on with the profession or trade of their ancestors as they are hoping to survive the onslaught the current economic situation is providing them with. Tribals have a broad knowledge of how to live sustainably. The indigenous knowledge may be integrated into the modern education system concerning the tribals and thereby promote sustainable lifestyle to them. This will also help them to retain their traditional knowledge and technical knowhow.

Tribals prefer traditional way of healing. In cases of health related issues, tribals seek help from specialists like Bhagat popularly known as Buva, Bhopa or Ojha. They generally use herbal remedies, cauterization, divination and exorcism, treated the more intractable cases. These people are highly respected in tribal societies and had considerable social power. Such is the popularity of these healing techniques that they are widely used and practices amongst the tribals even today. With the advent of modern form of medicine and healing techniques, the conventional tribal medical treatment has developed them to a hybrid form of healing that combines ritual with various quasi allopathic or complementary medical practices.

Tribal culture is unique in its own way as tribals prefer to have a simple life and filled with music, songs, liquor and merry making. Every tribal society has these three things in common. However, the cultural imbalance amongst tribals largely diminished because of foreign invasions upon tribal lands. There are many instances which suggest that the social, environmental, cultural and legal system of the tribes all across the globe where the British hegemony has been successful to flourish their business and trade and later their administration, has been detrimental to the system both in short term and long term. The man who works as a labor in the construction industry, the thousands of them involved in the big dream home projects and sky creepers, who work in the construction of big flyovers, bridges are those who have been either forced to leave their motherland or fled from the group which has lost its sustainability. Irrespective of these grave situations, the tribes in most part of the world has been successful in retaining their cultural traits within the clan or tribal community. They follow their own way of life, marriage, ceremonies, rituals, dialects, food and drinks. They regularly follow their cultural affiliations in almost all aspect of their life.

Another fundamental feature of tribal life is their code of conduct and their redress system. It is imperative to state that the tribals follow the primitive system of law. Customs have been the guiding stars for the tribals as far their laws are concerned. This has been acknowledged in a number of countries even today including India, Australia and United States of America. Customary laws form the basis of regulating their conduct. The tribals have been guided by their customary practices which have been guiding them for ages.

1.2. REVIEWING THE TRIBES IN INDIA

It is important to analyze the various tribes in India and also at the outset to know the problem in nomenclature.

1.2.1. PROBLEMS IN NOMENCLATURE

The indigenous peoples are vastly known as inter alia tribes, adivasis, jati, jana jati, natives or savages in Indian context. There has been long standing debate as to whether the term indigenous may be applied to their Indian counterpart as the latter has undergone a major transition during the last century under the colonial rule and have almost lost their basic indigenous identity and is in a form of a mixed category more aptly be termed as tribes or adivasis. At this outset, it is important to identify whether the word indigenous at all used in the Indian scenario.

India, from the very outset during 1984 stated that the scheduled Tribes of India are not indigenous. It was designated that India has long been a 'melting pot'. It was argued that it is now very difficult in India to come across communities which retain 'all their pristine tribal character'. However, if this logic is to be adhered to then there cannot be any tribal communities anywhere in the world.

The double standard reflected by India in the international forum when it was stated that the tribals survive but not as indigenous communities. However, this distinction took place at much later stage as India being a party to the ILO Convention of 1957 on Indigenous and Tribal Population. India supported the document at the early stages when it only used the term Indigenous. In a number of Government publication the term adivasis and aboriginal have been used interchangeably. The current rejection of the term indigenous developed in the context of the Working Group in 1984 and later in 1992.[57]

The term tribe has not been defined in the Indian Constitution. However, Art. 342 state that the Scheduled Tribes are the tribes of those communities, which the President may specify by Official Notification.

The international definition of the term indigenous peoples is indeed problematic in the Indian context as the population movement and the experience in India have been different from the new world. The benchmark being the territory where they live in, being the primary determinant of indigenous shall always be debated. However, the communities in question have considered themselves as indigenous as against those of other communities. They consider themselves to have prior and preferential if not surely an exclusive right over the territory where they lived either on account of their prior settlement or numerical or other dominance. Following this they aspired to promote and protect the interest and welfare of the community and confer on the members of their, special rights and privileges.[58]

To abate the debate the term tribe shall be given preference in this book. The object of this research book is not only to identify the tribals but to understand the problems faced by them and what leads them to frequent retaliation. There is overwhelming discussions relating to tribal rights movement in the era of human rights in the international forum. And this paper would try to explore the various difficulties of this section of the Indian populace. The issue is to identify tribes. Even when there is no clear identifier of tribes, some basic patterns are developed to incorporate them in the Fifth and Sixth Schedule of the Indian Constitution.

As a matter of fact, considering the term 'Adivasi' to be equivalent to the term 'Tribe' in India would be gross mistake. It may be stated that this reinforce the anti-Indian feelings and a sense of deviation from the main stream among many of the tribes inhabiting, North Bengal, Sikkim and other North-Eastern States.[59] The term will be considered pejorative and humiliating to most of them. It must be realised that the term tribe itself is a colonial construct and 'aboriginal' 'autochthon' precepts are outcome of colonial conquests.[60]

---

57 IWGIA, 1992 Report of the Working Group on Indigenous populations on the tenth session, Geneva, International work Group for Indigenous Affairs.

58 Supra Note 9

59 J.J.Roy Burman, "Adivasi Vs Indigenous peoples Adivasi: A Contentious Term To Denote Tribes As Indigenous peoples of India" 32, Mainstream, 1 (2009)

60 Ibid

The so-called 'friends of tribes' in India have been amateurishly trying to romanticise the term in the name of radical empowerment.[61] The tribal situation in India is extremely heterogeneous and a unified approach may not do justice to all the communities.[62]

Bijoy[63] (2003) writes:

> "The 67.7 million people belonging to 'Scheduled Tribe' in India are generally considered to be 'Adivasi', literally meaning 'Indigenous peoples' or original inhabitants, though the term 'Scheduled Tribe' (ST) is not coterminous with the term 'Adivasi'. Scheduled Tribe is an administrative term used for the purpose of 'administering' certain specific Constitutional privileges, protection and benefits for specific section of people historically considered disadvantaged and 'backward'. However, this administrative term does not exactly match all the people called 'Adivasi'. Out of the 5653 distinct communities in India, 635 are considered to be 'tribes' or 'Adivasis'. In comparison, one finds that estimated number of STs varies from 250 to 593."[64]

Bijoy[65] continues;

> "The application and use of the term adivasi or tribes in India is more of politics than of law. It has often been used to convey the position of exclusion of the tribes (Kumar: 2001: 4052-4054) and their subaltern status (Ekka: 2000-2001: 4610-4612).[66] The term Adivasi has been even used to focus the tribal rights (Dietrich: 2000), their resistance (Pati: 2001), protests (Viswanath: 1997), assertions (Hardiman: 1988, Rahul: 1998), struggles (Raman: 2002) and movements.[67] (Bijoy and Raman: 2003) The term in a way conveys a sense of 'empowerment' of the tribes.[68] This empowerment is being asserted by linking with the global indigenous peoples's movement."[69]

It is important to note that the tribes in India are not the only group to claim indigenous status.[70] Even many of the Dalit intellectuals have made similar assertions.[71] The concept of the term scheduled tribe has been intentionally made complicated by political intent by incorporating a few Brahmins[72] and Rajput[73] communities within its fold. The political version of the term tribe may again be established when the

---

61 Ibid

62 Ibid

63 *Ibid*

64 Ibid

65 Ibid

66 Ibid

67 Ibid

68 Ibid

69 Ibid

70 Ibid

71 (Massey: 1994)

72 Jaunsari in Uttarakhand

73 Kanaura in Himachal Pradesh

Government of India itself refuses to grant indigenous status to the tribes.[74] The term 'Adivasi' has various popular usage and connotations as it has various popularly use in various parts of India and specifically in a few in north eastern states.[75] At times it is popularly used to refer to the tea plantation labourers and at ties to identify the migratory population that inhibited during the Colonial invasion.[76] Santhal, Munda, Oraon and Ho are some of prominent examples in this regard. The local inhabitants, prior to the nomenclature like tribes or adivasi were never in favour of a terminology being imposed upon them as this literally outcastes and separates them from the mainstream.[77] The local tribes in these States also find it humiliating to identify them as 'Adivasi'.[78] The indigenous Rabha, Mech and Rajbansi tribes and ethnic groups in North Bengal prefer to identify themselves by their own names and not as 'Adivasi'.[79] It has been noticed that the use of the term adivasi or tribe has been used instead of their specific tribal names to those groups which used to migrate from other parts of the country to a distinct place for some work. One of the instances that may be given in this regard is the identification of the migrant plantation labourers from Chotanagpur as 'Adivasi' by the Sikkimese tribesmen.[80] Another instance being the Santhal, Oraon, Munda and Ho migrant tribes in the Sunderbans of West Bengal, working as agricultural labourers or cultivating small farms, are collectively referred to as 'Adivasi' by the local Bengali settlers, a majority of whom are Scheduled Castes.[81] The term 'Adivasi' therefore, remains a generic name in East and North-East India for identifying the migrant tribal labourers and small peasants from central India.[82]

In most places in North Bengal and North-East India, the adivasis are considered to be encroachers or intruders. During the Naxalite uprisal at Naxalbari in the late 1960s the Rajbansis en-block resisted the onslaught of the adivasi land grabbers. This lead to a complex and disturbing situation leading to a lot of ethnic clashes of various magnitude between the indigenous Bodos and adivasi encroachers in the Bodoland Territorial Council areas.

The situation became so antagonistic that in one incident there has been an onslaught of more than 100 Santhals by the dangerous Bodo militants. It has been documented that almost 40 per cent of the forests belonging to the Bodo areas have been the subject matter of encroached. It has also been seen that these encroachers are mostly the outsiders who migrated in these areas for shelter from various other adjacent areas and includes other tribals and non tribal communities. There has been a lot of disputes still unaddressed in these areas making this zone disturbed for quite some time. It may be referred in this regard that the government must take some logical steps to bring the situation under control and make the zone stress-free. It must be stated here that there are antagonistic relationship between the Boros and the adivasis in this area but the political intervention in the proper direction would mitigate the situation to a great extent.

---

74 Supra note 56

75 North Bengal, Sikkim, Arunachal Pradesh, Assam, Meghalaya, Nagaland and Tripura

76 Supra note 56

77 Ibid

78 Ibid

79 Ibid

80 Ibid

81 Ibid

82 Supra Note 50 at p 5

Another disturbing scenario notices because of infiltration of people of other areas in tribal zones is in Arunachal Pradesh. It is the indigenous Chakmas[83] who encroached the tribal lands of the tribes of Arunachal Pradesh as refugees. This led to a lot of disturbance in that area as well. Movements from the student wing of the local tribes were seen to be initiated against the encroaching Chakmas. The All Assam Tribal Sangha (AATS) comprising of various tribal organisations, including Bodo, Karbi, Dimasa and Tiwa student organisations are opposing the Adivasi demand for ST status of the Chakmas, alleging if granted, it would affect the interests of tribals of Assam. According to AATS, the Adivasis did not fulfil the requisite criteria of their inclusion in the ST list as they are not originally from Assam.[84]

The term 'indigenous peoples' itself appears to be contentious and subject matter of misuse in more than one ways. There have been many claimants to it. The Dalits[85], the Vaishnavite Meiteis[86] and the caste Hindus[87] have claimed themselves to be indigenous. It will perhaps be always better to avoid using the popular NGO nomenclature 'Adivasi' in the tenors of serious academic discourse when dealing with the notion of indigenous groups in the Indian context.[88]

The tribes in all quarters of the country are not aboriginals of the regions where they inhabit at present. It must be understood that indigenous must not be referred to the concept of the first man in the specific geographical zone. There have been various views in this context including that of the famous historian Kosambi (1956) who viewed that the tribes had migrated to the plain areas at a much later date only after the vegetation had thinned out and wild animals became less numerous making the area less dangerous for human habitation and fit for settled cultivation.

Archana Prasad (2003), the young scholar from Jamia Millia Islamia, Delhi, feels that the tribes practising settled cultivation in the plains were pushed to the hills and forests by the profligate Aryan invaders and later Hindu settled cultivators and the outside traders.[89] The Kukis in Manipur or the Luseis of Mizoram have migrated to their present areas of dominance from South China and Chin Hills only a couple of centuries back.[90]

The Kukis were settled by the British in the Naga predominant areas so as to create a buffer between the Nagas and the Vaishnavite Meiteis.[91] The Sailo chiefs belonging to the Lusei tribe were encouraged by the British to operate as labour contractors for constructing roads in the remote areas of Mizoram.[92] The aboriginal tribes of the State who were pushed to the western borders along Tripura are now known as Tuikuk.[93]

---

83 They have claimed to be indigenous and have applied in the international forum to declare them as indigenous.

84 Supra note 56

85 Claiming their Dravidian antecedence

86 Manipur

87 Assam

88 Supra note 56

89 Ibid

90 Ibid

91 Ibid

92 Ibid

93 Ibid

An interesting discovery in this regard is the policy of the Tripura tribal kings to invite other communities[94] not indigenous to the area to work on the production of cotton through the popular jhum cultivation and also in the cotton mills. Other examples similar to this trend are the Totos[95] of Totopara in West Bengal and the Bodos[96] in Assam. Totos (believed to be migrant criminal clans who were pushed out by the Bhutan kingdom) are now residing in Toto para, in the border of India and Bhutan in the northern part of West Bengal. The author has conducted an empirical study of the tribals in West Bengal where he visited Toto para and found that a large section of Totos works as daily labourers in the orange plantations in Bhutan.

The trend of moving from one place and settling in another is common in various parts of India including the matrilineal Khasis of Meghalaya. These groups belong to the Mon-Khmer linguistic group. Historical evidence as to their migration from the Kampuchea region to Meghalaya has been depicted in many writings. Again, the Denzong Bhutias[97], is said to have migrated from Tibet.

The Santhals similarly has migrated to various parts of West Bengal and started inhibiting various places in Birbhum and Midnapur. Originally, they were from the Rajmahal Hills which is now in Jharkhand.

Thus the concept of aboriginals or the first man has been disputed by many sociologists and political thinkers at various national and international forums in addressing the debate between the indigenous and the modern nomenclature of tribe or adivasis. The concept of 'tribe' has undergone changes. The change which was inevitable due to plethora of reasons has been thoroughly depicted in a number of research work carried out and in scripted in various forms.

To begin with, it must be mentioned that tribal population is present in almost all countries of the world including India. Tribal peoples form a major segment of the world population. They are found all over the world. Various nomenclatures have been used to identify them such as 'jana', 'primitive', 'indigenous,' 'tribal,' 'aboriginal,' 'native,' and so on. India has a large number of tribal peoples. According to R. C. Verma they "constitute about 8.08% of the total population. They would be about 6.78 crores out of the total population of 83.86 crores according to 1991 census". The major tribes speaking various languages reside in both rural and urban areas of the country and include primarily the Santhals, the Gonds, the Bhils, the Oraons and the Minas. Majority of these tribes are domiciled in the forests. Of late there have been incidents of large scale evacuation of forest land for so called developmental projects forcing the tribal mass to come and work as daily wage laborer in urban areas of the country. Again the assimilistic approach of the international convention of ILO 109 which was adopted by India has led to a considerable number of tribal populations integrating with non tribals in the semi urban and urban areas. The concentration of tribal population can be noticed in almost all the states of India but the majority of them exists in the state of Madhya Pradesh, Orissa, Bihar, Jharkhand, Chattishgarh, Maharastra, Gujarat, Andhra Pradesh, West Bengal and the Northeastern Region. The Andaman and Nicobar Islands are also inhabited by several primitive tribes such as the Great Andamanese, Sentenelese, Onges, Jarwas, and Sompens amongst others.

Tribal history is prehistoric and is culturally rich. In the absence of written inscription it is difficult for historians and anthropologists to portrait a clear picture of their past and glorious developments. This obscurity has led to a lot of debate and confusion which in turn created an illusion rather than a clear

---

94 Reangs and Chakmas

95 Totos live in Toto para which is in the district of Alipurduar, West Bengal, India.

96 Bodos are believed to be aboriginals of Bhutan who flocked in great numbers to Assam at a much later stage.

97 It is the Royal Sikkimese tribe.

idea of the development of tribal history in India. It is still uncertain from the excavation discoveries as to whether India had a pre historic past. However, according to Nadeem Hasnain:

> *"It has now become an established fact that the aboriginal tribes in India are, in most cases, survivals from the later prehistoric groups".*[98]

The Aborigines of India primarily comes from various regions of Asia and belongs to various races. In the absence of any constructive proof, the tribal history lacks its stability and a mere possibility based on presumption can be presumed. The existence of scripts of a much later stage merely helps to have a decent idea of the tribes in ancient India.

Some scholars believe that the builders of the Indus valley civilization might have been the aboriginal people. Their extinction is attributed to the disastrous alteration of the course of the Indus river resulting in destructive flooding of settlements and silting of fields. Another explanation put forward by Stephen Fuchs is as follows:

> *"the Aryan invaders might have destroyed the centres of Harrappan civilization and killed or dispersed its population. The discovery of unburied skeletons on the steps of a building in Mohenjodaro seems to support such an assumption"* (qtd. in Hasnain 8)

There is scanty information about the people who were destroyed. There are also no grounds to believe whether they spoke Dravidian languages.

The Vedic scriptures have some convincing information of the tribes in India. The inscriptions made it clear that the Aryans invaded from the Northwestern parts of India and fought against the non-Aryans.[99] As Hasnain says:

> *"The Asuras who captured the city of an Aryan sage Dabhiti were defeated by Indra and dispossessed of their booty"*[100]

The later Vedic period (1000 to 600 BC) witnessed the fusion of the Aryan and the non-Aryan. According to Kosambi,

> *"The process of Aryanisation of the tribals and tribalization of the Aryans was on".*[101]

---

98 Supra note 56.

99 In a research inscription it was noted that God Indra was invoked to smash the forts of the 'Dasyus.' He is described as casting his dart on the 'Dasyus' to establish Aryan supremacy. He is described as having killed both the 'Dasyus' and the 'Samyus.' Goddess Saraswati is again credited with having killed the Parvatas, a hostile tribe who dwelt on the banks of the Paushni. Vishnu conquered the bull-jawed Dasyus in his battles and together with Indra destroyed Sambara's cattles.

100 Supra note 56.

101 Ibid

1.2.2. REFERENCE IN EPICS.

Various tribes have got its reference in the great epics The Ramayana and The Mahabharata. Tribes such as Sudras, Ahiras, Dravidas, Pulindas and Sabaras or Saoras are common instances of this.[102] A Bhil boy, Ekalavya, in the epic Mahabharata is a very common example as he had to offer his thumb to Dronacharya as gurudakhchina for secretly learning the arts of war from Dronacharya. There has been many other reference of tribals in the Mahabharata.[103]

It can be studied from various texts that it was during this phase of history when the tribes were used for tasks of the lower order. This process may ultimately led to the creation of the lower caste referred to as 'Sudra.' The tribes however, did not lead an isolated life. As Hasnain points out, their participation in sub-Puranic and epic traditions of myths and folktales gives evidence that they were not an isolated lot. One can see the impact of epic heroes/heroines such as Rama, Sita, Lakshmana, Ravana, Bhima, etc., on some of the tribes in central India in their myths and lore. The present day Gonds call themselves children of Ravana.

Apart from the greater epics like Ramayana and Mahabharata, various ancient Sanskrit literary works such as Panchatantra, Kathasarita Sagara, Vishnu Purana, Kadambah, and Harsha-Charita give descriptions of the tribals.[104]

1.2.3. REFERENCE IN SMRITIS AND SUTRAS.

Texts such as the Dharma Sutra (600 to 300 BC) and Manusmriti (200 BC to 200 AD) mention the old process of fusion and assimilation of the tribes. The marriage between various tribals and non tribal peoples during this era brought germinated the caste system in India. The 'Nishadas' in these texts are cited as an example. Hasnain says:

> *"The Chandalas, a tribe, were absorbed into Hindu society and assigned the task of removing dead bodies of animals and human beings as also whipping and chopping off the limbs of criminals".[105]*

Thus the process of out casting of tribals as lower from the existing mainstream started and continued.

The invasion continued by the non tribals upon the tribal areas during the feudal period (400-1000 AD).

The most noticeable thing of this era was the process of Sanskritization. This, to a great extent affected the tribal culture and customs. The Brahmin priests prepared suitable genealogies for themselves and the ruling Brahmin class spearheaded the process of Sanskritization as expressed and popularized by M. N. Srinivas.

Srinivas says:

---

102 Sabari,' who was a tribal woman, is shown in the Ramayana as having offered fruits to Rama.

103 Some of the other instances being the Pandava prince Arjuna being married to a Naga princess Chitrangada. The Mundas and the Nagas claimed to have fought on the side of the Kurus against the Pandavas. It has been inscripted that Ghatotkacha was born out of Bhima's tribal wife.

104 The assimilation of tribal and non tribal peoples slowly and steadily created a new set of rules and customs for the society where both of them belong.

105

"Sanskritization may be briefly defined as the process by which a low caste or tribe or other group takes over the customs, rituals, beliefs, ideology, and style of life of a high and, in particular, a twice-born (dwija) caste. The Sanskritization of a group has usually the effect of improving its position in the local caste hierachy. It normally presupposes either an improvement in the economic or political position of the group concerned, or a higher group self-consciousness resulting from its contact with a source of the 'Great Tradition' of Hinduism such as a pilgrim centre or a monastery or a proselytizing sect."[106]

Virginous Xaxa was quick to points out in this regard that

"Though M.N. Srinivas had the so-called lower class in mind when he coined this term, it can be extended to the tribals as well. This process of social change is also termed as "Hinduization".[107]

1.3. INVASIONS IN INDIA AND TRIBAL CONFRONTATION

Historical inscription declares certain aspects of invaders being confronted by tribal peoples. One of the famous invaders was Alexander who wiped out tribal belts on the Northwestern border of India another invader Ajatasatru was incited to have destroyed the tribal republic of Vaisali.

1.3.1. VARIOUS MAJOR INVASIONS IN A NUTSHELL

The Muslim invasion also during the 11th and 12th centuries, witnessed some dethroned Rajput rulers, establishing their rule in various tribal areas. This process also led to the replacement of the tribal chiefs or the headman. Instances of such displacement are ample in the pages of the past. The Parmar Rajputs expelled the Cheros from Shahabad, and the Chandels replaced the Bhuinya in the South Monghyr district of Bihar. This also to a considerable extent led to the loss of the traditional and customary laws being followed by these tribes and a new set of rules and regulations generated from Rajput philosophy being incorporated amongst the tribals. Consequently assimilation took place leading to loss of indigenous features of the tribes.

During the Mughal rule (12-18th century), the tribal chiefs and the Hindu rulers in tribal areas of Central India and Bihar were forced to show their allegiance to the Turko-Afghan and Mughal rulers. In 1585 and 1616 A.D., the Mughal Muslim army marched into Chotanagpur and defeated the Raja of Khukra. Similarly, the tribal areas of Assam were also subjugated by another Muslim general. During this period, a number of tribes were converted into Islam in the Northwest frontier region. The Gond dynasty which had its 'Garha' near Jabalpur and ruled the region for more than two hundred years also faced defeat at the hands of the Muslim and Maratha rulers. The loss of their power compelled the tribes to convert to Islam, but some of them still retained their identity. The Muslims of the Lakshadweep Islands and the Siddi Muslims of Gujarat are the best examples of such conversion. R. C. Verma points out that

"when the Moghuls invaded South India, they forced the Banjaras, an enterprising tribe of Northwestern India to employ their cattle for transporting their supplies. That is how the Banjaras migrated to Andhra Pradesh and other adjoining areas in the South"[108].

---

106 Ibid

107 Xaxa Op.cit at p. 1519.

108 Ibid

But it was a common affair that religious reasons are given in many other cases amongst many other religions as well.

The tribals were also influenced by some streams of the Bhakti Movement. Some became followers of Chaitanya Mahaprabhu when they came in contact with him during his travels. There have been instances of complete loss of tribal traits by taking up Hinduism, Islam or Christianity in different period of history. For example, the Bhuiyans of Jharkhand, surrendered their tribal traits and converted to Hinduism. Tribal authority and cultural traits was substantially eroded by these influences.

Apart from cultural and social subjugation there have been instances of economic withering of tribal societies under the Zamindari and other colonial systems of administration.

There have been other instances of invasion that also to a considerable extent affected the customary life of the tribes in India. The Persians, the Greeks, the Sakas, the Huns and other hordes of nomadic invaders periodically invaded tribal areas in India from the Northwest.

In furtherance of the Doctrine of Discovery, the British invasion started and reached India through the East India Company. East India Company, authorized by the British penetrated into various tribal regions in search of resources. They used forest produces for their business. Ramachandara Guha and Madhav Gadgil in their essay "State Forestry and Conflict in British India" (1989) shows the commercial exploitation of natural resources of the tribes by the British colonial rulers. There has been indiscriminate felling of trees for timber. This lead to the loss of vital resources needed for sustenance of tribal life. The use of land for commercial cultivation like tea, rubber and coffee plantations have compromised on the naturally grown habitation, leading to the extinction of thousands of flora and fauna. New mode of transportation was built to transfer forest resources from tribal belts to the ports for transportation to Europe. In the process new inroads were made in forest areas. Routes from forest to sea coasts were built to transport goods on one hand and transfer armed forces to the forests in cases of conflicts on the other.[109]

In another article entitled "The Making of the 1878 Forest Act" Guha points out the following:

> "The early years of the expansion of the railway network, 1853 onwards, led to tremendous deforestation in peninsular India owing to the railways' requirements of fuel wood and construction timber. Huge quantities of durable timber were also needed for use as sleepers across the newly laid tracks. The Grand Trunk Road, which was built through tribal labour, helped in business, and there was an inflow of outsiders adding to the population."[110]

This change in the surroundings affected the tribes in India like never before. Loss of land led to a complete up-rootment of the self sustained economy of the tribal peoples and most of them had no other alternative for sustenance. This led to a number of armed conflicts where the tribals were easily overpowered by the more powerful settlers. There has been loss of tribal life. Instances of death by starvation became a common affair. The tribal peoples had little option left but to start working for the settlers as labourers.

The tribals were also cheated and adversely affected by the non tribal middlemen who operated between the new rulers and the tribals. Stories of exploitation of the tribals by merchants and moneylenders were

---

109 Ramachandra Guha and Madhav Gadgil, "State Forestry and Social Conflict in British India", 123 Past & Present, 150 (1989).

110 R Guha, "An Early Environmental Debate: The Making of the 1878 Forest Act", 27 IESHR 70 (1990).

common. Various literary works of eminent authors depicts the condition of tribal exploitation during this era. The outsiders started grabbing tribal land and property for personal economic gains. The condition of tribals deteriorated and pushed them more into the hills and forests. The cultural position of the tribes changed dramatically during this period as the tribal peoples were forced to take up the cultural practices of the non tribals. The so called and self created upper castes started their exploitation over poor tribals and led to the loss of rich and indigenous cultural features of the tribal peoples. This process is very close to the processes described by M.N. Srinivas in his book on Sanskritization.

Francis Gautier puts it as,

> *"The missionaries arrived in India on the heels of the British. And their first prey were the Adivasis, the tribal peoples who they promptly proceeded to name as the 'original' inhabitants of India, who were colonized by the 'bad' Brahmins, during the mythical Aryan invasion."*[111]

The Christian missionaries also came into the picture with the patronage of the British government. It is during this time the welfare provided by these missionaries in areas like health care, education and support, Christianity spread among the tribals. Christianity was an easy alternative to the caste ridden and complicated Hinduism as it preached less complicated beliefs and rituals and egalitarian principles.

After the Sepoy Mutiny in 1857, Christianity spread rapidly amongst the tribals with the patronage of the Government. In a case study with reference to the tribals of Chotanagpur region, Joseph Bara rightly points out that the Mutiny of 1857 temporarily jolted the official zeal. The specific tribal situation of Chotanagpur made the colonial rulers give the missionaries a signal to go ahead in full swing. This was part of a mission to civilize the most backward populations where the missionaries would prove expedient. Bara gives an instance of how a government official supported the missionary activity. For instance, as Bara points out: [...] Chotanagpur had an extraordinarily zealous official in E. T. Dalton (first as deputy commissioner of Ranchi and then as commissioner of Chotanagpur from 1857 to 1875) at Ranchi. Having realized the need of special treatment of the tribals in the scheme of colonial 'civilization', Dalton acted as a patron of the Mundas and the Oraons, and western education was one of his priorities.... Soon he found in the Christian missionaries, who were fast expanding their operation, a good companion which effectively meant placing the colonial government's educational responsibility on the missionary's shoulder. Thus, the western education and the Christian missionaries became a single vehicle as far as the tribals were concerned.[112]

Mahasweta Devi's novels, which are concerned with tribal history, elucidated that, the missionaries, with the patronage of the government, spread Christianity among the tribals and helped them with health care and education. Unlike Hinduism and Islam, Christianity spread widely in the tribal regions with the patronage of the British government and established a firm footing there. The result was a feeling of discontent and unrest among the tribals.

In 1871, the British Government of India 'notified' certain tribes as 'criminals' and passed the notorious 'Criminal Tribes Act of 1871'. Those who fell into this group, according to the British, were nomadic cattle grazers, wandering singers, acrobats, etc., and also those who resisted the British aggression from time

---

111 Francis Gautier, "Rewriting Indian History, Nalanda Digital Library", available at http://www.naturalresourceshub.org/ (Accessed on August 15, 2015)

112 Ibid

to time. This was done in an effort to subjugate these tribes and bring in larger areas under the British territorial rule.[113]

1.3.2. TRIBAL MOVEMENTS

At this stage, a number of movements took place, the Kherwar movement (1871 -80), the Birsa Munda Movement (1874-1901), the Bhil Rebellion (1879-80), the Sardari Movement (1881-95), the Bastar Uprising (1910-11), and the Tana Bhagat Movement (1920-35) raised voices against the oppression and exploitation by landlords and British rulers on the poor tribals.

The Santhal Insurrection which has a very convincing historical impact took place as a reaction to the atrocities of the non tribals upon the tribals. It all started when some non tribals got hold of santhal land in furtherance of some deal. This led to the payment of rent by the Santhals to the Hindu chiefs. As the Santhal tribals fail to pay the rent due they started losing their lands. Initially, the Santals did not pay much attention to the 'dikus' (aliens), but when their traditional economy was affected to such an extent, they stood against the administrator and the landlord. Around 1885, 'Santhal hul,' broke out. However this insurrection was short lived and the British troops put down the Santhal rebels at ease. Consequently, specific reformative measures in the Damin-i-koh and other crucial parts were taken up by the British. More powers were given to the administrators over tribal land alienation and indebtedness issues. The old rules and regulations gave way to the new policy of the administrators in the Santhal Parganas. The new regulations eroded the authority of the head man leading the Dikus to take up matters arbitrarily and compromised the interest of the tribes in the region. Frequently increase in rents on land holdings without any notice or consultation, imposition of fines on non payment of exorbitant rents was to name a few. The new judicial system also contributed to the destruction of the santhal status to merely serfs.

Such atrocious condition of the Santhals led to their protest in 1871. Two Santal brors, Sido and Kanhu, came to the forefront providing leadership for mass uprisings. Their objective was clearly stated:

> *"we should slay all the Dikus (aliens) and become rulers of ourselves... We should only pay eight annas (fifty paise) for a buffalo plough and four annas for a bullock plough, and if the rulers (both British and Indian aliens) did not agree we should start fighting..."*[114]

Another tribal movement which gained much popularity among the tribals was the Birsa Munda Movement (1874-1901). Ranchi and the Santhal Parganas were in the grip of exploitation in the closing years of the nineteenth century. The domination of the 'dikus' still continued. Around that time the Christian missionaries were also active in this region. There was a feeling of discontent and unrest among the tribals. At this stage Birsa, a Munda youth, organized his people to raise their voice against the oppression and exploitation by the landlords and the Britsh rulers. Today the Munda and other tribes of the Ranchi district hail Birsa as their God. They call him Birsa Bhagwan. Mahasweta Devi's novel, Aranyer Adhikar, is based on this movement. Like the Mundas, the Oraons of this region also launched a powerful movement known as the Tana Bhagat Movement. The Oraons had seen oppression and deprivation at the hands of the local Zamindars and policemen. Jatra Bhagat, an Oraon, proclaimed that he had a vision of Dharmu or God. He had received a revelation for the other fellow Oraons. His message swept over the country, and people from far and near began to come for his darshan. His followers gave up worshipping spirits (ghosts) and

---

113 Mahasweta Devi, "Year of Birth – 1871", available at http://www.indiatogether.org/bhasha/budhan/birth1871.htm (Accessed on December 3, 2015)

114 Quoted in Srivastava 13

stopped animal sacrifice. People gave up non-vegetarian food, wine, tobacco and group songs and dances. They were asked not to pay rent to the Zamindars and not to work for the aliens. Jatra warned his people in strong words that if they did not obey his orders they would soon perish. Acting upon Jatras's advice people began refusing to work for the landlords and disobeyed rules and regulations imposed by the British rulers who in turn issued orders for the arrest of Jatra and his close disciples. Jatra was imprisoned. After completing his term in jail, Jatra lived for a short period. The followers of Jatra are called 'Tana Bhagats' because 'tana' means pulling together. Jatra was trying to pull together all Oraons into his fold. Apart from these movements in the Chotanagpur regions, uprisings also took place in other parts as well. The Bastar Uprisings that took place in Central India in 1910-11 is such an example. The monopoly of the outsiders has been cited as the main reason for this uprising. K. S. Singh quotes a letter sent by B. P Standant, Chief Secretary and the Commisioner for the Central Provinces to the Secretary to the Government of India, Forest Department, Shimla. The letter cites the following reasons: [...] the inclusion in reserves of forest and village lands, highhanded treatment and unjust exactions on the part of Forest Officials, maltreatment of pupils and parents by school masters in order to extort money, forcible collection by school masters of money to purchase supplies for Tahsildar and Inspector, purchase by school masters of supplies at one-fourth of the market price, similar acts by the State Police, with the addition that they exact begar and beat village servants to compel the cheap supply of grain, the demand of excessive begar by the Tahsildar and non-payment for supplies in connection with the camps of officials, the exaction of excessive begar by Malgujars, interference with the rights of manufacturing intoxicating liquor, a practice of officials of getting houses built by begar, even compelling the labourers to feed themselves, exactions by the lessees of villages... and general oppression on the part of officials. The petitioners add that this oppression began with the advent of Rai Bahadur Panda Baijnath, that they had petitioned him without result, and that their present object was merely to ensure that some one should come and hear them. (Qtd. in Singh, Tribal Situations 178-179) Singh further says: It was a total revolt. The outburst was accompanied by murder, arson, looting and general savagery, it was a regular revolt against civilization, against schools, against forest conservancy, against the opening up of the country by Hindu settlers, in short it was a movement of Bastar state for Bastar forest dwellers. (179) It was during the colonial period that the tribals were studied by scholars and designated as 'tribals.' A number of administrators and anthropologists who were engaged in studying the tribes provided classified information about the tribals and their population.

The first Census of India took place in the year 1881. The term used to incorporate the indigenous communities was "forest tribes" and not merely tribes. This was incorporated as a sub-heading under the category of Agricultural and pastoral castes. In the Census Report of 1891, V.A. Bains, the Commissioner of Census, classified the castes according to their traditional occupations. As Verma records:

> *"Under the category of Agricultural and Pastoral castes; he formed a subheading called 'Forest Tribes.' The first nomenclature of the term tribe may be found in the Census of 1901 where these communities are termed freely as hill tribes, primitive tribes, savage tribes, backward tribes etc. In the Census Report of 1901, they were classified as 'Animists'*

> *In the 1911 census, the so called animists in the table for caste and ors have been incorporated by Gait, who was in charge of the 1901 and 1911 census. In 1911 they were termed as 'tribal animists' or people following tribal religion".*

Gaits predecessor Marten, who was in charge of the 1921 census, followed the same pattern to the exception of incorporating "tribal religion" from "animism". The British policy on tribes began with the first census in 1921. In the Census Report of 1921, they were specified as 'Hill and Forest Tribes' and in the 1931 census they are described as Primitive Tribes. The Government of India Act specified them as Backward Tribes.

However, the Census Report of 1941 classified them as 'Tribes' only. Thus, the term 'tribe' was designated by the British for these people.

The distinction on the basis of religion between tribes and other castes ere even carried forward by Hutton even though not very convincingly. The presumption of being a tribe as being an animist was however not the convincing distinction between tribes and castes. Keeping this dis-satisfaction in mind the census keepers they observed that there were difficulties in distinguishing the religion of the tribes from that of the lower strata of the Hindu society.

Keeping these observations in mind, Ghurye (1963:205) went to the extent of observing that the so called aboriginals who form the bulk of the scheduled tribes and who have been designated in the censuses as animists are best described as "backward Hindus".

Historical evidence establishes the existence of tribes or indigenous peoples in the territory of India. However, the term tribe was first used by the British to recognize these uncivilized[115] communities. It was during this time onwards the recognition of the term 'tribes' was officially recorded. Various classifications of tribes were initiated by the British administration to nomenclature these people according to their policies objected towards economic exploitation and territorial expansion. Some of the tribes were referred as primitive tribes, some as backward tribes and some as criminal tribes.

Jagannath Pathy in "The Idea of Tribe in the Indian Scene" tried to identify the term tribe and its origin. He states that before India was colonized, there was no equivalent indigenous word for the English term 'tribe'. The Sanskrit word atavikajana simply denoted an agglomeration of individuals with specific territorial kinship and a cultural pattern. The so-called tribes were called nations and people. The so-called tribals called themselves people and ors as outsiders. It was used to dominate and oppress the people and nations. Another term 'noble savage' was coined to divide the struggling people. The word indicates economic and political relations between the so-called tribal and the civilized capitalist world. It also denotes a special kind of social origin and a stage of evolution in human history. During the colonial expansion, the British faced opposition from non-Aryan and non-Muslim people. At that time

> "tribals were characterized as food gathering communities and animists and shifting cultivators were added to the list of tribes"[116]

It is pertinent here to mention that the line between the tribe and caste is very arbitrary. For people who are classified as tribe in one region are known by caste in other regions. It is worth mentioning the major debates that concern tribal development. K.S. Singh foregrounds the nature of the studies done by the British in this regard. He states: The ethnographers took a placid and synchronic view of tribal society. Their view was inspired by the then model in anthropology. Tribal communities were treated as isolates, tribals as Noble Savages, and their primitive condition was described as a state of Arcadian simplicity. (Singh, "Colonialism" 400) The anthropologists looked at the Sanskritization of tribal chiefs in negative terms and held the view that it was not good for the tribals. They also rationalized and justified the British rule. The administrators however, took a diachronic view of the tribal society and described the pattern of

---

115 Uncivilised, the term was used in rampant to identify the natives, aboriginals and tribals in various countries. Lately, the term has been subjected to debate and criticism as the question was raised as to the authority to determine the features of civilized communities. Currently the meaning of the term in the dictionary has also been changed and is no longer in use to identify these people.

116 Pathy 347

changes in the agrarian system, which suggested that primitive people were not immune to the impact of colonialism. There was a proposal by two administrator-anthropologists, J.P. Mills and G.H Hutton to keep the tribal areas under the direct control of British administration (Singh 1984: 405)3. The nationalists, on the other hand, expressed their apprehension saying that the new Constitution of fully excluded areas was an imperial design to separate the tribals from other communities and thus weaken national unity. The Indian National Congress at its session held at Faizpur felt that "this was yet another attempt to divide the people of India into different groups" (Qtd. in Singh, "Colonialism" 407). The isolationist school of policy makers comprised anthropologists and British members of the I.C.S of which G. H. Hutton was the arch-exponent. However, it was Verrier Elwin who got identified with the isolationist stance in the pamphlet the Loss of Nerve published in 1941. In this pamphlet, he recommended isolation of the tribals and suggested that the administration should be so adjusted as to allow the tribes to lead their life without interference from outside agencies. He said in conclusion: I am not one of those who advocate a policy of absolute isolation, but I do urge a policy of isolation from debasing and impoverishing contact. The aboriginal cannot remain as he is-but is it necessary for him to pass through a long period of degradation before he emerges as the civilized man of the future? Could we not keep him in his innocence and happiness for a while till "civilization" is more worthy to instruct him and until a scientific age has learnt how to bring development and change without causing despair? (Qtd. in Singh, "Colonialism" 408). In another pamphlet, The Aboriginal, Elwin reiterates his thought: I advocate, therefore, for the aboriginals a policy of temporary isolation and protection, and for their civilized neighbors a policy of immediate reform... The essential thing is not to uplift them into a social and economic sphere to which they cannot adapt themselves, but to restore to them the liberties of their own countryside [...] But whatever is done, and I would be the last to lay down a general programme, it must be done with caution and above all with love and reverence. The aboriginals are the real swadeshi products of India, in whose presence everyone is foreign. These are the ancient people with moral claims and rights thousands of years old. They were here first; they should come first in our regard.[117] He was attacked by "A.V. Thakkar, who propagated the idea of assimilation of the tribes instead of isolation" (Guha, "Savaging" 2382).

Elwin later denied having been an isolationist. He explained that his idea was of

> "a temporary isolation for certain small tribes, but this was not to keep them as they were, but because at that time the only contacts they had with the outside world were debasing contacts, leading to economic exploitation and cultural destruction"[118]

He said that he had condemned the policy of isolation. But the confusion arose out of the inept phrase, 'the National Park,' that he coined in the late thirties to underline the need for the protection of the tribes against exploitation. As there were negotiations for transfer of power, the administrators and anthropologists were active to ensure the protection of tribal interests. As Singh mentions: Sir John Hubbock prepared a note on the backward tribes. He was of the opinion that the British interest in tribal affairs should continue even after the transfer of power. Hubbock also suggested the formation of a group of anthropologists, and administrators and missionaries which would do more for the hill tribes than an anthropological dictator of the kind suggested by Elwin. Sir John Hubbock and Sir Kenneth Fitze who had served in Western and Central India showed concern that with the transfer of power the missionaries would not be able to do good work. They were also critical of Elwin's aim to Hinduize the tribes. The Secretary of State was also critical of the isolationist stance. (Singh, "Colonialism" 410) In all these debates tribals were nowhere in

---

117 Quoted in Singh, "Colonialism" 408

118 Elwin, "The Tribal Perspective" available at

http://shodhganga.inflibnet.ac.in:8080/jspui/bitstream/.../14_references.pdf (Visited on August 15, 2015)

the picture. They were the objects of the critical gaze. The Adibasi Mahasabha and its leader Jaipal Singh did not attract any notice. K. S. Singh writes: "Hubbock was of the opinion that Jaipal Singh's influence did not extend beyond the Mundas" ("Colonialism" 412). Thus, the British felt that the tribals were their responsibility and the former formulated policies for the tribals. The principle of partial and full exclusion was later embodied in the Indian Constitution. Constitutional guarantees of protection had to be combined with programmes of rapid development which did not find any place in the colonial framework. After Independence, the government chalked out a number of provisions to safeguard the interests of the tribals and their development without hampering their culture. It is pertinent here to mention Nehru's views on this issue. His policy was to approach tribal life with respect. He said:

> *"The Tribals may be allowed to develop on their own genius and we should not impose anything on them"*[119]

He wanted them to advance, but at the same time not "lose their artistry and joy in life and the future that distinguishes them in many ways" (qtd. in Elwin, "The Tribal Perspective" 220). The Indian Constitution adopted by the Constituent Assembly on 26 January 1950 visualized a policy of progressive acculturation of tribal communities. Thus the former policy of their isolation and segregation was finally abandoned. According to the Constitutional provision certain tribes were listed as Scheduled Tribes and special facilities were to be provided for their uplift and education. The main criteria adopted for specifying certain communities as Scheduled Tribe include, as Verma points out: (i) traditional occupation of a geographical area, (ii) distinctive culture which includes whole spectrum of tribal way of life, i.e. language, customs, traditions, religious beliefs, arts, crafts etc., (iii) primitive traits depicting occupational pattern, economy etc. and (iv) lack of educational and techno-economic development. (Verma 6) There was a suggestion by Jaipal Singh that the term 'adibasi' should be used instead of' Scheduled Tribe' but Dr. Ambedkar, Chairperson, Drafting Committee of the Constitution, said that

> *"the word Adivasi is really a general term which has no specific legal de jure connotation. Whereas, the word 'Scheduled Tribe' has a fixed meaning, because it enumerates the tribes".*[120]

It has to be mentioned here that all aboriginal people are not included in the list of Scheduled Tribes. Verma says that there are about 360 Scheduled Tribes (sub-tribes being many more) speaking more than 100 languages. Tribals have come a long way. Their situation has been changing. With the facilities available to them, their situation is improving to some extent. Some of them are in public positions as doctors, engineers, academics, legislators and so on. They are becoming aware of their reality. Some of them arc engaged in research studying what has been said about them. Therefore one has to be careful in using terminology. The fact that term like 'tribals', 'primitive', 'native' etc. as Edward P. Dozier says,

> *"are often placed within quotation marks and indicate the shaky and unsure ground upon which they rest as designation for the societies which are studied".*[121]

From the foregoing account it seems safe to infer that tribal history is marked by struggle and subjugation by outsiders. These are some of the views available on the tribals from sociological accounts but to complete the picture it would be pertinent to look at a few literary texts in order to know how imaginative perceptions of the tribals have contributed to understanding. These divisions are made by scholars like H.H. Riseley,

---

119 Quoted in Verma

120 (Verma 6)

121 Ibid

B.S.Guha, D.N.Majumdar and ors. The Banjaras are called Lambadas in Andhra Pradesh and Sugali in Karnataka. The British Government decided on a policy of segregating tribes into special areas where their lives and interests would be adequately protected. An Act was passed in 1874 to specify tribal areas into scheduled regions. In 1935 provisions for special treatment of tribal areas were incorporated by constituting partially excluded areas. In the subsequent years up to 1947, a number of acts and regulations were promulgated.[122]

1.4. COLONIAL PERIOD AND TRIBES

The colonial era perhaps has witnessed the worst that has ever happened to tribals in India. Tribals and other indigenous communities of various parts of the world also faced similar situations. The various enactments and systematic destruction of the indigenous functioning of various tribes in India was initiated by the colonial rulers.

1.4.1. COLONIAL PERIOD LAWS AND TRIBALS

Some not so well known groups of people including nomadic cattle grazers, acrobats, wandering singers etc were for the purpose of territorial expansion and administrative policies been declared as Criminal Tribes and an Act was passed in furtherance of such declaration commonly known as the notorious Criminal Tribes Act of 1871. Those groups which resisted the British aggression were also included within this group of criminal tribes. This Act was intended to even incorporate the children and women under its purview. This was done in an effort to subjugate these tribes and bring in larger areas under the British territorial rule.[123] Even after passing of this draconian law, the British administration faced a lot of retaliation in their process of expansion of territories for the purpose of drainage of wealth. Whenever any sacred or heritage place of the tribals have been encroached, the colonial rulers faced retaliation from the tribes causing bloodsheds on either side. This led to the change of strategy of the British administration as they started to camouflage their objective under the garb of developmental projects. "The Thirteenth Schedule to the Govt. of India (Provincial Legislative Assemblies) Order, 1936 specified certain tribes as backward in the then provinces of Assam, Bihar, Orissa, Central Provinces and Berar, Madras and Bombay." A Census was conducted as the first attempt to list 'primitive tribes' in India in 1931. The discriminatory terms such as 'backward' or 'primitive' were 'Eurocentric' and imbibed a cultural bias in its application. Certain so called development schemes were practically imposed upon these communities and on their land. Even studies of the culture of these tribes made it easier for the colonial rulers to formulate their exploitative schemes. Ethnographic studies were conducted for the first time in 1931 to collect cultural profiles of the tribal masses in India.[124] The cultural profiles of the tribes gave valuable information about their, religion, language, geographic habitation, etc. The 1931 Census uses the term 'Hinduised tribes' for Koch, Mech, Poliya, etc. The use of 'Hinduised tribes' signifies the fact that some of the tribes had started worshipping Hindu Gods[125] and were interacting with non-tribes. Likewise, the 1931 Census also used terms such as 'Munda speaking tribes' for those staying in the Chota Nagpur plateau and Santhal Paraganas, 'border tribes' for

---

122 Elwin. op.cit. at p. 25

123 Later in 1952, the Government of India officially "de-notified" the stigmatized ones.

124 Post-independence such studies were resumed in 1961.

125 When asked about their religion, when it was found that some of the traits are common to Hinduism, they were brought under the said religious category even when they were not Hindus in the strict sense of the term. The broad interpretation of Hinduism also was responsible for such assimilation.

tribes in Baluchistan, 'jungle tribes' in Western Ghats or 'forest tribes speaking Dravidian[126] language', and 'hill tribes' for Khonds, Sawaras, etc. This information also played a crucial role in formulating State policies for the British administration and constructing their legal framework with the objective of encroaching upon the tribal land. The classification of tribes made reflected the geographical habitation of tribes. Such geographical locations were primarily forests, hills and certain plateaus. The use of tribes in different ways in the 1931 Census also signifies the geographical habitation of the tribes. Hence, it can be inferred that the tribes were concentrated in the forests, hills and plateau.[127]

The official use of terms such as 'primitive' or 'backward' tribes put forth the necessity of development for the tribes. And the development agenda for the tribes was supplemented by development activities by the European missionaries. Francis Gautier puts it as,

> *"The missionaries arrived in India on the heels of the British. And their first prey was the Adivasis, the tribal peoples who they promptly proceeded to name as the 'original' inhabitants of India, who were colonised by the 'bad' Brahmins, during the mythical Aryan invasion."[128]*

However, the tribes were exposed to education and the outside world through the missionaries.[129] It is during this phase that the tribal religion got diluted as the tribals chose the options available to them in furtherance of their situation. Some converted to Christianity or Hinduism while the ors carried on their tribal religious affairs. Infrastructural development was one of the significant steps towards the transportation of wealth in the form of raw materials from primitive areas to the British Headquarters where the factories were situated to convert them to finished goods and to transport them to various parts of the world. In order to achieve higher goals substantive changes were made to the legal system of the country. In order to acquire land and forest the British passed The Land Acquisition Act, 1897 and The Forest Act, 1978 respectively. The concept of 'patta' was first initiated to create a reservation over the land or inhabiting the forest. The Forest Act, 1878 clearly gave the State authority over the forests for the purpose of protection and reservation of forests and to prohibit or permit shifting cultivation. Moreover,

> *"in the case of a claim to a right in or over any land, other than a right of way or right of pasture, or a right to forest produce or a water-course, the Forest Settlement-officer shall pass an order admitting or rejecting the same in whole or in part".[130]*

This process slowly and steadily infringed the right over forest produce of the tribes which no longer remained within their exclusive domain. The modes of utilization over the land and forest resources vary a lot from the way it was used by the tribals. Mining, deforestation for timber in building roadways and railways created a permanent destruction to the natural environment that was protected by tribal inhabitants for centuries. The Explosives Act, 1884 was enacted to provide exclusive right to use the land for mining and prohibits the free use of the natural resources by the tribes. Special licenses were created for tribals to enter and use certain specified resources upon their own ancestral land. The Explosives Act, 1884 also put restriction on possession, manufacture, transport and importation of substances categorized as 'explosives'.

---

126 The Dravidian language family has two branches. Gondi-Kui and Telugu. Tribes such as Koya, Samantha and Chenchu belongs to this language family

127 Chota Nagpur plateau, Western Ghats, tribal areas in Baluchistan and North-West frontier province

128 Hasnain Nadeem, *Tribal India*, (Palaka Prakashan, Delhi. 1991).

129 It has been a general practice of Christian missionaries all across the globe.

130 Census of India,1931

This Act became very significant in the mining areas which were rich sources of metals and minerals. This act was later used to displace the tribes form their land and resources. The displaced and poor tribals looking for alternative source of sustenance were very easily used by the colonial rulers as cheap and bonded labour for India and other colonial countries. The ever growing exploitation of the tribals led them further up the hills or more into the denser part of the forests to save themselves from the civilized rulers. The British administration was efficient to demarcate the Scheduled Areas for the purpose of administration of tribal inhabited areas. These Scheduled Areas underwent change according to the administration's needs of the Crown. While the Scheduled Districts Act, XIV, 1874 gave more autonomy to the local government, section 52-A(2) of Government of India Act, 1919 curtailed this autonomy since it gave the Governor-General in the Council overriding power. The British had also enacted a few legislations which secured tribal rights only by giving the authority on rights of permission to the district administration.

The Acts were not full-fledged measures and were rather token measures which could be used according to need.

> *"The Bombay Province Land Revenue Code, 1879 prohibited transfer of land from a tribal to a nontribal without the permission of the district collector. In 1901, in Gujarat, some measures of protection were provided (when it formed part of the Bombay Province) by amendment of Section 73-A and 79-A in the Bombay Land Revenue Code, 1879 and a ban on transfer of land of tribes in those scheduled villages in which survey and settlement had not been introduced, without prior permission of the collector. In Bihar, the Chhotanagpur Tenancy Act, 1908 prohibited transfer of lands by sale, etc., except with the sanction of the deputy commissioner."[131]*

By giving the authority to the district collector to prohibit transfer of tribal land into the hands of non-tribes, it limited the scope of right of control over forests of the tribes and gave space to arbitrariness while taking such decisions. The British policies nevertheless officially recognised the tribes and tried to look at tribal life through various studies and missionaries.

1.4.2. POST-COLONIAL PERIOD AND TRIBALS IN INDIA

Even after Independence, interests of the majority took precedence while formulating policies. Though tribal friendly legislations such as Schedules V and VI, etc., were introduced, often the interests of the tribes took a backseat. For instance, The Coal Bearing Areas Act,1957 guards the economic interest of the Central Govt. by giving rights over land containing coal or likely to contain coal to the State while alienating the land rights of the native tribes. Likewise, Entry 56 of the Union List empowers the Central Government to exercise control over regulation and development of inter-State rivers and river valleys. One of the primary consequences of such control is construction of dams to use water resources for commercial as well as domestic purposes. Construction of dams has witnessed large scale displacement of tribes in India. The Land Acquisition Act, 1894 has been used to procure such land, which emphasized on 'pattas' despite the fact that tribal land was common property resource and was not necessarily owned through 'pattas', essentially an individual ownership phenomenon. Such legal measures ignore the economic interests of the tribes. Apart from economic interests of the mainstream society, there have been instances wherein environment interest was given precedence over the tribal rights. The Wildlife Protection Act, 1972 empowers the State to declare a forest area as a sanctuary, national park or closed area and thereby, restricts activities within The Scheduled Districts Act, XIV of 1874 gave special powers to the local Government to specify the enactments supposed to be in force in a specially administered area. Without an enactment by the local government,

---

131 Tribal Land Rights: Myth or Reality, available at http://www.indlaw.com/ActionAid/?Guid=f7ef1f2e-db9c-4327-b648-b43949e9bff4 (Accessed on July 20, 2015)

the acts meant for British India could not be enforced in the Scheduled Districts, which were primarily inhabited by the tribes. Section 52-A(2) of the Government of India Act, 1919 gives the Governor-General in Council the power for special modified administration of various areas, regarded as backward, thereby exempting these areas from administration under the provisions of this Act. For instance, in a declared sanctuary area, the State empowers the collector of the area to acquire land. The collector has the authority to 'proceed to acquire such land or rights, except where by an agreement between the owner of such land or the holder of rights and the Government the owner or holder of such rights has agreed to surrender his rights to the Government, in or over such land, and payment of such compensation, as is provided in the Land Acquisition Act, 1894 (1 of 1894)".[132] Once again the Land Acquisition Act is being used for procuring as well as compensating the land which is insensitive to the rights of the tribes. Further, there was no policy of resettlement and rehabilitation for long after Independence. Yet the State policy has evolved over the years and continues to be so and thereby, strives to address the rights of the vulnerable and the deprived in society. It has acknowledged the need for giving autonomy to the tribal areas, while working towards tribal development. "The Panchsheel of Pandit Jawaharlal Nehru which laid the foundation of State Policy towards tribal development aimed at providing an enabling framework for the tribal peoples to move according to their own genius in a system of self-governance while sharing the benefits of development, retaining the best elements of their tradition, cultural life and ethos."[133] This balanced approach encouraged development while preserving cultural heritage. The Tribal Sub-Plan strategy was introduced for the first time in the Fifth Five Year Plan for the rapid socio-economic development of tribal peoples. And the State or an UT plan undertook the welfare and development measures for tribals, which is called a sub-plan. The benefits given to the tribals and tribal areas of a State or a UT from the TSP are in addition to what percolates from the overall Plan of a State or an UT. At the same time, the Constitutional provisions and protective legislations (reservation in education, employment, legislature, etc.) encouraged active participation of the tribals in mainstream society. These policy measures laid the foundation for subsequent policies for tribal development. The Government made efforts to give autonomy to the tribal areas for better administration. The Fifth and Sixth Schedules of the Constitution define the administration of Scheduled Areas and give the respective State and its Governor the primary responsibility of ensuring so the Fifth Schedule applies to scheduled areas and scheduled tribes in States other than Assam, Tripura, Meghalaya and Mizoram and it made provisions for the Tribal Advisory Council (TAC). The TAC is crucial while implementing any specific State or central Act in a scheduled area.

The Sixth Schedule applies to control and administration of scheduled areas in Assam, Tripura, Meghalaya and Mizoram. The Sixth Schedule introduced the district councils and regional councils for the administration of tribal areas. The district councils gave rise to autonomous district councils later which gave more power in the hands of the local administration. In precise, post-Independence, the State policy was a mix of positive as well as negative measures from the viewpoint of tribal identity and rights.

In the post independence period, the distinctions between tribes and castes have been categorized with much needed clarity.

---

132 Kumar, B.B., *Re-organisation of North-East India,* (Omsons Publications, New Delhi, 1996).

133 National Tribal Policy Draft, Ministry of Tribal Affairs, Govt. of India, New Delhi, July 2006

1.5. CASTE AND TRIBES: RELATIONSHIP[134]

Castes and tribes are assumed to belong to two different set of social organization. Caste being regulated by the hereditary division of labour, hierarchy, the principle of purity and pollution, civic and religious disabilities, etc, and tribes on the other hand are devoid of these attributes suffered by the castes.

The tribes and the castes are being seen to be governed by two different set of principles relating to social organization. It is said that kinship bonds govern tribal society where every member of the community is believed to be equal to the ors. The lineage and clan tend to be the chief unit of ownership as well as of the production and consumption. In contrast, inequality, dependency, and subordination are integral features of caste society. Again the tribes are not so sharply differentiated like that of the castes on the basis of various religions. The next difference lies in psychological disposition of members. The tribals are said to take direct unalloyed satisfaction in the pleasure of the senses, like food, drink, sex, dance and song whereas the caste people maintain certain ambivalence about such pleasures. Tribals again have a homogeneous society and not heterogeneous like the caste people.

1.5.1. CASTES[135]

The Indian society is highly stratified and is divided into castes, scheduled castes, scheduled tribes etc. It should be understood at the outset that our intention is not to give the detailed account of individual castes, their ceremonies, and their machinery for regulating their relation with other castes, nor of their own internal conduct, but to examine caste in terms of Mendelian population groups. Hindu caste system is a highly complex institution, though social institutions resembling caste in one respect or other are not difficult to find elsewhere, but caste as we know it in India, is an exclusively Indian phenomenon. The word 'caste' comes from the Portuguese word 'casta', signifying breed, race or kind. Risley (1915) defines it as "a collection of families or groups of families bearing a common name; claiming a common descent from a mythical ancestor, human or divine; professing to follow the same hereditary calling; and regarded by those who are competent to give an opinion as forming a single homogeneous community' is generally associated with a specific occupation and that a caste is invariably endogamous, but is further divided as a rule, into a smaller of smaller circles each of which is endogamous (this is called Jati), so that a Brahman is not only restricted to marrying another Brahman, but to marrying a women of the same subdivision of Brahmans." The internal exogamous division of the endogamous caste is 'Gotra'. There are several stages of groups and the word 'caste' is applied to groups at any stage. The word 'caste' and 'sub-caste' are not absolute but comparative in significance. The larger group will be called a caste while the smaller group will be called a subcaste. These divisions and subdivisions are introduced on different principles. At theoretical level, Gotra or Got is derived either from the Gotrakara rishis of early Vedic time or from Gotra of some Brahman priests who ministered to a non-Brahman caste. In reality, Gotras are exogamous units of various kinds, territorial, occupational, totemistic and so forth.[136]

The feature of the castes are: hierarchy; endogamy and hypergamy (male of higher caste marrying a female of lower caste) occupational association; consciousness of caste membership and restriction on food, drink

134 Shambhu Prasad Chakrabarty, 'Tribes and Indigenous peoples vis-à-vis the Caste People: A Legal Analysis to Demystify the Two', Nepal Bar Council Law Journal 2014/15, Nepal Bar Council, pp 419-438

135 Ibid

136 M. K. Bhasin, "Genetics of Castes and Tribes of India: Indian Population Milieu", 6(3): International Journal of Human Genetics, 252 (2006).

and smoking; distinction in dress and speech and confirmation to peculiar customs of particular caste; ritual and other privileges and disabilities; caste organization and caste mobility.

The essence of the caste is the arrangement of socio-economic hereditary groups than hierarchy. The popular impression of the hierarchy is derived from the idea of Varna with Brahman at the top and scheduled caste at the bottom. Only the two opposite ends of the hierarchy are relatively fixed, in between and especially in the middle regions, there is considerable room for debate regarding mutual positions. In a dispute over rank each caste would cite as evidence of its superiority the items of its diet, the other caste groups from which it accepted or refused to accept food and water, the ritual it performed and the custom it observed, its traditional privileges and disabilities and the myth of its origin. This fact of mutual position and arguments regarding it permit social mobility in certain areas. Mobility is not a recent phenomenon, but is restricted. All Hindus regard scheduled castes as being at the bottom of the ladder, but the category of scheduled castes is not homogeneous. In each linguistic area there are a few scheduled castes which form a hierarchy.[137]

1.5.2. CLASSIFICATION OF CASTES[138]

Castes may be considered as the biggest curse that Hindu religion brings to its followers. The classification may be stated as follows:

(1) Based on Colour: It is generally believed that in the early Vedic period there were no castes in Punjab. Only the fair skinned invaders called themselves Aryans and they called the dark skinned aborigines as Dasyus, Dasas or Asuras. The term Varna (colour) is often confused with caste (Jati, Jat), though it is far from having the same meaning. The Rig vedic society was divided into four classes on the basis of Varna, hree categories of twice-born (Dvija)—Brahman, Kshatriya and Vaishya, and fourthly the Sudra below whom were the outcastes.

(2) Based on Purushukta: In the Purushukta of the Rig-Veda, there is a mantra interpreted by scholars as such: "The Brahmans were born from the mouth of God, the Kshatriyas from his arms, and the Vaishyas from the thighs and Sudras from his feet." Some people regard this Mantra as the basis of the caste system.

(3) Based on Division of Occupation: After the Aryan invasion into Ganges valley, the stratification in the Indian society began. Social mechanisms were built up in order to carry on the organization of production and supply of services. One such well known mechanism was caste. Caste was not wholly an economic structure. Yet undeniably, it was built up on the basis of monopolistic guilds which were endogamous, each of these guilds grew up into separate caste. Exchange of goods and services was a highly stratified affair and each caste specialized in certain type of industry or delivery of goods. So each unit in the economic structure was virtually a monopoly of one caste and every tribe if possible was brought into more than one caste according to their specialization. Each caste or tribe was allowed to preserve its diverse socio-cultural pattern as long as it did not give rise to conflicts with Brahmanical priesthood. Brahmans were trying for the uniformity of the rites and practices at a community level, local communities were allowed to carry on their modified version at family level. Traditionally, each caste was associated with hereditary occupation and had a limited monopoly over it e.g. Brahmans (priestly and learning); Kshatriyas (warrior and aristocracy); Vaishyas (land owners and traders); and Sudras (crafts and service). It is not true to say that every member of the caste practised the associated occupation exclusively. It can only be said true of castes like Dhobi (washerman) and Kumhar (potter). However, generally speaking most practised agriculture

137 Ibid at pg 253.

138 Supra note 135

along with their traditional occupation. Even agriculture as a single occupation cannot be associated with castes, as agriculture also means number of things: land ownership, tenancy and labour. Often the artisans and servicing castes do not earn enough from traditional occupation, so they augment their income by working as casual labourers or tenants on land. An analysis of the occupational statistics for 84 selected castes in 1931 showed that only 45 per cent of their members were following the traditional occupation.[139]

Occupations practiced by high and low castes are considered high and low, respectively. Manual labour is looked down and certain occupations like swine-herding and butchery are considered to be polluting and low. Castes are governed by their own organization of authority. A greater uniformity has been retained at the economic level of caste than perhaps in relation to customs regulating marriage in particular. Though, there is a wide prevalence of the above model in all parts of non-tribal India, the system of economic inequalities has been encapsulated so to say, in regional moulds.

The Saryuparis of Avadh (Uttar Pradesh), Namboodaris of Kerala, Chitpavans of Maharashtra, Chattopadhayas of Bengal and Iyengars of Tamil Nadu are all Brahman, but these categories are essentially regional. In the same way, the Jats of Haryana, the Bhumiyars of Bihar, the Reddys of Andhra and Vakilagas of Karnataka are cultivating castes, but the regional structure imposes boundaries which are generally recognised especially for inter-marriages. The Chamars of Uttar Pradesh, the Balais of Bengal, the Magirs of Gujarat, the Mahars of Maharashtra, the Malls of Andhra or the Adi-Dravidas of Tamil Nadu are all toiling scheduled castes but they are all highly concentrated in specific regions. It is, therefore, clear that, in spite of its wide prevalence, the caste system is, in many ways, also a regional phenomenon. The status and position of every caste group may be determined on an All India scale of social hierarchy, but the caste group itself, in many important respects is also a regional category.[140]

The concept of tribes in India has been derived from these perceptions developed through research and study of decades by various anthropologists and sociologists from India and abroad. Lately there has been efforts from the tribals themselves to self describe themselves, their features and characteristics. The tribals in their own way and language through their literature through poetry, songs and folklores, political texts articulated their relationship with the larger society. One is stuck by the magnitude of such endogenous effort to define and sustain tribal identity in various ways[141]. One has to visit the exhibitions organized by the tribal peoples themselves covering the entire gamut, their life and culture, in order to understand how they perceive their identity in its multiple forms and project it at various levels and how they are keen to preserve it.[142] This reflection of the tribals may be in furtherance of their effort to reach out to non tribals and the larger society but on their own terms and conditions. This may also be considered to be an effort to adapt with the changing socio-economic scenario of the country.

Parallelly the international community through various conventions has tried to come to a reasonable and logical understanding of the tribals and indigenous communities of the world. The ILO Convention no 189 has played a significant role in identifying the rights and liberties of these communities and provides them a respectable position on the international stage.

---

139 Census of India, 1931, Vol. 1, Part 2, pp. 416-19

140 M. K. Bhasin, 'Genetics of Castes and Tribes of India: Indian Population Milieu', Int J Hum Genet, 6(3): 233-274 (2006) at pg. 259

141 K.S.Singh, The Emerging Tribal Scenario, India International Centre Quarterly p 85

142 Id. at p 86

1.5.3. TRIBAL-CASTE CONTINUUM[143]

To start with, tribes enjoy a class less society unlike that of castes which is the basis of Hinduism.

Tribe and caste are very different from each other from the perspective of their origin. Tribes are unique to the land they have been living for ages. Castes, on the other hand, are necessarily non tribals, and within the religious fold of Hinduism. Tribals have their own distinctive religious affiliation in most cases which is somewhat close to that of nature worship.

Another important aspect of tribes is their nature to be secluded from the world different to theirs which is not so in case of castes. From the purview of language, tribes follow their inherited dialects unlike that of castes. Tribals have been within their land and been enjoying self sustaining economy contrary to the castes who have been subjected only to certain lower category functioning in non tribal society.

One of the common aspects that the tribes and castes share is the need of care and protection of both these communities from the various atrocities being practices against them. Another similarity that has come up of late is that they are interdependent. Another major similarity is the dilution of tribes and castes due to marriage, conversion of tribes to Hinduism etc. it has been noticed of late that the electronic media has played some influential role in conversion of tribes to Hinduism.

Tribals are free to choose any profession or business they want but that is not possible in most cases as caste system specifically identifies people of the religion with certain functioning.

According to Bailey tribe and caste should be viewed as continuum. [144] He seeks to make distinction not in terms of totality of behaviour but in more limited way in relation to the political economic system.[145] Briefly Bailey's argument is that a caste society is hierarchical while a tribal society is segmentary and egalitarian.[146] But in contemporary India both caste and tribe are being merged into a different system which is neither one nor the other.[147]

The ethnographic records establish that the contacts varied from semi-isolation to complete assimilation. Many castes amongst the Hindus have actually emerged out of the tribal stratums. The recent studies of tribes of Himalayan western and middle India have left no doubt that some of the tribes are Hinduized to the extent that they have been assimilated with the different castes at different levels in the caste system.[148]

1.6. TRIBES IN INDIA: CLASSIFICATION

The Anthropological Survey of India under the People of India project has identified approximately 461 tribal communities and 174 of them are sub groups. The entire country has broadly been classified into

---

143 Supra Note 134

144 Tribal-Caste Continuum, available at, http://www.sociologyguide.com/tribal-society/tribal-caste-continuum.php (Accessed on August 15, 2015)

145 Ibid

146 Ibid

147 Ibid

148 Ibid

five tribal regions which are widely spread in terms of population density, level and pace of change and development and social formations including political and agrarian structures. The heterogeneous nature of the tribals in their language, culture and physical features are prominent in these five areas.

- Firstly, the North Eastern Tribal region
- Secondly, the tribal Middle India which stretches from Gujarat to West Bengal across Madhya Pradesh and upper regions of Andhra Pradesh.
- Thirdly, The Southern Pockets comprising of the Nilgiri Hills and other adjoining hilly areas. The homeland of the most backward and isolated tribes of the mainland of the country.
- Fourthly, the North-Western Himalayas incorporating the border areas of Himachal Pradesh and Uttar Pradesh comprising of the poorest and backward and low populated tribes.
- Fifthly, the Andaman and Nicober Islands where there are two groups:

The Onges, Jarawas and the Great Andamanese and

The Great Nicoberese who are the richest of all these groups due to their coconut trade. Amongst them Laccadive, Minicoy and Aminidivi Islands having the largest concentration of tribals with high level of literacy.

1.6.1. TRAITS OF INDIAN TRIBES

India with about 1000 million people has the second largest population in the world and it is one of the world's top twelve mega diversity countries and has vast diversity of human beings, fauna, flora and environmental regimes. Its present population includes stone-age food gatherers, hunters, fisher-folk, shifting cultivators, peasant communities, subsistence agriculturists, nomadic herders, entertainers, as well as those engaged in mechanized and chemicalized agriculture, mechanized fishing, tapping offshore oil and natural gas, running atomic power plants and producing computer software. India has been peopled by human groups carrying a diversity of genes and cultural traits. We have almost all the primary ethnic strains Proto-Australoid, Mediterranean, Mongoloid, Negrito and a number of composite strains. It is homeland of over 4000 Mendelian populations, of which 3700 endogamous groups are structured in the Hindu caste system as 'jatis'. Outside the preview of caste system there are a thousand odd Mendelian populations which are tribal autochthones and religious communities. Like any other plural society, India offers a cauldron where the processes of unification as well as of fragmentalisation are unceasingly taking place. This presents a situation of cultural, biological and environmental richness and diversity, and one where the constant interactions between communities are aiding the formation of bridges, thus creating a sense of unity. It is in these terms that India offers an ideal case for examining unity in diversity both biological and socio-cultural perspectives.[149]

1.6.1.1. DRAVIDIAN

The Mediterranean people form a bulk of the tribal population and are generally known as the Dravidians. These are found in large numbers in various parts of the world including the southern part of India. Because of the typical tongue of the language, which includes Telegu, Tamil, Kannada and Malayalam, are easily noticeable. Apart from the southern part of the country these people are present in some parts of central and eastern India as well. In certain remote places in India a few scheduled tribes are also noticed to be inheriting this language family. They are the Gond tribes and Kurukh. Dravidian language family can also be found in Northern part of Sri Lanka, some parts of Pakistan and Bangladesh as well. In some places

---

149 Supra Note 94 at p 234-235

in Malaysia and Singapore, this language family is fairly visible.[150] It is often considered that Dravidian languages are native to India.[151] This language family has been considered to be present since the second century BC. It has been found that there are only two Dravidian languages, the Bhurui[152] and Dhangar[153], which is not found in India.

Verma says: "Dravidians are again divided into two parts [groups]—Kolarians who speak a dialect called Mundari, and the Dravidians proper".

Historical texts written by various Indian and foreign historians indicates that the Aryan invasion has lead to the end of Dravidian supremacy in India. The conquest[154] resulted to the arrest and practice of slavery over a considerable Dravidian population which was termed as 'Sudras' and the ors fled to the forests and hills to protect them from the invasion. It is considered that the Dravidian communities are the forerunners of various tribes and tribal communities in India.

1.6.1.2. PROTOAUSTRALOID

The term Proto-Australoid was first used by Roland Burrage Dixon, a notable social scientist in his book 'Racial History of Man' which was published in the year 1923. According to him, the Proto-Australoids' were an ancient hunter-gatherer people. They have descended from the first major wave of modern humans to leave Africa estimated by anthropologists and scientists about 50,000 years ago. These people have certain typical features which distinguish them from the ors like their dark skin, curly black hair on their long heads with broad flat noses, typical gracile body, etc.[155]

- Negritos Element[156]

It is generally accepted that the Negritos represent the oldest surviving type of man and it is possible that they even preceded Neanderthal man by whom, according to Grifth-Taylor, they were displaced and disposed. They are considered to be the first inhabitants of South East Asia. These people are present in the southern part of India. Some of the forest tribes found in the higher hills of the southern part of the country are quite similar to some found in certain inaccessible areas of Assam and Bengal. In Myanmar (Burma), they are also found with certain distinctive features like dwarf stature, combined with frizzy hair. It is presumed that this is because of the recent admixture of pure Negritos stock of the Andaman with blood from the main land of India or Myanmar (Burma).[157]

---

150 Barbara A. West, *Encyclopedia of the People of Asia and Oceania*. 713 (Infobase Publishing New York, 2009)

151 Burjor Avari, 'Ancient India: A History of the Indian Sub-Continent from C. 7000 BC to AD 1200,' Routledge Taylor &Francis Group, 2007. p 252

152 Present in Pakistan

153 Present in Nepal

154 It is believed that with the advent of the Aryans, there was a protracted struggle between the Aryans and the Dravidians, then referred to as the 'Dasyus.'

155 Their long heads and broad flat noses are very much like the people of Modern day Africa.

156 The Negritos are several ethnic groups who inhabit isolated parts of Southeast Asia. Their current populations include Andamanese people of the Andaman Islands, Semang people of Malaysia, the Mani of Thailand, and the Aeta, Agta, Ati, and 30 other people of the Philippines.

157 Kashyap et al. (2003)

Research conducted for decades reveals that the aboriginal groups found in the Great Andamanese and Jarawas have distinct genetic identity of the aboriginal populations of the Andaman Islands and other Asian and African populations. Research reports identifies that there is nuclear and mitochondrial DNA diversity in these people. From the said study it may be summed up that:

(i) Either the aboriginals of Andaman are one of the surviving descendents of settlers from an early migration out of Africa who remained in isolation in their habitat in Andaman Islands, or

(ii) They are the descendents of one of the founder populations of modern humans.

Various anthropological studies suggest that the earliest stratum of Indian populations was a long-headed, dark skinned, broad nosed people. Certain physical features of these people matches with the modern aborigines of Chota Nagpur, Central India and the primitive tribes of South India. Many represent these people as the 'Adi' people of India or the original inhabitants. Vedic[158] inscriptions addressed them in its hymns as 'Dasa'[159] or 'Dasyu'[160]. They have been commonly described as 'Anas' as well because of their typical facial and other physical features[161]. These people does not worship Vedic gods. It has been identified that these people were the first barrier to the Aryan speaking tribes when they entered India.[162] It was Lapicque who in the year 1920 used the term Pre-Dravidian to represent these people. Guha (1937) used the term 'Proto-Australoid' to identify the indigenous peoples of India. The nomenclature was created to identify the various racial affinities Indian tribes share with Australian Aboriginals.[163]

1.6.1.3. MONGOLOID ELEMENT

The Mongoloid[164] is the general physical type of some or all of the populations in central, eastern and southeastern part and some northeastern part of Asia. Apart from their presence in Asia they are found in the eastern part of Russia. Mongoloid also has a considerable presence in America, the Pacific Islands and the Arctic. Individuals within these populations are generally found to have certain common phenotypic traits. Some of the prominent common features are epicanthic folds, sinodonty and neoteny. In terms of population worldwide, it is the most widely distributed physical type, constituting over a third of the human species.

The term "mongoloid" was introduced by early ethnologists. The primarily objective of such introduction was to describe various central and East Asian populations. It is considered to be, one of the proposed three major races[165] of humanity. This term was also used by certain anthropologists, scientists and sociologists in the context of criminal justice and in consequence to that the term is now considered derogatory by most anthropologists due to its association with disputed typological models of racial classification.[166]

---

158 Rigveda the oldest sacred texts of the Hindus

159 Barbarians

160 ugly, sub-human

161 'a-nas' = noseless or 'an-as' = without a mouth), Krishnagarba (Dark skinned), 'Mridhravak' (Hostile speech).

162 from Transcapia

163 The Papuas of New Guinea and the Australian aborigines of Oceania are often called Australoids. Perhaps Guha was inspired by this

164 Christopher Beckwith. *Empires of the Silk Road: a History of Central Eurasia from the Bronze Age to the Present.* 58-59 (Princeton University Press, Princeton and Oxford, 2009)

165 Caucasoid, Mongoloid, Negroid

166 Keevak Michael, *Becoming Yellow: A Short History of Racial Thinking,* (Princeton University Press, Princeton, 2011)

In India, the presence of this race is identified in the sub Himalayan region with two major divisions:

    a. The Palaeo Mongoloids: The Palaeo Mongoloids are represented by the tribes living in Assam, Meghalaya, Mizoram, Nagaland and Manipur. and

    b. The Tibeto Mongoloids: The term came into existence with the belief that these people migrated from Tibet. These people have their presence in Sikkim and Arunachal Pradesh.

As already stated the Mongoloids are primarily noticeable in the northern and north eastern zones of the Himalayan ranges, valleys and the eastern frontiers. Regarding the Mongoloid element, Hutton is of the view, that

"It may be said to fringe upon the area to Indo-European languages. There is very considerable overlap in the places. In all the overlapping areas the Indo-European languages are definitely intrusive and the Mongoloid element in the population is strong enough to retain its own languages. It is possible that the extension of Mongoloid physical elements has gone a good deal further than the present range of their language would suggest. One of the Mohenjodaro skulls has been identified as definitely Mongoloid and from the lowest stratum of the excavation have been recovered terracotta figurines with unmistakable Mongoloid features having the typical sloping narrow eyes of caricatures of that type." [167]

On the other hand, Eastern Bengal is strongly suggestive of mixed Mongoloid and Proto Australoid strain. Buxton suggests that the Pareoean element extends to southern India. Burma, of course, is almost completely Mongoloid and though the existence of other strains is not doubted, they are no longer easy to isolate. There are Proto-Australoid elements too. In some of the hill tribes and on the Assam side a Melanesian strain is to be expected. Mongolian features have been observed among the tribes of Central and Eastern India, the tribes occupying the States of Bihar, Orissa, Madhya Pradesh and Andhra Pradesh, in the latter state in areas adjoining Orissa and Madhya Pradesh. The list includes almost important Mundari speaking (Munda Group of Austro-Asiatic Family) tribes like the Munda, Santal, Ho, Juang, Saora, Gadaba etc. and number of Central Indian Dravidian speaking tribes like the Maria, Muria, Kondh, Oraon etc. The occasional presence of Mongolian features among the central and eastern Indian tribal groups foetalized derivative's of Australian types as suggested by Rakshit (1965).

1.6.1.4. CAUCASOID

Caucasian race (also Caucasoid[168] or Europid) has historically been used to describe the physical or biological type of some or all of the populations of Europe, North Africa, the Horn of Africa, Western Asia, Central Asia, and South Asia.[169] The term was used in biological anthropology for many people from these regions, without regard necessarily to skin tone.[170] First introduced in early racial science and anthropometry, the taxonomy has historically been used to denote one of the three proposed major races (Caucasoid, Mongoloid, Negroid)

---

167 Puja Mondal, "Classification of Indian Races – Essay", available at
http://www.yourarticlelibrary.com/sociology/classification-of-indian-races-essay/4007/ (Accessed on December 15, 2015)

168 Supra Note 103 at p 115

169 Carleton Stevens Coon, *The Races of Europe*, pp. 400–401 (The Macmillan Company, New York, 1939).
This third racial zone stretches from Spain across the Straits of Gibraltar to Morocco, and thence along the southern Mediterranean shores into Arabia, East Africa, Mesopotamia, and the Persian highlands; and across Afghanistan into India[...] The Mediterranean racial zone stretches unbroken from Spain across the Straits of Gibraltar to Morocco, and thence eastward to India[...] A branch of it extends far southward on both sides of the Red Sea into southern Arabia, the Ethiopian highlands, and the Horn of Africa.

170 Grolier Incorporated, Encyclopedia Americana, Volume 6, (Grolier Incorporated, 2001), p.85

of humankind.[171] Although its validity and utility are disputed by many anthropologists, Caucasoid as a biological classification remains in use,[172] particularly within the field of forensic anthropology.

A detailed study of the various tribal traits present in India has been made in chapter 3 of this book.

1.6.2. MAJOR LANGUAGE FAMILIES IN INDIA.

Again the Indian tribals belong to all the major language families.

The languages spoken by the people of India belong to the following four language families:
1. The Austro-Asiatic Language Family (Nishada),
2. The Tibeto-Chinese Language Family (Kirata),
3. The Dravidian Language Family (Dravida), and
4. The Indo-European Language Family (Aryan).
5. Andamanese.

1.6.2.1. AUSTRO ASIATIC

The Austroasiatic languages, in recent classifications synonymous with Mon–Khmer,[173] are large language family of continental Southeast Asia, also scattered throughout India, Bangladesh and the southern border of China. The name Austroasiatic comes from the Latin words for "south" and "Asia", hence "South Asia". Of these languages, only Khmer, Vietnamese, and Mon have a long-established recorded history. Vietnamese in Vietnam and Khmer in Cambodia have been designated an official status. The rest of the languages are spoken by minority groups. Ethnologue identifies 168 Austroasiatic languages. These form thirteen established families (plus perhaps Shompen, which is poorly attested, as a fourteenth), which have traditionally been grouped into two, as Mon–Khmer and Munda. However, one recent classification posits three groups (Munda, Nuclear Mon-Khmer and Khasi-Khmuic)[174] while others have abandoned Mon–Khmer as a taxon altogether, making it synonymous with the larger family.[175]

1.6.2.2. TIBETO-BURMAN

The Tibeto-Burman language family is very popular and has been followed by a huge population in and around Tibet and Burma. More than four hundred varieties of this family can be found in practice in these areas. The renound Anthropologist Van Driem suggests that the Sino-Tibetan family should be replaced by the taxonomy of Tibeto-Burman than the existing practice. Pai-lang, is considered to be the oldest attested Tibeto-Burman language of the 3rd century.

---

171 Robert Pickering, *The Use of Forensic Anthropology*, 82 (CRC Press. 2009) available at https://en.wikipedia.org/wiki/Caucasian_race (Accessed on December 15, 2015)

172 Diana B. Smay and George J. Armelagos,
"Galileo Wept: A Critical Assessment of the Use of Race in Forensic Anthropology", 9 Transforming Anthropology, 22 (2000)

173 Bradley (2012) notes, MK in the wider sense including the Munda languages of eastern South Asia is also known as Austroasiatic.

174 Diffloth 2005

175 Sidwell 2009

1.6.2.3. DRAVIDIAN

Dravidian languages are a language family spoken mainly in southern India and in parts of eastern and central India. This is also common in northeastern Sri Lanka, Pakistan, Nepal, Bangladesh, Malaysia and Singapore. The Dravidian languages with the most speakers are Telugu, Tamil, Malayalam, and Kannada. There are also small groups of Dravidian-speaking scheduled tribes, who live beyond the mainstream communities, such as the Kurukh and Gond tribes[176]It is often considered that Dravidian languages are native to India.[177] Epigraphically the Dravidian languages have been attested since the 2nd century BC. Only two Dravidian languages are exclusively spoken outside India, Brahui in Pakistan and Dhangar, a dialect of Kurukh, in Nepal.

1.6.2.4. INDO-ARYAN

Indo-Aryan or Indic people are an ethno-linguistic group referring to the wide collection of people united as native speakers of the Indo-Aryan branch of the Indo-Iranian language family, and is in turn a member of the larger Indo-European language family. Today, there are over one billion native speakers of Indo-Aryan languages, most of them native to South Asia, where they form the majority. The Indo-European family has two language branches known as Eastern Hindi and Chattisgarhi respectively. They are found in India amongst the Baiga people.

1.6.2.5. ANDAMANESE

The Andamanese languages are the indigenous languages of the Andaman Islands, spoken by the Andamanese Negritos. There are two clear families of Andamanese languages, Great Andamanese and Ongan, as well as Sentinelese, which is unknown and therefore at present unclassifiable.[178]

A SUM UP

This chapter identifies and surveys thorough the various interpretations and definitions of the term tribes and finds out the various dimensions of the term tribe. In order to do so, the researcher has undergone various sources to find out these interpretations made by various researchers both in the national and international front. Various researchers have identified various aspects or features of these people.

The features emanated out of these interpretations have been verified to be at par with the features laid down by the United Nations Organization (UNO) in its interpretation of indigenous and tribal peoples.

The study also identifies the reason why the term indigenous has not been used in the Indian context.

The study also reveals the various invasions made by various invaders in India and how these people had been adversely affected.

---

176 Supra Note 99

177 Burjor Avari, *Ancient India: A History of the Indian Sub-Continent from C. 7000 BC to AD 1200*, (Routledge, London, 2007)

178 Blevins Juliette "A Long Lost Sister of Proto-Austronesian? Proto-Ongan, Mother of Jarawa and Onge of the Andaman Islands" 46 (1), Oceanic Linguistics, 154–198, (2007)

The study also reveals the reason behind the current geographical location chosen by the tribes to carry on their livelihood.

The study finds out the logical reasons for the overlapping areas of confusion to indentify who a tribe is.

The study specifically identifies the politics involved in declaring a person or category as tribal. Sad to say, the position of tribals in India is more of politics than of law.

Assimilation of tribals with other non tribals has not been an easy affair. The researcher was astonished to identify the plethora of conflicts between the tribals and non tribals and also the tribals and the government in the study made in this chapter.

The study makes it clear that tribes and castes are not the same even when there are overlapping areas. Caste system is purely a matter integrated with the Hindu religion. Tribals have been converted to various religious affiliations including the Hinduism, Christianity and Islam.

The study also reveals that even when Buddhists and Jains are Hindus and are guided by the Hindu personal law, they are clearly different as they developed and gained popularity because of their anti Hindu principles. It is pertinent to state that there are many tribal in India who has been converted to Buddhism.

Irrespective of assimilation with various other religions, tribals tend to carry on their own distinct features much different from other non tribal communities.

Majority of these people who have been approached by non tribals have been subjected to various acts of atrocities and intolerance.

An analysis of these features and characteristics identifies the crisis created by the absence of a proper definition of the term in the legal parlance which is absent till date.

CHAPTER 2

CIVIL AND ECONOMIC RIGHTS OF TRIBALS: THE INTERNATIONAL PERSPECTIVE

AN OVERVIEW

The majority of world community has respected the rights of indigenous and tribal peoples but at a very later stage. The first instance of such effective effort was shown in the representation of indigenous voice in the League of Nations in the year 1923 by Chief Deskaheh of the Cayuga Nation. However such voice was not recognized as it should have done. But this led the indigenous communities to follow the vision of this great activist and succeeded in carrying on the indigenous movement in the world stage in the years to come.

The first significant step towards the protection of the tribal and indigenous peoples from atrocities and to provide certain rights was the adoption by the General Assembly of the United Nations (UN) the International Labour Organization (ILO) Convention 107.[179] This convention was ratified by India.

It shall be relevant to mention in this regard that the ILO may be considered to be the only organ of the United Nations who has contributed to the highest extent for the protection of the rights of the indigenous and tribal peoples since its inception in the year 1919 as a part of the then League of Nations. It was through the ILO that the discriminatory labour practice has been addressed amongst the independent states relating to indigenous peoples. A significant research work led to the ILO Convention 29[180] which came up in 1930 on labour practice. This is because of the considerable number of labourers being the members of the indigenous communities across the world. A research work took place by the ILO thereafter on indigenous peoples and a comprehensive report was drafted in 1953 entitled "Indigenous peoples: Living and Working Conditions of Aboriginal Populations in Independent Countries"[181].Then comes the ILO Convention 107 with the assimilationist approach with the objective to bring them (the indigenous and tribal peoples) with the larger community of the society with respectable right of self reservation of land resources etc of the indigenous and tribal peoples. However with the passage of time this approach was seen to be of an embarrassment to the UN prompting them to reconsider the ILO 107 to formulate a more updated and comprehensive Convention which led to the development of ILO 169[182].

In the decade of 1970-1980 there has been significant development in the position of indigenous peoples because of the groundbreaking study of the United Nations Special Rapporteur Jose Martinez Cobo. He provided crucial information on the state of these communities across the world to the United Nations.

---

179 C107 - Indigenous and Tribal Populations Convention, 1957 (No. 107)

Convention concerning the Protection and Integration of Indigenous and Other Tribal and Semi-Tribal Populations in Independent Countries (Entry into force: 02 Jun 1959)Adoption: Geneva, 40th ILC session (26 Jun 1957) - Status: Outdated instrument (Technical Convention).

180 C029 - Forced Labour Convention, 1930 (No. 29)

Convention concerning Forced or Compulsory Labour (Entry into force: 01 May 1932) Adoption: Geneva, 14th ILC session (28 Jun 1930) - Status: Up-to-date instrument (Fundamental Convention).

181 Indigenous peoples: Living and Working Conditions of Aboriginal Populations in Independent Countries, available at, http://www.worldcat.org/title/indigenous-people-living-and-working-conditions-of-aboriginal-populations-in-independent-countries/oclc/869643, (Accessed on December 4, 2015).

182 Convention No. 169

Convention No.169 is a legally binding international instrument open to ratification, which deals specifically with the rights of indigenous and tribal peoples. Today, it has been ratified by 20 countries. Once it ratifies the Convention, a country has one year to align legislation, policies and programmes to the Convention before it becomes legally binding. Countries that have ratified the Convention are subject to supervision with regards to its implementation. (http://www.ilo.org/indigenous/Conventions/no169/lang--en/index.htm) (Accessed on December 4, 2015)

In the year 1982 the Working Group on Indigenous populations is formed. This is perhaps the most significant step so far taken by the world community for the protection of *inter alia* civil and economic rights of these communities. The work of this group was to develop international standards on indigenous peoples's rights.

As stated in the going discussion, there has been long standing criticism on the ILO Convention no. 107 as being assimilationist. There was a need for the necessary changes to the said convention and this led to the undated Convention Concerning Indigenous and Tribal peoples in Independent Countries commonly known as ILO Convention 169 in the year 1989.

In the year 1993 the United Nations declared the year as the "International Year of the World's Indigenous peoples". This was done bearing in mind that one of the purposes of the United Nations, as set forth in the Charter, is the achievement of international cooperation in solving international problems of an economic, social, cultural or humanitarian character, and in promoting and encouraging respect for human rights and for fundamental freedoms for all without discrimination as to race, sex, language or religion.[183] The primary purpose of making this as the "International year of the World's Indigenous peoples" is to strengthen the international cooperation for the solution of various problems faced by indigenous communities in areas such as human rights, environment, development, education and health.[184] Recognizing the value and the diversity of the cultures and the forms of social organization of the world's indigenous peoples is also one of the primary objectives of this declaration. One of the primary objective of this declaration was to give recognition to the values and the cultural diversity of the indigenous peoples. It was also worth mentioning that the objectives also included the respect of the diversified forms of social organisation of these people.

On the decision of the United Nations General Assembly, the world celebrates 9th August every year as the International Day of the World's Indigenous peoples. The date marks the day of the first meeting, in 1982, of the UN Working Group on Indigenous Populations of the Sub commission on the Promotion and Protection of Human Rights.[185]

It must be stated in this regard that the indigenous movement was successful to secure their cultural integrity and status through this development and was in the right direction to meet the challenges to come in the twenty-first century. This achieved the much desired objective of initiating a new relationship based on mutual understanding between the States on one hand and the indigenous peoples on the other.[186]

A voluntary fund was created by the UN Secretary General. This fund was to be used for various educational and cultural events. Every member states were invited to contribute fund in this regard in furtherance of the celebrations of the said International Year for the World's Indigenous peoples.[187]

In order to address various issues of indigenous and tribal peoples, the UN Permanent Forum was demanded to be created. The creation of this permanent forum was the subject matter of discussion at Vienna, Austria at the world conference on Human Rights. It shall be prudent in this regard to mention

---

183   UN General Assembly, 85th Plenary Meeting; A/Res/47/75; 14th December 1992

184   Ibid

185   Background, available at, http://www.un.org/en/events/indigenousday/background.shtml (Accessed on August 14, 2015)

186   Who Are The World's Indigenous peoples, available at, http://www.ciesin.org/docs/010-000a/Year_Worlds_Indig.html (Accessed on August 14, 2015)

187   UN General Assembly, 85th Plenary Meeting; A/RES/47/75; 14TH December 1992

in this regard that a similar recommendation was made by the Vienna Declaration. A proposal was given for its establishment within the Decade of the World's Indigenous peoples. A working group was formed and various other meetings took place that led to the establishment of the permanent forum by the UN ECOSOC Resolution 2000/22 on 28 July 2000.

In furtherance of such recommendation as referred above, a Draft Declaration was formulated by the said Working Group on Indigenous peoples.

The year 1994 can be remembered as the initiation of the First International Decade of the World's Indigenous peoples (1995-2004).

2002 was the year that will also remain in the pages of History as for the very first time indigenous peoples, as indigenous-nominated (or government nominated) experts, speak for themselves as full-fledged members of a United Nations body (at the inaugural Session). The primary reason for the establishment of the United Nations Permanent Forum on Indigenous Issues (UNPFII)[188] was to advise Economic and Social Council (ECOSOC)[189] on various aspects of indigenous and tribal population. The issues are mostly concerned with the social and economic development of these people with special reference to Human Rights. After the establishment of UNPFII, another interesting development may be stated to be the announcement in the year 2004, the second International Decade[190] of World's Indigenous peoples.

Ultimately, United Nations Declaration on Rights of Indigenous peoples (UNDRIP)[191] was adopted by the UN General Assembly. The adoption of UNDRIP reinstated the contention and reaffirmation of the commitment of the international community to protect various rights of the indigenous and tribal peoples across the world.

Much water has flown down the river since then and a tremendous development has been seen in the upliftment and preference of the rights and liberties of the indigenous communities across the continents. The international arena has worked together so far in collaboration with the member states to formulate a basic guideline as to the modes of the protection of *inter alia* civil and economic rights of the indigenous peoples of the world in whatever name so called.

2.1. THE CONCEPT OF INDIGENOUS AND TRIBAL PEOPLES UNDER INTERNATIONAL LAW

The term "indigenous peoples" is a common denominator for more than 370 million people, spread across some 90 countries around the world (DESA, 2009: 1). Such diversity made it near impossible to have a unified definition of the term indigenous peoples however, there is also a consensus accepted internationally that a universal definition is neither necessary nor desirable. On the other hand the approach of self identification has been emphasised to identify indigenous peoples and communities. This became the

---

188 The United Nations Permanent Forum on Indigenous Issues (UNPFII) is an advisory body to the Economic and Social Council (ECOSOC), with a mandate to discuss indigenous issues related to economic and social development, culture, the environment, education, health and human rights.

189 ECOSOC is the United Nations platform on economic and social issues.

190 2005-2015.

191 UNDRIPS(Adopted on 13th September 2007)was the outcome of a long struggle and debate on various levels. The outcome was however rewarding.

recommended approach accepted by most indigenous groups across the world. It has been identified that there are more than 5000 indigenous and tribal groups possessing unique distinctive features living on this planet at this day. Their presence can be felt across all geographical locations and all social systems from primitive to ultra modern cities.

Irrespective of the geographic positioning, they can easily be distinguished from others by their distinctive cultural presence with special attachment with their land.

With the advent of western dominance on the planet through the process of colonisation, slowly and steadily the indigenous culture and society started the process of evolution towards westernisation with the initiation of the process of traditional and cultural erosion.

Large scale displacement of tribals started in lieu of the process of developmental projects and industrialisation. With this started the process of resettlement in urban and semi urban areas by these uprooted population which became easy victims of discrimination and exploitation in the hand of non tribals. Lack of state initiative to protect this vulnerable class, instances of atrocities increased leading them to be marginalised amongst all the people of the world.

Those who decided to fight the odds in or around their displaced habitat found their slow and inevitable death due to the absence of their economic system as that was directly related with the land and resources inherent in such land. [192] The one sided battle left the indigenous communities' strangers in their own land and marked as criminals and offenders against the state. Their struggle ended with the loss of lives of their leaders and forced assimilation of the rest in the lower strata of the urban and semi urban societies. There has been evidence of large scale increase in the unskilled labour market due to the continuous and never ending influx of indigenous and tribal peoples from their displaces habitat.

This large scale displacement followed with various instances of atrocities plagued indigenous life and their sustainable economy irretrievably and permanently changed their harmonious and peaceful life of isolation and dignity. In a very short of span of time indigenous peoples across the world became arguably the most vulnerable and disadvantageous group on this planet.

A brief study of such brutality portraits some interesting facts relating to these people.
1. Most of the indigenous and tribal peoples in the world are below the poverty line of their respective countries.
2. The mortality rates in comparison to the non tribals are lesser by more than 10% on an average with a low of 18% which is notices in Russia as of late.
3. Irrecoverable loss of indigenous knowledge and knowhow
4. Massive destruction of natural resources and reduction of forest land at an alarming rate.
5. Massive increase in unemployment across the world.

The process of forced assimilation has certain inherent limitations. Due to the large scale displacement in forest and hilly areas of the planet, there has been a massive increase in the demand of basic facilities in the semi urban and urban areas. This has consequently increased the demand for basic amenities like food, education and housing in these areas.

---

192 How Many Indigenous peoples Are There, And Where Do They Live? Available at, http:// www.NativeNet%gnosys.svle.ma.us@tamvm1.tamu.edu, (Accessed on August 16, 2015)

It can be asserted in this regard that a number of indigenous groups has got extinct and along them their rich cultural heritage.

Under the said situation there has been a growing demand for justice for the indigenous peoples across the world. This ultimately led to the unification of the world community to pass one of the most significant conventions in the form of ILO Convention No. 169.

Convention No. 169 of the International Labour Organization (ILO) provides a set of subjective and objective criteria, which are jointly applied to guide the identification of indigenous peoples[193] in a given country. According to these criteria, indigenous peoples:

a) Identify themselves as indigenous peoples in whatever name so called and to remain so.
b) Indigenous peoples' rights to lands, territories, and resources.
c) Having a special relationship with their land and natural resources.
d) They were descent from populations who inhibited the geographical region at the time of conquest, colonization or establishment of current state boundaries.
e) Have been a history of oppression and ongoing conditions of non-dominance.
f) Retaining their social, economic, political, cultural and customary institutions.
g) Distinguishing social, cultural and economic condition from the broader populace of the country.
h) Having distinctive customs and laws to regulate themselves.

These characteristics immediately underline the importance of land, territories, and resources for indigenous peoples. The territories they have traditionally occupied, and which have shaped their distinct identities, livelihood practices, and knowledge systems, have been submerged into nation-states that often do not respect their customary tenure systems. Thus their history and, in many cases, their current situation is marked by continuous loss of control over lands, territories, and resources. It is this situation of discrimination that the international framework for the recognition of indigenous peoples' rights attempts to remedy.[194]

While the term "indigenous peoples" is the common denominator used in international instruments, these people are often known in national or local contexts by terms such as adivasis, aboriginals, hill tribes, hunter-gatherers, etc., or simply by the name of the specific people.

2.2. INDIGENOUS COMMUNITIES OF THE WORLD

Such is the diversity of indigenous and tribal population across the planet that they can be noticed in almost all countries of the planet. It must be stated that many countries deny the existence of indigenous peoples in that country as they argue that due to the change and evolution these people have undergone, they have lost their tribal and indigenous characteristics which was there before. India, Bangladesh and even Russia stood on this standpoint for a long period of time till they lose their battle to the international acceptance, as if this argument is to be taken then there shall be no indigenous peoples on this planet. Amongst the 5000 strong indigenous and tribal groups consisting of more than 370 million people of this planet, most of them are habituated in over 70 countries.

---

193 The Convention uses the inclusive terminology of "indigenous and tribal peoples" and ascribes the same set of rights to both groups. In Latin America, for example, the term "tribal" has been applied to some Afro- descendant communities.

194 Birgitte Feiring, "Indigenous peoples' Rights to Lands, Territories and Resources" *ILC*, Rome 15 (2013)

The indigenous peoples are distinctly found inter alia in Australia, New Zealand, America, Canada, China, India and Myanmar. This vast population of the tribals and indigenous communities have great variations in their culture, economy and law but they tend to have very similar problems that needed to be addressed in a very practical legal framework.

The indigenous communities can be found in almost all continents of the world. Primarily they have their presence in Asia, Middle East, Africa, North America, Arctic, Latin America and Oceania/Pacific.

2.2.1. LATIN AMERICA

Latin America is a multi–ethnic and multi-cultural region with over 650 indigenous peoples currently recognised by states, over half of whom are settled in tropical forest areas (ECLAC, 2006: 143) In total, they are estimated to number approximately 40 million people (IWGIA[195], undated), constituting numerically small but highly diverse minorities in countries such as Brazil (over 200 distinct groups, totalling approximately 1% of the population) but majority populations in Bolivia and Guatemala. Territorially and demographically, "these people are highly diverse and their socio–political status within the countries they inhabit varies widely. Their common denominator, however, is the structural discrimination they suffer in the form of marginalization, exclusion and poverty" (ECLAC, 2006: 143). According to World Bank figures, 12.76% of the entire American population and approximately 40% of the rural population is indigenous.[196]

Descendants of the populations that inhabited the region prior to the European colonisation form the majority of indigenous population in Latin America. These include, for example, the Quechua and Aymara people of the Andean highlands, the Guaraníes, the various Maya groups in the Meso-American region, the Naua in Mexico, and the Mapuche in the southern part of South America.[197] Further, building on the similarities in terms of cultural features (existence of distinct cultures, knowledge systems, customary law and institutions, attachment to territories) as well as socio-economic and political conditions (widespread poverty and marginalisation, including in terms of participation in decision-making), some Afro-descendant communities are recognised as collective rights-holders with the same rights as other indigenous peoples under national and international law. This, for example, is the case with the Garífuna in the Caribbean region.[198]

The International Work Group for Indigenous Affairs (IWGIA) estimates that there are approximately 200 indigenous groups in isolation in the Americas, numbering approximately 10,000 people[199].These comprise "indigenous peoples or segments of indigenous peoples who do not maintain or have never had regular contacts with the population outside their own group, and who tend to refuse contact with such outside persons"[200]. As noted, "Unlike other rights-holders, indigenous peoples living in isolation by definition cannot advocate for their own rights before national or international forum. Therefore, the protection of their life and culture become particularly relevant for the Inter-American system of human rights".[201]

---

195 The International Work Group for Indigenous Affairs

196 Indigenous peoples In Latin America - A General Overview, available at http://www.iwgia.org/regions/latin-america/indigenous-people-in-latin-america (Accessed on December 4, 2015)

197 Supra note 9 at p.62

198 Ibid

199 IWGIA; 2013: at p. 8

200 Ibid

201 Ibid at p.9

In some parts of the Andean highlands and parts of Central America, indigenous peoples are categorised as campesinos[202]. While this has reference to the sedentary agriculture that is the main livelihood strategy of these communities, the denomination in occupational rather than ethnic terms is largely a result of land reforms that took place in the 1950s and 1960s. For example, in Peru, through the agrarian reform in 1969, the country's semi-feudal system was abolished and large landholdings on the coast and in the highlands were divided up and handed over to indigenous labourers, resulting not only in land reforms but also in citizenship rights[203] While this was a "turning point for wider processes of democratization and recognition of citizenship rights for the deprived rural indigenous population"[204], it also led to the individualisation of land rights and, to some extent, the hiding of ethnic and cultural identity. It is only in the past decade that the campesino communities in some parts of Bolivia and Peru have reframed their struggle with regards to the international instruments for recognition of indigenous peoples' collective rights. Still, for example, the Ministry of Energy and Mines in Peru questions the identity of the Campesinos communities as indigenous, with an intention to limit these communities' rights to consultation and consent (see e.g. CAOI, 2013).[205]

In contrast, most indigenous peoples of the lowlands and forested areas of Latin America are numerically smaller communities of hunters-gatherers and shifting cultivators. They had practically no recognised land rights until the 1980s. When they started making their claims heard, these were from the outset framed by the claim for collective rights to territories. These historical processes provide for highly diverse patterns and trends with regards to recognition of land, territories, and resources in the different countries and eco-regions of Latin America, ranging from individual titling to recognition of territories.[206]

Latin America has witnessed legal progress in regard to Constitutional and legal recognition of rights of indigenous peoples. Fourteen countries in the region have ratified ILO Convention No. 169. Majority of the Latin American countries have enacted legislation to recognise various rights of the indigenous peoples *inter alia* lands, territories, and resources.

Contrary to the declarative and legal achievements of the indigenous social movement, the security of their territory and resources has been affected adversely in recent times. After the recent ratification on the part of Chile and Nicaragua few countries in the region have yet to ratify Convention 169 of the International Labour Organization (ILO). The effective application of some of the rights that emanate from its provisions is, however, postponed.[207] The struggle between the indigenous peoples and the governments regarding the right to be consulted and express their free, prior and informed consent, another manifestation of the right to self-determination, exhibits the gap between the recognition and enforcement of indigenous rights.[208] In Peru, Brazil, Colombia, Nicaragua, Guatemala and other countries, the lack of political will to carry out consultations before initiating large-scale projects with expected impacts has led to a series of conflicts not only with the indigenous peoples, but also with the international institutions in charge of monitoring compliance with human rights.[209]

---

202 campesinos means peasants.

203 CEPES, 2009 at p. 21.

204 Ibid

205 Supra note 9 at p.62

206 Ibid

207 Supra Note 18.

208 Ibid

209 Indigenous peoples in Latin America - a general overview, available at, http://www.iwgia.org/regions/latin-america/indigenous-people-in-latin-america (Accessed on August 15, 2015)

2.2.2. AFRICA

The fifty million indigenous peoples living in Africa are mostly nomadic and semi-nomadic pastoralists and hunter/gatherers who live in situations of marginalization and discrimination.[210] The principles laid down in the ILO 107 and its assimilistic approach has been the general trend in Africa. Irrespective of these hindrances, various indigenous peoples's organization in Africa is trying to open up in their endeavor to make their voice reach the international stage.[211]

As per the conceptualization of the African Commission on Human and People' Rights (ACHPR) and international mechanisms dealing with indigenous peoples' rights, indigenous peoples in Africa live in situations of marginalization and discrimination.[212]

On a report[213] on Indigenous Populations/Communities in Africa issued in 2005, a recommendation was made to make an approach to identify rather than define indigenous peoples. The said report emphasised the following characteristics for identification of African indigenous peoples:
1. Their cultures and ways of life differ considerably from those of the dominant society;
2. Their cultures are under threat, in some cases on the verge of extinction;
3. The survival of their particular way of life depends on access and rights to their traditional land and resources;
4. They often live in inaccessible, geographically isolated regions; and
5. They suffer from political and social marginalisation and are subject to domination and exploitation within national political and economic structures[214].

Practically, in Africa the term "indigenous peoples" is applied mainly to pastoralists and hunter-gatherers. The majority of these communities are Maasai, Ogiek, Turkana, Sengwer, Endorois, Touareg, Samburu, Hadzabe, Mbororo, El Molo, etc. of West and East Africa, the San of Southern Africa, and the Pygmies of the Central African region. Both the pastoralists and hunter-gatherers are non-permanent use and occupation of lands, which have made their traditional lands and territories appear unoccupied to the outsider. This has resulted in a plethora of land related injustices upon them throughout history.

In spite of the contextualisation of the concept provided by the ACHPR, the issue of definition or identification is still ongoing in many African countries. Far from being an academic debate, this has grave consequences in terms of failure to address the desperate situation of many indigenous peoples in the region. On the positive side, there is growing recognition of African hunter-gatherer communities as "indigenous peoples". For example, a survey undertaken by the OHCHR in seven countries in the Central African region shows that there is common acceptance of the existence of indigenous peoples in all the countries concerned (Burundi, Cameroon, Central African Republic, Chad, Gabon, Republic of Congo, Rwanda) (OHCHR, forthcoming).[215]

---

210 Ibid

211 Ibid

212 "Report of the African Commission's Working Group of Experts on Indigenous Populations/Communities". 2005

213 Working Group under the African Commission on Human and People' Rights (ACHPR) 2005

214 Ibid

215 Supra note 9 at p.44

In contrast, the application of the concept to pastoral communities is still disputed by many governments and international agencies. For example, the World Bank remains reluctant to systematically apply its Operational Policy 4.10 to pastoralist communities in Africa. Also, there are differences with regards to the self-identification as "indigenous" of pastoralist people in Africa, depending on the situation and history of a given country and people. For example, while the Mbororo in Cameroon and the Maasai in Tanzania and Kenya identify themselves as indigenous, pastoralists in Benin have not come forward to do the same.[216]

The non-recognition of indigenous peoples in Africa also leads to a lack of specific data on their situation, which again hampers the possibility of devising adequate legislative and policy responses. According to IWGIA (undated) there are approximately 50 million indigenous peoples in Africa and where data is available, often through case studies, it provides a grim picture of their situation, which is frequently characterised by severe poverty, marginalisation, discrimination, and human rights violations (see, for example, ACHPR 2005; ILO and ACHPR, 2009).[217]

The condition of tribal peoples in Africa has gone from bad to worse in the last century. This extreme condition is basically due to bad governance, corruption, impunity, violent conflict and poverty. Because of these situations in the African continent, and indigenous peoples are among the groups suffering the most. It is quite astonishing that most of the African countries have denied recognizing the existence of indigenous peoples. In the last decade, however, this situation is gradually improving and several central African countries now recognize the existence of indigenous peoples in their countries. Countries such as Kenya and Namibia are also gradually become vocal towards the rights of the indigenous communities. However, widespread lack of recognition persists in all other parts of Africa.[218] Compared to other regions of the world, the indigenous movement is very weak in Africa, and the few indigenous organizations which do exist lack the teeth needed in this situation.[219]

Irrespective of international recognition of indigenous peoples's participation in decision making process concerning them, indigenous peoples in Africa are often poorly represented in decision-making bodies at both local and national level and their participation in decision-making processes is nearly negligible. Consequently, the lack of representation and participation doesn't allow indigenous peoples to advocate their cause and determine their own future development. The only existing pan African organization for indigenous peoples in Africa is the "Indigenous peoples of African Coordinating Committee" (IPACC) which has its secretariat in South Africa and which has member organizations from all the regions of Africa.

Because of their colonial past, most African states follow European-oriented modernization and development strategies based on the policy of drainage of wealth and there has been complete disregard to the traditional African indigenous interest.[220]

The main problem faced by indigenous peoples in Africa like most of the other indigenous communities of the world is encroachment over tribal and indigenous land, for instances declaration of national parks and conservation areas, declaring a rich mineral area as reserved for extraction and the like. Consequently, the

---

216 Ibid

217 Ibid at p.45

218 Supra note 30

219 Ibid

220 Ibid

loss of land disturbs the entire socio economic condition of these communities leading to impoverishment and their existence.

The ways of protecting the indigenous peoples through law making has been very far and few. Even it has been notices that the laws have been flouted at will to encourage economic gains. Policies have been compromised and the indigenous peoples been thrown to the brink of extinction.[221] Indigenous peoples have been subjected to severe compromise by the state in many a cases. It has been a regular affair to grant lands and resources belonging to indigenous peoples to non indigenous forces by the state. This joint exploitation has led to violent conflicts. In eastern and western Africa there are numerous violent conflicts between nomadic pastoralists and sedentary farmers as well as inter-community conflicts between pastoralists themselves.[222] Continuing decrease in natural resources and the growth of population has increased the completion over natural resources. On the other hand the climate change has poised even a harder condition for the tribal communities over resources leading to mass displacements, leading to great suffering amongst all the sections of these communities.[223] Another important factor for the growing suffering of tribal peoples is the increase of armed militia groups in clusters causing great loss of ethnicity of these peoples. Another factor of mass violation of human rights of the indigenous peoples is the abuse of military in these areas.[224]

2.2.3. AUSTRALIA (OCEANIA/PACIFIC)

Indigenous peoples have been considered by many as the first people to have been connected with the Australian landscape, including marine and coastal areas. Some estimates maintain that this relationship has endured for at least 40,000 years. There has been many scientific evidence of this in the vast landscape. It was estimated that during the time when the colonial settlers entered Australia, the number of indigenous population may have been up to 1.5 million people.[225]

In June 2011, Indigenous peoples were estimated to make up 3.0% of the Australian population, or 670,000 individuals.[226]

There has been evidence of the existence of human population involving Aboriginal people in all parts of Australia. However, the majority of modern aboriginal people live in regional centres (43%) or cities (32%), although some still live on traditional lands.[227]

The Australian Bureau of Statistics (ABS) Corrective Services report recently noted that the number of Aboriginal men in prison had risen by 8% and women by 12% in the past year, compared to a national prison population increase of 6%. Aboriginal and Torres Strait Islander people now comprise 30% of the prison population.[228]

---

221 Ibid

222 Supra note 18

223 Ibid

224 In countries such as Niger and Burkina Faso the situation is extreme involving organized massacres of entire villages.

225 Indigenous peoples in Australia, available at http://www.iwgia.org/regions/oceaniapacific/australia (Accessed on December 4, 2015)

226 Ibid

227 Ibid

228 Ibid

One of the concerns of indigenous population in Australia relates to their health. Despite recent minor improvements, the health status of Indigenous Australians remains significantly below that of other Australians. Rates of infant mortality among Indigenous Australians remain unacceptably high at 10-15% and life expectancy for Indigenous Australians (59 for males and 65 for females) is 17 years less than that of ors. Recent suicide figures report 105 deaths per 100,000, for Indigenous males between the ages of 25 to 34 years, as compared to 22 deaths per 100,000 for their non-Aboriginal counterparts.[229]

According to the ABS, there were 996 suicides reported across Australia between 2001 and 2010 among Indigenous peoples.[230] 1.6% of all Australians die by suicide but, for Aboriginal people, this rate is more than 4.2%, or one in every 24 Aboriginals or Torres Strait Islanders.[231]

The 1975 Racial Discrimination Act has proved a key law for Aborigines but was overridden without demur by the Howard government in 2007 when introducing the Northern Territory Emergency Intervention (see The Indigenous World, 2008).[232]

States and Territories also have legislative power on rights issues, including Indigenous rights, where they choose to use them and where these do not conflict with national laws. Australia has not ratified ILO Convention 169 but, although it voted against the UN Declaration on the Rights of Indigenous peoples (UNDRIP) in 2007, it went on to endorse it in 2009.[233]

2.2.4. HAWAII (OCEANIA/PACIFIC)

Ka Pae Aina o Hawaii (the Hawaiian Archipelago) is made up of 137 islands, reefs and shoals, stretching 1,523 miles south-east to north-west and consisting of a total land area of approximately 6,425 square miles. Kanaka Maoli, the indigenous peoples of Ka Pae Aina o Hawaii, represents approximately 20% of the total population of 1.2 million.[234]

In 1893, the Government of Hawaii, led by Queen Liliuokalani, was illegally overthrown and a Provisional Government formed without the consent of Kanaka Maoli and in violation of treaties and international law. Since 1959, Hawaii has been a state of the US.[235]

Kanaka Maoli continues to struggle and suffer from the wrongs that were done in the past and continue today. In 2010, the US finally endorsed the UN Declaration on the Rights of Indigenous peoples (UNDRIP). The UNDRIP guides the actions and aspirations of the indigenous peoples of Hawaii, together with local declarations such as the Palapala Paoakalani[236]. The U. S. Census Bureau report 2000 identified around 401,162 people who identified themselves as 'Native Hawaiian". Two-thirds of the said population lives in

---

229 Ibid

230 Supra note 18

231 Ibid

232 Ibid

233 Ibid

234 Indigenous peoples in Hawaii, available at, http://www.iwgia.org/regions/oceaniapacific/hawaii, (Accessed on December 4, 2015)

235 Ibid

236 Ibid

the State of Hawaii while the other one-third is scattered among other states, with a high concentration in California.

2.2.5. BOUGAINVILLE (OCEANIA/PACIFIC)

The history of Bougainville dated back to 28,000 years back when people from New Ireland first settled there. Historians believe that about three to four thousand years ago the Austronesian people entered this landscape with domesticated dogs, chicken and pigs. Scientists also believe that it is during this time when obsidian tools first entered Bougainville.

In 1768 the French explorer arrived and later in 1899 the German claimed this island as their own. The English arrived in the island in 1902.

Under the League of Nations mandate, Australia occupied German New Guinea, including Bougainville, taking it over during World War I.

In 1942 during World War II, Japan invaded the island, but allied forces launched the Bougainville campaign to regain control of the island in 1943. Following the war, Bougainville returned to Australian control. Bougainville became part of an independent Papua New Guinea in 1975.

Civil war broke out, and the independence of Bougainville was declared twice, once in 1975 and once in 1990. Peace talks brokered by New Zealand began in 1997, leading to autonomy for the island.

The colonial history of Bougainville follows the histories of Papua New Guinea (PNG) and the Solomon Islands closely. Geographically and culturally, Bougainville is part of the Solomon Islands chain. Politically, it has been part of PNG, as "North Solomon Province", since the country gained independence from Australia in 1975 and claimed Bougainville.

It has, since 2005, had separate status with an Autonomous Bougainville Government (ABG) although military, external and judicial powers have been reserved by PNG. The first government was established in June 2005 following elections in May 2005 that were overseen by international observers.[237]

The majority of the 175,000 inhabitants of Bougainville (approximately 85%) still survive on subsistence farming. Cocoa and copra are produced for cash cropping. The people live in numerous small, traditional societies and belong to about thirty language groups. Women play strong leadership roles and some degree of customary land rights still exists, supported by ABG policy.[238]

During the first year of Joseph Kabui's term as President of the ABG, several avenues for economic development have been explored, including cruise-line tourism and mining.[239]

---

237 Indigenous peoples in Bougainville, available at, http://www.iwgia.org/regions/oceaniapacific/bougainville, (Accessed on August 16, 2015)

238 Ibid

239 Ibid

2.2.6. ARCTIC

The Arctic region is a vast area with approximately 13.4 million square kilometres of land within the AMAP boundary. [240] This extensive area is home to various groups of indigenous peoples that have a diverse set of cultural and historical background and basis of economy. The indigenous peoples of Alaska include the Inupiat, Yup''ik and the Aleut. The Inuit are considered as indigenous peoples in the Canadian Arctic and Greenland.[241] In Northern Russia there are dozens of indigenous peoples, including the Chukchi, Nivkhi, Saami, Even, Evenk and Nenets. The indigenous peoples in Fennoscandia are the Saami.[242] Out of the total population of 4 million people in the Arctic, only 10 percent are indigenous.[243] The majority of the Arctic people live in communities with more than 5,000 residents. Despite the fact that in most of the Arctic region indigenous peoples have been encouraged to live in fixed settlements, there are still some groups that lead a nomadic way of life (e.g. Nenets in Northern Russia).[244]

Indigenous communities throughout the Arctic face various social problems, a fact which needs to be taken into consideration when studying the impacts of climate change.

Generally speaking, newcomers to the Arctic, usually Europeans, have introduced new lifestyles, culture, educational systems, technology, food and diseases for centuries. Cultural changes, modern transport, western way of living and implementation of state policies have increasingly affected all features of indigenous peoples'' lifestyles at least from the beginning of the 20th century.[245]

Indigenous peoples of the Arctic have to live on ice and have adapted accordingly over centuries. Their history, traditions, economy and lifestyle is uniquely distinct and separate from all other indigenous peoples on the planet. These people are generally used to fishing, hunting, herding, and gathering wild plants. To protect themselves from the harshest of weather conditions they have developed and transmitted their knowhow and traditional knowledge from generations to generations. They learned the skill to hunt on ice and the knowhow to make clothes and travel on ice. Arctic people used to live in small, scattered communities. However with the change in their lifestyle in recent years, most communities are moving towards a modern and bigger settlement.

2.2.7. ASIA

It is estimated that approximately two-third of the worlds indigenous peoples live in Asia, with the majority in India (80-100 million), followed by China (60-80 million) and Indonesia (50-70 million).[246]

There are over 260 million indigenous peoples in Asia and most of them are culturally diverse. Along with this diversity there lies a plethora of problems. Denial of self-determination, loss of control over their land and forests, resources, discrimination, marginalization, heavy assimilation pressure and violent repression

---

240 AMAP, A State of the Arctic Environment Report: *Arctic Pollution Issues* (1997)

241 Nuttal, 2000, p. 377

242 Ibid at p. 2

243 AMAP, *Arctic Pollution Persistent Organic Pollutants, Heavy Metals, Radioactivity, Human Health, Changing Pathways*, (2002)

244 Ibid; AHDR, 2004, pp. 30 - 31

245 AHDR, 2004, p. 49; Nuttall, 2000, pp. 377-378, 405-406; Nuttall, 2002, pp. 53-54

246 Data presented by Asia Indigenous peoples Pact, 2013

by state security forces are a few to note. In Asia they are found in countries like Bangladesh, Burma, Cambodia, China, Nagalim, Nepal, Philippines, Sri Lanka, Taiwan, Thailand, Tibet, India, Indonesia and Vietnam

In India there are 461 ethnic groups which are recognized as Schedule Tribes. The estimated population of scheduled tribes in India is about 8.2 percent of the nation's population which is about 84.3 million.

The estimated tribal groups in India are more than 635 even when they are not officially recognized. The government of India has appreciated the importance of UNDRIP and has voted for it and made it applicable in the Indian Territory. It shall be relevant in this regard to state that the Indian government has not acknowledged the concept of indigenous peoples and instead termed these communities as tribals or adivasis. However it shall be important to state that this deviation from the term indigenous by India in the international sphere is of recent practice. It all started in the year 1984 Working Group when the representative of India has protested the similarity between tribals and the indigenous communities in India. They contended India to be a Melting pot and that there has hardly been any community which still possesses the pristine tribal culture and features. This statement was further uplifted by the Indian representative in the Working Group in the year 1992 when he removed his glasses to show the various traits he possesses in his physical appearances because of inter caste and inter sect marriages. However this opposition was never seen before in India as the word aboriginals were supported by India during the drafting of the ILO Convention 107 in 1957. At this point India had no problems in accepting the notion of tribals in the lines of aboriginals.

Secondly the contention of the Indian representative cannot be taken to the fullest extent as if this demarcation is to be taken into consideration to distinguish indigenous and tribals then there would hardly be any indigenous communities of the world as almost all of these groups have gone through the process of adaptation and there can hardly be any community which has upheld all the features and ethnicity that their ancestors have upheld thousands of years ago.

In July 1992, ILO representatives attended the round table in New Delhi in the presence of the central, state governments, the governmental and nongovernmental organizations. The objective was the utilization of the technical assistance provided by the ILO for various projects in some states of India like Bihar, Orissa etc.[247]

India was able to participate at the ILO Convention 169 because it dealt with both indigenous and tribal populations.[248]

In India the decolonization has two vivid reflections. First, the India that was colonized was never the same after de colonization because of the partition. And secondly, the princely states which have been recognised by the British merged with the rest of India. They were never given an opportunity or a choice to decolonize as an Independent jurisdiction. Thus the minority indigenous population never got any recognition.[249]

---

247 Sanders Douglas, "Indigenous peoples on the International Stage" 43 *Social Action* 6 (1993)

248 Ibid

249 Ibid

2.3. CATEGORIES OF INTERNATIONAL MOVEMENTS

The entire international movements relating to the indigenous communities may be analyzed in the following categories:
1. Directly related to indigenous communities and
2. Other Human Rights instrument of great importance which upholds the rights of these communities.
3. Other conventions affecting the indigenous peoples.

There are primarily three conventions which are directly related to the indigenous peoples:
1. The United Nation Declaration on the Right of Indigenous peoples which was adopted in 2007
2. ILO Convention No. 169 on Indigenous peoples adopted in 1989 and
3. ILO Convention No. 107 of 1957 concerning Indigenous and Tribal Populations

There are primarily seven conventions relating indirectly to Indigenous peoples and is of significant importance to the tribals.
1. International Covenant on Civil and Political Rights which came up in the year 1966
2. International Covenant on Economic, Social and Cultural Rights of 1966
3. International Convention on the Elimination of all forms of Racial Discrimination 1963
4. Convention on the Rights of the Child 1989
5. Convention on the elimination of all Forms of discrimination against Women, 1979
6. Convention against Torture and other Cruel, Inhuman or Degrading treatment or Punishment, 1984
7. Convention on the prevention and Punishment of the Crime of Genocide, 1948

There are two conventions which relate to the tribals and indigenous communities to a considerable extent.
1. Convention on Biological Diversity 1992 and
2. Convention on International Trade in Endangered species of Wild Flora and Fauna, 1975

There is a set of UN Resolutions concerning indigenous and tribal peoples. They are as follows:
1. International Convention on the Elimination of All Forms of Racial Discrimination Committee (ICERD)
2. Committee for economic, Social and Cultural Rights (CESCR)
3. Committee for Civil and Political Rights
4. Permanent Forum on Indigenous Issues

Twelve indigenous peoples' organizations have consultative status with the United Nations Economic and Social Council (ECOSOC).[250] These are: Four Directions Council, Grand Council of the Crees (Quebec), Indian Council of South America, Indian Law Resource Center, Indigenous World Association, International Indian Treaty Council, International Organization of Indigenous Resources Development, Inuit Circumpolar Conference, National Aboriginal and Islander Legal Services Secretariat, National Indian Youth Council, Nordic Saami Council and World Council of Indigenous peoples.[251]

---

250 Who are World's Indigenous peoples? Available at, http://Race.Eserver.Org/Indigenous.Html (Accessed on December 3, 2015)

251 Ibid

The United Nations plays a pivotal role in the protection of indigenous and tribal communities across the world. The United Nations Working Group on Indigenous Populations is the centre of indigenous rights activities within the United Nations system. The Working Group:

a) reviews Government policies covering the protection of the human rights of indigenous peoples;

b) makes recommendations to the United Nations Sub-Commission on Prevention of Discrimination and Protection of Minorities and to the United Nations Commission on Human Rights, which promote action on issues related to indigenous peoples; and is drafting, as part of its mandate to develop international standards concerning the rights of indigenous peoples, a Universal Declaration on the Rights of Indigenous peoples, which is expected to be completed in 1993.[252]

In Latin America and Africa, regional human rights mechanisms have been instrumental in addressing indigenous peoples' rights, particularly to lands and territories. In South-East Asia, the recently adopted Human Rights Declaration of the Association of Southeast Asian Nations (ASEAN) is noted to fall "below international standards on human rights particularly on the duties and responsibilities of states in upholding the universality and non-derogability of and the enjoyment and exercise of human rights by citizens" (AIPP, 2012).

Further, it does not include recognition of indigenous peoples as "distinct from the majority and systematically discriminated and exploited through the non-recognition and violation of [their] collective rights" (AIPP, 2012). Fortunately, while there is no immediate prospect of addressing indigenous peoples' rights through regional mechanisms in Asia, national human rights institutions are increasingly addressing their situation. In Malaysia, for example, the national human rights institution (SUHAKAM) has undertaken a comprehensive national inquiry into the land situation of indigenous peoples.[253]

2.4. RIGHTS OF INDIGENOUS PEOPLES

There has been growing disparity between the indigenous and other communities across the globe in the last few decades. The primary issues that concern indigenous peoples are:

1. land and resources
2. human rights
3. internal colonization
4. self-government
5. self-development
6. environment
7. discrimination
8. health
9. education
10. language
11. cultural survival
12. intellectual property rights
13. social and economic conditions

In almost all parts of the world, there is growing recognition of the importance of protecting indigenous peoples right, as an integral element of the promotion of human rights, democracy, good governance, sustainable development, and environmental protection. This global commitment was clearly expressed in 2007, when

---

252 Supra note 14.

253 Supra note 9 at pg. 31

144 governments voted in favour of the adoption of the UN Declaration on the Rights of Indigenous peoples (UNDRIP)[254]. The African Commission on Human and People' Rights (ACHPR) has also undertaken groundbreaking work to contextualise the concept of indigenous peoples to the African region (see ACHPR, 2005). However, some governments, particularly in parts of Africa and Asia, are still reluctant to acknowledge the existence of indigenous peoples within their states, in yet another denial of these peoples human rights.

Most indigenous peoples have highly specialized land use practices and livelihood strategies, developed over generations and embedded in knowledge and belief systems that are often undocumented and governed by customary institutions that often remain unrecognised. In the midst of the financial, environmental, and climatic crisis facing many countries, there is growing recognition of the contribution of indigenous peoples' traditional knowledge to sustainable development and ecosystem management, biodiversity conservation, and climate change adaptation.[255]

The rights of the indigenous and tribal peoples have been a continuous development rather than recognition by the outside world to these minority sections of the world population. The ever growing struggle of these people has made a dramatic change in the outlook of the way world have recognized them.

A comparative study between the ILO Convention No. 107 and No. 169 depicts the achievement of the indigenous movement. The UNDRIPS and its acceptance by various countries have even strengthen the position of these communities in their respective countries. However there has been shortfall in the protection of the rights of these people in a number of cases. Even the language in which the ILO Convention No. 169 has been written has the capacity of dual interpretation.

In the light of such vulnerability, some of the rights of the indigenous peoples may be discussed and analyzed in some details for a better understanding of the position of tribals and indigenous peoples of the world. These rights are needed for the basic sustenance of tribal life. Various international agreements have been drawn in this regard both formally and informally. These rights have been the integral part of tribal and indigenous peoples life.

2.4.1. LAND AND RESOURCES

Indigenous peoples see themselves as the legitimate claimants to their territories and natural resources, and consider control over local economy, social planning, land use and taxation essential to their existence.[256] Thus they are seeking greater degrees of autonomy and self-rule.[257] The lives of the 50 million indigenous peoples who inhabit the world's tropical rainforests are threatened by deforestation.[258] But while indigenous peoples are on the frontlines of environmental degradation, they also have a vital role to play in environmental protection. For centuries, they have engaged in sustainable land management and land-use in the areas in which they live.[259]

---

254 The United Nations Declaration on the Rights of Indigenous peoples was adopted by the United Nations General Assembly on 13 September 2007 with 144 votes in favour, 11 abstentions and four States against (Australia, Canada, New Zealand and the United States of America). Later, other states including the four who opposed it endorsed the said Declaration.

255 Supra note 9 at p.15.

256 Supra note 71.

257 Supra note 14.

258 Supra note 71.

259 Ibid

Various international conventions have acknowledged the role of land in the life and sustenance of indigenous communities of the world and how such communities have erodes, their sustainability have been destroyed due to encroaching of their land by the state and non state entities for various so called developmental projects etc. Land has been the heart of every indigenous community and has been the sole provider of tribal welfare in terms of their economy and social solidarity. The entire resources arising of the land has been the backbone of tribal and indigenous economy and sustenance. A study of various international instruments also indicates the acceptance of this right in more way than one. The ILO while drafting the Convention No. 107 in 1957 addressed the land right of the indigenous peoples in Part II of the said Convention vide Articles 11 to 14. Article 11 uplifts the right of ownership of the members of the population concerned either individual or collective, which these populations traditionally occupy.[260] Article 12 of the said Convention states the right of these people from being removed without their free consent from their habitual territories except for certain specified reasons. In such specified exceptional circumstances where removal of these people are made, just and equitable compensation has been recommended in terms of land or in some cases money.[261] Prohibitions and restrictions have been made in case of transfer of such land to other members of non tribal communities.[262] Article 14 of the Convention seeks for National Agrarian programmes which shall secure these people treatment equivalent to that accorded to other sections of the national community.[263]

Article 13 to 19 of the ILO Convention No. 169 provides the right to land and resources to the indigenous and tribal communities. Article 13 has been divided into two clauses. Clause 1 states that in applying the provisions of this Part of the Convention that is Part II which deals with land, the governments shall respect the special importance for the cultures and spiritual values of the people concerned of their relationships with the lands or territories, or both as applicable, which they occupy or otherwise use, and in particular the collective aspects of this relationship.

Clause 2 of the article interprets the term land used in Articles 15 and 16 to include the concept of territories, which covers the total environment of the areas which the people concerned, occupy or otherwise use.

Article 14 is divided into three clauses. Clause 1 declares that the right to ownership and possession of the people concerned over the land which they traditionally occupy shall be recognized. Additionally, measures must be taken in appropriate cases to safeguard the right of the people concerned to use lands not exclusively occupied by them, but to which they have traditionally had access for their subsistence and traditional activities. The provision further states that particular attention shall be paid to the situation of nomadic people and shifting cultivators in this respect.

Clause 2 of the article directs the concerned Governments to take necessary steps to identify such lands which these people traditionally occupy and also to guarantee effective protection of their rights of ownership and possession.

Clause 3 directs the governments to take adequate steps to incorporate the procedures in this regard in their respective national legal system in furtherance of resolving land claims by the people concerned.

---

260 Article 11 of the Convention concerning the Protection and Integration of Indigenous and other Tribal and Semi-Tribal Populations in Independent Countries (No. 107) (Entered into force: 02:06:1959; Date of adoption: 26:06:1957)

261 Ibid at Article. 12.

262 Ibid at Article. 13.

263 Ibid at Article. 14

Article 15 is divided into two clauses. Clause 1 states that the rights of the people concerned to the natural resources pertaining to their lands shall be specially safeguarded. These rights include the right of these people to participate in the use, management and conservation of these resources. The participation of the indigenous peoples in these activities was unprecedented and this article may be considered to be a very significant step in furtherance of providing significant rights relating to land and resources to these people.

Clause 2 states that in those cases in which the State retains the ownership of mineral or sub-surface resources or rights to other resources pertaining to lands, governments shall establish or maintain procedures through which they shall consult these people, with a view to ascertaining whether and to what degree their interests would be prejudiced, before undertaking or permitting any programmes for the exploration or exploitation of such resources pertaining to their lands. The people concerned shall wherever possible participate in the benefits of such activities, and shall receive fair compensation for any damages which they may sustain as a result of such activities.

Right not to be removed from the land which they occupy have been provided in Article 16 of the Convention. The provision also provides the right to relocation with appropriate representation in the decision making process. The right to return is also very much there in the said provision in case of secession of the ground for relocation.[264] In case where such return is not possible the said Article provides monetary compensation to the community thus relocated.[265] In case of any loss or injury occasioned due to relocation, the indigenous and tribal peoples are also entitled to compensation.[266]

UNDRIPS has been the next step in the movement of indigenous rights globally. In the year 2007, the UNDRIPS laid down the right of indigenous and tribal peoples in respect of their land. Article 10 states that Indigenous peoples shall not be forcibly removed from their lands or territories. No relocation shall take place without the free, prior and informed consent of the indigenous peoples concerned and after agreement on just and fair compensation and, where possible, with the option of return. This provision is to be read with the right to remedy in case of violation of this specific right which has been also provided in the said Declaration. The mechanism set out in the Convention No. 169 for effective redress can also be taken into consideration.

Nature and scope of indigenous peoples' right to land, territories, and resources UNDRIP and ILO Convention No. 169 enshrine a series of fundamental principles to determine the scope of indigenous peoples' rights to lands, territories, and natural resources, as follows.

The concept of territories[267]:

Indigenous peoples do not have rights only to the land they directly cultivate or inhabit, but to the broader territory, encompassing the total environments of the areas which they occupy or otherwise use, inclusive of natural resources, rivers, lakes, and coasts. Their rights to land and natural resources require special attention, as these are fundamental to securing the broader set of rights related to self-management and the right to determine their own priorities for development.

---

264 Article 16 clause 2 and 3 of ILO 169.

265 Ibid at clause 4.

266 Ibid at clause 5.

267 UNDRIP art. 26; C169 art. 13.2.

Collective rights[268]

The rights of indigenous and tribal peoples are both individual and collective in nature. In other words they have rights to enjoy the land and resources individually as well as jointly with other members of the community. The ways by which these people enjoy their land is customary in nature. This includes certain collective aspects like the right to self determination, right against discrimination etc. These collective rights reflect cultural integrity and development as distinct people.

Traditional occupation, ownership, or use[269]

Indigenous peoples are considered to be the traditional owner, occupier and user of their land and resources and thus "the traditional occupation and use which is the basis for establishing indigenous peoples' land rights, and not the eventual official recognition or registration of that ownership"[270].

Natural resources pertaining to their lands[271]

Indigenous peoples have rights to the natural resources of their territories, including the right to own, use, develop, and control these resources. As a basic principle, "these resources comprise both renewable and non-renewable resources such as timber, fish, water, sand and minerals"[272]. In cases where states retain ownership over mineral and sub-surface resources, Convention No. 169 (article 15.2) stipulates that indigenous peoples have rights regarding consultation, consent, and participation in the benefits of resource exploitation, as well as compensation for damages resulting from such exploitation.

Lands not exclusively occupied by indigenous peoples[273] Many indigenous peoples have traditionally had access to and used lands, territories, or resources that are also used by other communities or population groups. The ILO elaborates: "This is especially the case with grazing lands, hunting, fishing and gathering areas and forests, which may be used by nomadic pastoralists, hunters or shifting cultivators on a rotational or seasonal basis. In other cases, certain communities may have rights to certain types of resources within a shared territory, as they have developed complementary livelihood strategies. Also such non-exclusive land rights are established on the basis of traditional occupation" (ILO, 2009: 95).

Cross-border contacts and co-operation[274] Due to processes of conquest, colonization, or establishment of state boundaries, many indigenous peoples have been involuntarily separated by state borders that run across their territories and hamper contact. States should engage in international agreements to facilitate contact and cooperation.

---

268 UNDRIP preamble, art. 25; C169 art. 13.1; C107, Art. 11.

269 UNDRIP art. 25, 26.1, 26.2; C169 art. 14.1; C107 art. 11.

270 ILO, 2013: 21

271 UNDRIP art. 26; C169 art. 15.1.

272 ILO, 2009: 107

273 C169 art. 14.

274 UNDRIP art. 36; C169 art. 32

2.4.2. CULTURE, RELIGION AND LANGUAGE

Indigenous peoples are identified through their culture. Every aspect of their life is guided by their unique culture. Various aspect of their life is controlled and guided by their customs and cultural diversity. Their art, dresses, lifestyle reflects their culture which they have been carried on through ages. Various artefacts symbolises the distinct indigenous traits. The high quality of indigenous artworks and cultural artefacts generates great demand for them. However, theft and unauthorized sale of indigenous items robs the creators of both money and their cultural patrimony. Thus indigenous peoples are looking to secure the right to their cultural property.[275]

Without a doubt, UNDRIP is a milestone of indigenous empowerment.[276] Still, legally speaking, United Nations declarations, like almost any other resolution by the General Assembly, are of a mere hortatory nature: they are characterized as 'recommendations' without legally binding character.[277] Even when 'declarations' are not binding upon the member states, greater authority of declarations have been the subject matter of demand in the international forum. In 1962, the Office of Legal Affairs of the United Nations, upon request by the Commission on Human Rights, clarified that '[i]n United Nations practice, a "declaration" is a formal and solemn instrument . . . resorted to only in very rare cases relating to matters of major and lasting importance where maximum compliance is expected'.[278]

To the outside world, and oftentimes also within indigenous communities, indigenous peoples' cultural distinctiveness is considered to be one of their defining features.[279] Giving expression to the right to cultural equality, the Declaration contains numerous provisions to protect against discriminatory and adverse treatment on cultural grounds as well as positive measures to support indigenous peoples cultures.[280] These include their right not to be subjected to assimilation or destruction of their culture; the right to practise and revitalize their cultural traditions and customs, to teach their cultural mores, and to the repatriation of human remains; and the right to "maintain, control, protect and develop" their cultural heritage, traditional knowledge and traditional cultural expressions.[281] Given the centrality of culture to many indigenous peoples' identity, the Declaration also recognizes the right of indigenous individuals to belong to an indigenous community or nation in accordance with their community or nation's traditions and customs.[282]

The most important aspect of every tribal population is their distinct culture. Their unique religious belief and their mode of communication make them one of their kinds. The UNDRIPS has recognised this and provides a set of provisions to protect the rights of these people. Part II and III of the UNDRIPS which comprises of Articles 8 to 10 and 11 to 17 respectively dedicates themselves to provide the necessary rights to indigenous and tribal peoples.

---

275 NativeNet%gnosys.svle.ma.us@tamvm1.tamu.edu

276 Anaya and Wiessner, Supra note 1

277 UN Charter, Arts 10, 11. The one formal exception, referring to budget allocations to member states (Art. 17(2) UN Charter) does not apply here

278 Economic and Social Council, Report of the Commission on Human Rights (E/3616/Rev. l), (Mar-Apr. 1962)

279 http://www.ohchr.org/Documents/Publications/fs9Rev.2.pdf at pg 7

280 Ibid

281 Ibid

282 Ibid

Rights not to be subjected to forced assimilation or destruction of their culture has been recognised and has been incorporated in Article 8 of the Declaration. Apart from providing this right the Declaration provides direction to the concerned States to take effective action to prevent such deprivation or to harm their integrity as distinct people.[283] Irrespective of the said protection there has been a systematic violation of rights in all tribal populated areas.

Right to belong to a distinct community is yet another basic rights that makes the tribal life more fulfilling has been recognised in UNDRIPS in Article 9. The said Article also provides the right to exercise their traditions and customs in furtherance of their right to belong to such indigenous community or nation.[284] Land rights are yet another integral part to enjoy and exercise cultural rights which have been continuing for ages. Thus rights not to be removed from their ancestral lands have been incorporated in Article 10 of the Declaration.[285] The tribals have their own and unique right to maintain, protect and develop their cultures. They must have the right to practice and revitalize their cultural traditions and customs.[286] This right was objected to help them retain their society at large.

Right to manifest, practise, develop and teach their spiritual and religious traditions, customs and ceremonies; the right to maintain, protect, and have access in privacy to their religious and cultural sites; the right to the use and control of their ceremonial objects; and the right to the repatriation of their human remains are some of the basic cultural rights required for a simple tribal life.[287] The rights to revitalize, use, develop and transmit to future generations their histories, languages, oral traditions, philosophies, writing systems and literatures, and to designate and retain their own names for communities, places and persons are some very important rights of the tribals and indigenous peoples which has got its due recognition.[288] Absences of these rights in many cases have proved fatal leading to conflicts.

---

283 UNDRIPS Article 8. 1. Indigenous peoples and individuals have the right not to be subjected to forced assimilation or destruction of their culture. 2. States shall provide effective mechanisms for prevention of, and redress for: (a) Any action which has the aim or effect of depriving them of their integrity as distinct people, or of their cultural values or ethnic identities; (b) Any action which has the aim or effect of dispossessing them of their lands, territories or resources; (c) Any form of forced population transfer which has the aim or effect of violating or undermining any of their rights; (d) Any form of forced assimilation or integration; (e) Any form of propaganda designed to promote or incite racial or ethnic discrimination directed against them.

284 Ibid at Article 9 Indigenous peoples and individuals have the right to belong to an indigenous community or nation, in accordance with the traditions and customs of the community or nation concerned. No discrimination of any kind may arise from the exercise of such a right.

285 Article 10 Indigenous peoples shall not be forcibly removed from their lands or territories. No relocation shall take place without the free, prior and informed consent of the indigenous peoples concerned and after agreement on just and fair compensation and, where possible, with the option of return.

286 Ibid at Article 11 1. Indigenous peoples have the right to practise and revitalize their cultural traditions and customs. This includes the right to maintain, protect and develop the past, present and future manifestations of their cultures, such as archaeological and historical sites, artefacts, designs, ceremonies, technologies and visual and performing arts and literature. 2. States shall provide redress through effective mechanisms, which may include restitution, developed in conjunction with indigenous peoples, with respect to their cultural, intellectual, religious and spiritual property taken without their free, prior and informed consent or in violation of their laws, traditions and customs.

287 Ibid at Article 12 Clause 1

288 Ibid at Aricle 13 clause 1.

Education has been one of the significant rights of the tribals that too in their own language. In order to provide this right to the indigenous and tribal peoples ILO Convention No. 107[289] and 169 as well as the UNDRIPS has made relevant provisions. The ILO Convention No 107 was assimilate in nature and was subsequently replaced by ILO 169. Part VI of the Convention deals with the educational rights of the indigenous and tribal peoples. Education of these communities must be in furtherance of their own history, culture their traditional knowledge, their techniques their value systems and their future goals in furtherance of their social, economic and cultural aspirations.[290]

Children must be taught the language of the ancestors for continuation of the distinct mode of communication exclusive to the community. This will help them to carry on the unique war of developing their medium of communication and plays a very significant role in their community.[291] The UNDRIPS has in explicit language upheld this right of these people in Article 14. It states that Indigenous peoples have the right to establish and control their educational systems and institutions providing education in their own languages, in a manner appropriate to their cultural methods of teaching and learning. It further states that, Indigenous individuals, particularly children, have the right to all levels and forms of education of the State without discrimination. States shall, in conjunction with indigenous peoples, take effective measures, in order for indigenous individuals, particularly children, including those living outside their communities,[292] to have access, when possible, to an education in their own culture and provided in their own language.[293] Importance of mother tongue as the means of imparting education to children of these communities has been one of the significant rights provided by ILO Convention No 107.[294] The imparting of general knowledge and skill that is necessary for proper participation in their own community shall be the objective of education of tribal children.[295] It shall be relevant in this regard that the government must adopt measures appropriate to the traditions and cultures of the people concerned. Also to make known to them their rights and duties amongst other things.[296]

Indigenous peoples have the right to the dignity and diversity of their cultures, traditions, histories and aspirations. These attributes must be reflected in education and public information.[297] Indigenous peoples have the right to establish their own media in their own languages and to have access to all forms of non-indigenous media without discrimination.[298] States shall take effective measures to ensure that State-owned media duly reflect indigenous cultural diversity. States, without prejudice to ensuring full freedom of expression, should encourage privately owned media to adequately reflect indigenous cultural diversity.[299]

---

289 Article 21 of ILO Convention No. 107 states that measures shall be taken to ensure that members of the populations concerned have the opportunity to acquire education at all levels on an equal footing with the rest of the national community.

290 ILO 169 at Article 27 clause 1.

291 Ibid at Article 28 clause 1.

292 http://www.zulunation.com/all-laws/ (Accessed on December 3, 2015)

293 UNDRIPS Article 14 clause 2 and 3

294 ILO 107 at Article 23

295 ILO 169 at Article 29

296 Ibid at Article 30

297 UNDRIPS at Article 15 clause 1

298 Ibid at Article 16 clause

299 Ibid at clause 2

2.4.3. CITIZENSHIP

Citizenship rights reflect the status of a person recognized by law as being a member of a state. This vesting of citizenship rights imposes a plethora of responsibilities upon the granting states upon the citizen. The concept of citizenship is of recent origin if compared to the existence of indigenous and tribal communities present in various parts of the world. The modern division of state is more of politics than of any other thing. And the problem that many indigenous and tribal communities face is that they are in a position of multiple or dual statehood. At times they are even in the position of enclaves. At times the indigenous and tribes find themselves in a stateless position bereft of any citizenship. Access to state protection in the time of need becomes a subject of debate and deprival. Gross human rights violation of these vulnerable sections of the society follows. Indigenous and tribal peoples must not be in a position of subalterns. Every indigenous and tribal peoples must have all the basic rights that are conferred upon a citizen of a country. Certain special measures in terms of providing certain rights must also be provided to them for their survival. However, conferring such special measures taken by the state must not in any way prejudices the citizenship rights of these people. Thus discrimination must not be exercised against these communities as they are also equally entitled to all the other benefits that are available to another non tribal or indigenous person.[300] The incorporation of certain measures to protect these people shall also not lead to any hindrance to their enjoying any right of a common citizen.[301] The UNDRIP also in Part I of the Declaration clearly provides the right to be free of discrimination. In other words, the state governments must ensure that indigenous peoples are treated the same way as ors, irrespective of any variation.[302] Indigenous peoples have a right to be citizens of the country in which they live.[303] Irrespective of such international instruments recognizing the citizenship rights of these communities, a major section of these vulnerable people suffer various discrimination by the non tribal communities. Even at times the domestic laws fail to provide certain basic rights to these people. It has been a matter of disgrace that states at times intentionally does not accept the basic rights of the indigenous peoples.

2.4.4. SELF DETERMINATION

Self identification as indigenous or tribal is one of the fundamental criteria for determining the group he belongs.[304] The self identification process is however not very simple and it has been a matter of debate for its political use. In certain countries, these communities have not come forward to bring them under certain conventions. Again in some countries, the government has not recognised some of these communities as indigenous or tribals. For example Russia has not recognised a large part of their indigenous community neither did India and Bangladesh amongst many ors.

The United Nations General Assembly has affirmed that indigenous peoples have the right to self-determination. Consequent to the adoption of the Declaration, the indigenous and tribal peoples have the right to freely determine their political status and freely pursue their economic, social and cultural development.[305] Self-determination is considered by the indigenous peoples as a central right recognized

---

300 ILO 169 at Article 4 clause 3.

301 ILO 107 at Article 3 clause 3.

302 UNDRIP at Article 4

303 Ibid at Article 33.

304 ILO 169 at Article 1 clause 2.

305 Article 3 of UNDRIP and Article 1 of the International Covenant on Civil and Political Rights and the International Covenant on Economic, Social and Cultural Rights.

at the international level. The right to self determination actually brings with it a host of other rights with it which is equally important for these communities. As the rights conferred by the Declaration is interrelated and interwoven, the right of self determination also gets a parallel status to other rights. Thus the interpretation of the rights of indigenous and tribal peoples should also be made from the perspective of self determination of these communities. In relation to indigenous peoples right to autonomy or self-government, the declaration states: "indigenous peoples, in exercising their right to self-determination, have the right to autonomy or self-government in matters relating to their internal and local affairs, as well as ways and means for financing their autonomous functions."[306] As far as the right to autonomy, indigenous peoples have the right, to "promote, develop and maintain their institutional structures and their distinctive customs, spirituality, traditions, procedures, practices and, in the cases where they exist, juridical systems or customs ...."[307]

There is a close nexus between the right to self-determination and the political rights of the Indigenous and tribal peoples. These include their right to participate in decision-making in matters that would affect their rights. It also creates the duties on the States to consult and cooperate with them to obtain their free, prior and informed consent before adopting and implementing legislative or administrative measures that may affect them. The right that comes with the right of self determination is the right to participate through their own respective institutions.[308] A proper and systematic strategy is needed to be developed in almost all tribal populated countries.

The United Nations Expert Mechanism on the Rights of Indigenous peoples undertook a detailed study of indigenous peoples and the right to participate in decision-making from 2009 to 2011 and the Special Rapporteur on the rights of indigenous peoples has focused on indigenous peoples' participation rights in reports on both thematic issues and country issues. The work of the Expert Mechanism and the Special Rapporteur reinforces the growing jurisprudence on the topic by, for example, the Human Rights Committee and the Inter-American Court and Commission on Human Rights. Consistent themes in this evolving understanding of indigenous peoples' participation 6 rights are that their consent must be sought for activities that have a significant impact on them and their lands, territories and resources.[309]

2.4.5. HUMAN RIGHTS

Rights inherent to human life is called human rights. These rights are essential for enjoying the full measure of human life. Various international instruments have accepted the need of conferring the indigenous and tribal peoples these basic human rights and fundamental freedom without hindrance and discrimination.[310]

Every indigenous person is born with the right to life, liberty and security. This right also extends to them as a group apart from an individualist right.[311]

---

306 UNDRIP at Article 4.

307 UNDRIP at Article 34

308 UNDRIP at Article 18

309 Expert Mechanism on the Rights of Indigenous peoples, advice No. 2: indigenous peoples and the right to participate in decision-making (A/HRC/18/42, annex).

310 ILO 169 at Article 3 clause 1.

311 UNDRIP at Article 7

2.4.6. CONSULTATION AND PARTICIPATION

While doing anything with or upon an indigenous community, it is essential that their participation and consultation is must. Such consultation must be undertaken however in good faith with the objective of achieving consent or agreement.[312] This right to be consulted and participate in their own affairs has also been recognized in international instruments.[313] It shall also be relevant to consult with the members of these communities in formulating legislation upon them or while taking any administrative measures that may affect them directly.[314] Participation in decision making process affecting them shall be considered a specific right of these people and which shall include the right to select who would represent them.[315] A few legislations in India incorporated these rights.

2.4.7. HEALTH

Tribal peoples have their own traditional knowhow to treat themselves in cases of health issues. They have the right to use traditional medicines and heath practices that they find suitable.[316] It shall also be up to them to access any other form of modern health care practices without any hindrance. State shall take appropriate measures that these people have the same right to health as anyone else.[317] It shall be the responsibility of the government for providing adequate health services for the indigenous and tribal peoples.[318] Special efforts taken by the Government of West Bengal in this regard has seen significant increase in the population of Toto community, a Particularly Vulnerablr Tribal Group in the border of Bhutan in the district of Alipurduar.

Minoo Parabia, in his paper presented at the Centre for Social Studies, Surat, and the Centre for the History of Medicine, University of Warwick, UK, in March 2007, argued that there are more than 2000 species of medicinal plants. He further estimated that in India tribes use about 6000 species of plants and its products in their healing. He even stated that a rich resource that is being underutilized specially as there is evidence that some of these plants can treat conditions that are considered incurable in allopathic medicine. As it is modern development is leading to a rapid deterioration in the tribal environment, with a resulting destruction and loss of many of these plants. He himself is working on the scheme and grants them plots of land where these plants may be grown, processed and practices from a special centre at Ahwa in the Dangs.[319]

2.4.8. ECONOMY, EDUCATION AND INTELLECTUAL PROPERTY RIGHTS

Tribal economy is based on land and its resources they live upon. The economy is generally self sustaining. The process of storing is generally absent in tribal economic setup except in certain cases. Their education,

---

312 Ibid at Article 6 clause 1 sub clause a.

313 Ibid at Article 2 clause 1.

314 Ibid at Article 6 clause 1.

315 UNDRIP at Article 18

316 Ibid at Article 24

317 Ibid

318 ILO 169 at Article 20 clause 1.

319 David Hardiman, 'Healing, Medical Power and the Poor: Contests in Tribal India', Economic and Political Weekly, April 21. 2007.pp 1404-1408 at p.1405

knowhow and transformation of skills are the basis of their economic setup. However, with the encroachment on their land, their economy has faced serious challenges forcing the current generation to seek other modes of sustenance.

Vocational training and other training programs must be provided to protect these communities. These training programs should have traditional values and interest of these communities.[320]

Indigenous peoples want to maintain their distinct cultures and transmit their cultural heritage to subsequent generations. Thus they are demanding the right to educate their children in their own languages, with their own textbooks and school material.[321]

The annual market value of drugs derived from medicinal plants discovered, developed and passed from generation to generation by indigenous peoples exceeds $43 billion.[322] Drug companies tap into this indigenous knowledge basis but rarely share the profits with indigenous peoples. Thus indigenous peoples are attempting to gain greater protection for their intellectual property.[323]

A SUM UP

In the last few decades, there has been a significant improvement amongst the indigenous and tribal peoples across the world. Even when tt is nor at par with the other non indigenous communities but still the situation has improved to a great extent. Many counties have accepted the existence of tribal and indigenous peoples in their territories which they have denied for long in the international stage. This acceptance leads them to have a legal status. However, there is need of further improvement in the areas of enforcement and implementation. Thus to sum up a set of recommendation may be provided.

Indigenous peoples will be nowhere in the absence of their ancestral lands. Thus, the first thing that the international regulating body should do is to provide a substantive along with a procedural or implementation system to protect the indigenous and tribal peoples from being displaces from their land. The international movement must also be tunes in the way of returning the lands to these poor people at the earliest in consultation with these groups.

The goal of international movements should be in furtherance of protecting the culture and language of these people. There should be international cooperation to allow groups of similar communities to develop relationship with each other. The best way to protect these groups would be to protect and safeguard their cultural identities beyond political divisions of statehood. There is need to provide special status to identify the most vulnerable groups in the verge of extinction and there should be proper international guidelines of cooperation between various segments of these people. It must be understood that the culture and language of these people are inextricably linked with their traditional way of life. It must also be prioritised that their language be used to provide their wards their way of education and proper care be given in furtherance of the same.

---

320 ILO 107 at Article 17

321 Supra Note 71

322 Ibid

323 Ibid

Indigenous communities include both individuals and a collective whole. To provide welfare to indigenous peoples means welfare to both of them. Indigenous philosophy is based on group ownership and this must be respected by modern international movements. As individual cannot live without the community, a community cannot survive without its members, both influence each other. Legal framework is essential by keeping this in mind.

Misunderstandings have arisen regarding the claims of indigenous peoples, particularly those to land and natural resources as well as those to self-determination. These claims can be properly understood only by linking them to their raison d'être, i.e., the cultural survival and flourishing of indigenous peoples. Cultural rights thus include not only rights to culture narrowly conceived, i.e., protection of language, customs, and traditions, but also the culturally bounded right to property and the culturally grounded right to self-determination.[324]

As their traditional lands are critical to the survival of the culture of indigenous peoples, the legal status of these properties ought to reflect this essential purpose. As the purpose of individual property law protections has been redefined from the maximization of economic benefits to the flourishing of humans beyond the accumulation of wealth, the protection of indigenous cultures through collective property rights has to be guided by similar criteria of the blossoming of people. The management of indigenous property rights, properly understood, would thus be guided by the culture of the people holding them, dynamic as this concept is. This would, in some cases, as in the US in the absence of formal ownership rights which are often held by the federal government, mean a right to use coupled with an obligation of stewardship toward the resource, for the benefit of future generations of the community and for the planet. In other cases, as Saramaka taught, full ownership might be the solution.[325] Even then, the Court trusts in the use of this collectively held land to the benefit of the community long-term.[326]

Indigenous self-determination also is best understood from its cultural foundation. As Vine Deloria Jr. said, the purpose of the sovereignty of an indigenous peoples is to protect its cultural integrity. The indigenous community should govern itself, in order to continue the life of its culture and its members and have it flourish. This would inform the exercise of its authority and control. The structures of decision making also could be tied to the culture, as they would sanction the authority and control of, say, traditional elders without the need of periodic democratic reaffirmation, by ballot, of their leadership role. As part of a global community, though, indigenous self-government would still be bound, as to the substance of their decisions, by the outer limits any sovereign experiences, i.e., universal standards of human rights.[327]

The international movement for the protection of indigenous rights must understand that it is up to these communities to decide their fate. It is up to them to decide whether they wish to continue their life the indigenous way or otherwise. The condition in some parts of the world has led to the formation of living museums and a place of tourist attraction. Governments should not indulge in this practice.

This chapter deals with various international instruments creating various international obligations on the part of the member states. This chapter is the outcome of the study made by the researcher to understand the position of indigenous and tribal peoples across the globe including that of India.

---

324 Siegfried Wiessner 'The Cultural Rights of Indigenous peoples: Achievements and Continuing Challenges' 22 *EJIL* 140 (2011)

325 Ibid

326 Ibid

327 Ibid

It has been observed that the various international instruments have been the outcome of long struggle and sacrifice by many members of indigenous communities.

These international movements have gained momentum with the passage of time mostly in the 21st century with a host of international and regional instruments taking place which related directly and in some instruments indirectly the indigenous and tribal communities of the world.

Credit must also go to the UN for its contribution for the protection of various socio economic rights of the tribal and indigenous peoples amidst a plethora of criticisms faces by them.

India being a signatory of the UN must also respect and implement the promises made by them in the international forums as far as possible. However, it has been identified that India is still following the principles and rules as formulated by the UN in ILO Convention No. 107, even when it has been scrapped by the UN as being assimilate in nature.

A new Convention came up in the form of ILO No. 169 which replaced the ILO No. 107.

India has not been up to date with the international obligations towards indigenous and tribal peoples in India. The study reveals the persisting problems of such outdated policy and how irretrievable the position would be if this outdated policy is continued.

India has not adhered to UNDRIPS which contains the current guidelines for the protection of civil and economic rights of the indigenous and tribal peoples.

India has avoided the acceptance of the tribes in its territory to be indigenous even when in the initial period of its dealing with the international community, India have used terms like aboriginal etc.

The United Nations Organisation has made the submission of Universal Periodic Review compulsory for all member states which are to be submitted every four years. In the previous two reports submitted by India in the year 2008 and 2011 respectively, India has mostly avoided its obligation to the indigenous communities of the country. The third report was due for submission in the first quarter of 2016. On January 18th 2017 the report was finally submitted and India like the earlier reports did little to protect the rights of the tribal peoples of the country whose human rights have been violated by various acts of the non tribals and governmental policies. Part IV of the UPR with the heading 'Rights of Specific Persons or Groups' consists of para 123 to 130 which includes within its purview women, children, persons with disabilities, older persons, sexual orientation and Gender Identity, Minorities and lastly SC and STs. The three aspects reflected in the report are:

1. Robust Affirmative Action, which is more of politics than of law and have reitarated stark contrast to the international movement to protect the tribal peoples. It is in direct conflict with ILO 169.
2. Amendment to SC and ST Act 1989 where new chapter for SCs are incorporated. This does very little to contribute to protect the tribal peoples and communities as such.
3. State Government to take steps to prevent and punish atrocities. This approach to shred off the responsibility and decentralize the punitive measures also have a negative impact as it would only invoke the blame game politics into the stage with little to do something positive to protect the rights of these people.

The government of India must take this matter very seriously and must adhere to the international standard that has been developing with time in the international sphere. The right of indigenous and tribal peoples must be acknowledged in furtherance of the ILO 169 rather than ILO 107. As the effectiveness of the earlier convention has been accepted as outdated and subsequently been rejected by the UN itself. All the activities going on in India in furtherance of tribal welfare and protection are in tune with ILO 107 and will be redundant once the new convention becomes enforceable in India. Thus earlier, the better for the policy makers to welcome the principles laid down in ILO 169.

CHAPTER 3

CIVIL AND ECONOMIC RIGHTS OF TRIBALS: THE INDIAN PERSPECTIVE

AN OVERVIEW

In order to understand the socio economic aspects of the indigenous and tribal peoples in India, a thorough and in depth study of the anthropological development of these people must be made. This chapter seeks to address who these people originally are starting from pre historic era to the historical records of modern researchers. The study of these people from 50,000 years ago till date should ideally provide a clear picture of these communities in existence in various parts of the country with various ethnic features. It will also make the study more effective as the study would ideally highlight the social and economic position of these people among other things. Apart from the historical development, the geographical positioning of these people contributes to a great extent towards their social and economic development. The study would also try to analyze the same in this chapter.

Aboriginals refer to the first man on land. The study should ideally address whether that man actually existed on the Indian soil and if it did, how its evolution took place in the next 50,000 years. The geographical, historical, anthropological and scientific explanations relating to tribals in India must be explored to understand who these people are and how they lived all these years and what rights they should have even after such revolutionary journey all through these years on this planet.

The chapter may also try to identify through this study as to why the Indian government has tried to avoid the nomenclature of indigenous and prefer the term tribe instead.

Tribal economic rights are largely dependent on the land they inhabit. However, because of the legal and policy loopholes, the tribals are gradually losing their right to land and consequently, their economic rights.

Because of pro majority policies of the government, tribals are victims of exclusion and marginalisation. The biggest loss of the tribes is their economic exclusion, which initiates with large scale displacement from ancestral lands and the resources emanating out of it. Tribal economy in India is largely dependent on various resources of the land including cultivation. The loss of rights over forests and lands destroys the very basis of their economy. Absence of accessibility of forest produce has also left the tribal women with loss of their economic activities. It was however revived with the enactment of Forest Rights Act 2006. Industrial and mining industries along with large scale hydro projects and construction of dams have left the tribals with little choice of sustaining life and livelihood. A lot of migration of non tribals in the tribal areas have made the situation worse for the socially and deprived tribes of India.

3.1 INDIAN POLITICAL DIVISION

India has a massive population of 1,210,193,422 people spread across 29 states and 7 union territories, in the census[328] that covered 640 districts, 5,767 tehsils, 7,933 towns and more than 600,000 villages. A total of 2.7 million officials visited households in 7,933 towns and 600,000 villages, classifying the population according to gender, religion, education and occupation[329] according to the 2011 Census report.

3.1.1 VARIOUS POLITICAL DIVISIONS OF THE COUNTRY AND TRIBAL EXISTENCE

The ethnic and political zones of India have been categorised as follows:[330]

---

328 15th Census of India, 2011

329 C. Chandramouli "Census of India 2011 – A Story of Innovations", Press Information Bureau, Government of India 23 August 2011.

330 Bhasin 1988

1. North India 2. West India 3. East India 4. Central India 5. South India 6. Islands

Himalayan Region may be divided into three divisions[331], i.e,

A) Western Himalaya B) Central Himalaya and C) Eastern Himalaya

There are various tribal communities living in almost all states of India and union territories. Their social and economic conditions vary according to their geographical variations and their cultural traits. The tribals are found in a great numbers in the Himalayan region where they rely upon the plantations for sustenance and inclement living conditions as a natural barrier from non tribal inhabitants. The tribal communities in these areas have successfully retained their culture and economic setup for ages. However with the advent of colonial rulers and independent India's developmental projects like construction of Dams, mining etc, the tribal economy in these regions have hit an all time low. There are instances of discontinuation of tribal culture because of large scale displacement and various other factors primarily created by non tribals.

3.1.2 ETHNIC GROUPS AND TRIBAL TRAITS

Ethnic groups[332] in India involve Castes, Tribes[333], Scheduled Castes and Scheduled Tribes and other Communities[334]. India has been a country of great diversity comprising of a plethora of various ethnic groups. The various ethnic groups have their own unique features and characteristics. These features have to a great extent distinguishes one from the other. A brief discussion of these groups is essential to identify the basic socio economic characteristics of these groups. The differences prevalent to these groups have been subject matter of debate as with the passage of time they have retained some of their originating features and some ors features have been discontinued due to the change time brought along with it.

3.1.2.1 CASTE SYSTEM IN INDIA AND ITS ORIGIN

Caste system in India is basically an exclusive Indian phenomenon based on Hindu religion. It is a complex and diversified institution having its existence in various parts of the country with variable applicability. The term caste is from the Portuguese term 'casta' which symbolise the race or breed of a person.

Risley (1915) defines caste as follows

---

331 I. North India: (A) Western Himalaya (S. No. 1, 2) and (B) Central Himalaya (S.No. 8): (1) Jammu and Kashmir, (2) Himachal Pradesh, (3) Punjab, (4) Chandigarh (U.T.), (5) Haryana, (6) Delhi, (7) Uttar Pradesh, (8) Uttaranchal, and (9) Rajasthan II. West India: (1) Gujarat, (2) Maharashtra, (3) Goa, (4) Daman and Diu (U.T.) and (5) Dadra and Nagar Haveli (U.T.) III. East India: C) Eastern Himalaya: (S. No.1 to 8 and Darjeeling District of West Bengal) (1) Arunachal Pradesh, (2) Assam, (3) Nagaland, (4) Manipur, (5) Mizoram, (6) Tripura, (7) Meghalaya, (8) Sikkim, (9) West Bengal, (10) Bihar, (11) Jharkhand and (12) Orissa IV. Central India: (1) Madhya Pradesh (2) Chhatisgarh V. South India: (1) Karnataka, (2) Andhra Pradesh, (3) Tamil Nadu, (4) Kerala and (5) Pondicherry (U.T.). VI. Islands: (1) Lakshadweep (U.T.) and (2) Andaman and Nicobar Islands (U.T.).

332 The aggregation of biological and socio-cultural characteristics constitutes an ethnic group.

333 All tribes have not been incorporated in the Schedule to the Constitution of India. It has been more of politics than of law when it comes to such incorporation.

334 Community is generally referred to a group of people who may have occupational, linguistic, religious or regional characteristics (Bhasin et al. 1992, 1994; Bhasin and Walter 2001); Also see Ghurye 1969; Hutton 1981

"a collection of families or groups of families bearing a common name; claiming a common descent from a mythical ancestor, human or divine; professing to follow the same hereditary calling; and regarded by those who are competent to give an opinion as forming a single homogeneous community' is generally associated with a specific occupation and that a caste is invariably endogamous, but is further divided as a rule, into a smaller of smaller circles each of which is endogamous (this is called Jati), so that a Brahman is not only restricted to marrying another Brahman, but to marrying a women of the same subdivision of Brahmans."

The internal exogamous division of the endogamous caste is 'Gotra'.[335] Apart from castes there are sub castes[336] which are in existence in various parts of India.

A greater uniformity has been retained at the economic level of caste than perhaps in relation to customs regulating marriage in particular. Though, there is a wide prevalence of the above model in all parts of non-tribal India, the system of economic inequalities has been encapsulated so to say, in regional moulds.[337] The various castes existent in various Indian states vary in their socio economic conditions and their status may be determined on a social platform in most of the cases.

3.1.2.2 COMMUNITIES IN INDIA AND TRIBAL EXISTENCE

India has more than 8.6 percent of its population in the form of Scheduled Tribes according to the Census report 2011. However, the number will increase if all the tribal communities been taken into consideration irrespective of those incorporated in the schedule to the Constitution of India. A vast portion of Indian subcontinent includes a lot of aboriginal and indigenous traits. Tribal existence can be noticed in most of the states and union territories and also in extreme villages. These primitive communities are able to sustain their customary way of life mostly because of their sustainable economic system.

In the Indian censuses prior to 1931, information was collected and published for each caste or tribe separately. In the 1931 census, data for individual communities was limited to (i) Exterior Castes (ii) Primitive Castes and (iii) all other castes with the exception of (a) those whose members fall short of four thousand of the total population and (b) those for which separate figures were deemed to be unnecessary by the local government.[338]

In the 1941 census, 'group totals' were tabulated for scheduled castes, tribes and AngloIndians. For selected individual tribes separate tables were furnished. By 1951 census, community distinctions based on caste were being discouraged. It was decided to enumerate population on the basis of race, caste or tribe only to the extent necessary for providing information relating to certain special groups of the people who are referred to in the Constitution of India. The Scheduled Castes and Scheduled Tribes were enumerated from 1951 census onwards. The President by a special order scheduled particular castes among Hindus and Sikhs in particular areas for special treatment that also applies to tribes irrespective of their religious persuasion. The Scheduled Castes and Scheduled Tribes have been specified by 15 Presidential Orders issued under the

---

335 M. K. Bhasin, 'Genetics of Castes and Tribes of India: Indian Population Milieu',
Kamla-Raj 2006 Int J Hum Genet, 6(3) (2006): 233-274 at p 253

336 The word 'caste' and 'sub-caste' are not absolute but comparative in significance. The larger group will be called a caste while the smaller group will be called a sub-caste

337 Supra at 7

338 Ibid

provisions of Articles 341 and 342 of the Constitution. They are listed in Scheduled Castes and Scheduled Tribes Orders (Amendment) Act 1976.[339]

All the groups incorporating the scheduled castes, scheduled tribes, other backward classes, Denotified Nomadic and Semi Nomadic communities, Punjabis, Bengalese, [340] Hindus, Muslims, Sikhs,[341] Tamil, Telegu[342] etc have been classified under the category of community.

3.1.2.3 TRADITIONAL OCCUPATIONAL GROUPS

India has been divided on the basis of occupational groups. There are traditional guilds incorporated in the 'chatur varna' system with its various divisions. The Brahmins, Kshatriya, Vaishya and Sudra are the four groups divided on the basis of occupational differences. The Brahmins being the priest, Kshatriyas the warriors, Vaishyas the traders and land owners and Sudras the labouring caste. This stratification of occupation has a gradation incorporated in it. The manual labour manual labour is looked down upon and those dealing with swineherding, scavenging (removal of night soil) butchery are regarded as polluting.[343] It shall be relevant to state in this regard that the tribal communities of India has to some extent diluted with the labour force of India due to large scale displacements and has taken up the status of the lower castes prevalent in Indian caste system.

3.1.3 MARRIAGE

The concept of marriage is dependent on the concept of private ownership of resources and the concept of inheritance. Tribal groups and communities generally live a life of seclusion from other communities. The concept of private property was not known to them and they believe in community resources. The advent of private property and ownership bought with it the evil of inheritance as one wants to enjoy his property even after his death. This may be achieved while the said resources are used by his or her heirs. This development eventually led to the concept of inheritance, which is the process of depriving of the community of one's own properties to the exclusive enjoyment and ownership of the heirs.

It was difficult to really identify who the heirs are as women in the community were able to have free sexual relationship with more than one man. To determine the paternity of a child born in the community, the concept of marriage evolved. The process of restricting women to only one man to identify the paternity of the child born is the ultimate objective of marriage.

In India tribes live in small groups and marriage is usually exclusive in such group itself. However, marriage with other groups is not new in historical past. The reason behind the marriage within the same group or close knit social circle is the sharing of similar likes and dislikes. Marriage patterns may be considered from the three aspects: the field of selection, the party to selection, and the criteria of selection. The restrictions posed among some tribes and communities in the field of selection are preferential and obligatory marriage.[344]

---

339 Ibid

340 On the basis of Region

341 On the basis of Religion

342 On the basis of Language

343 Supra at 7

344 Ibid at p 259

Till the industrial revolution in Indian society, the Hindus have both endogamous and exogamous rules limiting the selection of their spouse. The Hindu society is divided into a number of endogamous caste groups each of which is further divided into endogamous groups based in terms of locality. This multiplicity of groups thus restricts the choice of mate within a boundary. Caste exercises a great influence on the social life of a man. The breach of caste endogamy was a punishable offence till recently. People were excommunicated by caste panchayat.[345] As stated above the industrialization opened the door for choosing profession and widened the scope of social intercourse. The growth of inter caste and inter religious marriage became a regular affair. However, this led to a lot of confusion and indifference amongst many. In order to validate and regularise the social position arising out of these marriages new laws were formulated. The Special Marriage Act, 1954 followed by the Hindu Marriage Act, 1955 brought in several revolutionary changes in the Indian social and legal system.

The post World War II developed a change from *lassiez faire* to welfare state and India witnessed a plethora of welfare legislation in this period of time. Various legislations were incorporated to regulate the marital relationship amongst various communities of India with exceptions created to safeguard tribal marriages. The concept of cross cousin marriages amongst the tribal population in various part of the country has been allowed to continue as local custom but marriage between uncle and niece has been prohibited.

During Vedic period the favored marriage pattern was monogamy. Instances of polygynous[346] and polyandrous[347] marriages were also present in this age. This form of union was once practised by the people of the Cis-Himalayan tract in Northern India and among some tribes of the Pre-Dravidian or Dravidian groups in South India. Though polygyny was allowed by the Hindu ideal of marriage it was resorted to only when no male child was born to the first wife within the first few years of marriage.[348]

The tribes in India has their own and unique system of marriage and has to a great extent been influenced by the various practices of the non tribals especially after the industrial revolution. The process further was alleviated by large scale displacement and mixing in various semi urban and urban areas of the country.

3.1.4 INBREEDING IN INDIAN SOCIETY AND TRIBAL DILUTION

In India each of the endogamous castes, tribes and religious communities has distinct and well-defined cultural norms, which include varied marriage customs/practices. Generally speaking, most of the Indian communities follow endogamy, but marriage within relatives is not permissible up till the seventh generation. However, a few groups prefer marriages between related individuals like cross-cousins[349], parallel cousins, uncle-niece[350] etc. The types of preferential marriages vary across the country and different communities.[351]

---

345 Ibid

346 Polygyny is that form of union in which a man has more than one wife at a time (e.g., two wives being two sisters).

347 Polyandry is a form of union in which a woman has more than one husband at a time, or in which brors share a wife or wives in common

348 Supra at 7 p 260

349 Instances of cross cousin and parallel cousins are seen in Muslims of Northern India

350 Instances of cross cousin and parallel cousins are seen in Hindus of Southern India

351 Ibid

Instances of consanguineous [352]marriages are also practices in various parts of India including the tribal areas of India. One of the prominent reasons behind this is the economic unity and occupational preference of the community concerned. Other reasons[353] for this type of marriage may be summed up as under:

(a) To keep the cultivable land in larger pieces for growing food crops,

(b) The parental domination in arranging the marriage,

(c) The mutual knowledge of families,

(d) The relatives are better suited for economic and other reasons, to fit into the Hindu joint family system etc.

But with the passage of time the concept of consanguineous marriages have decreased. Education, industrialization and urbanisation have contributed to such decrease with certain exceptions in some tribal areas of India.

3.1.5 RELIGIOUS GROUPS AND TRIBAL RELIGION IN INDIA

Religion has played from time immemorial a great role in the unification of human habitat in various part of the globe. India has been the home of various religious groups for centuries including various religious practices of the tribes and tribal communities for ages.

3.1.5.1 HINDUISM AND TRIBALS

It has been construed by a number of experts that a lot of Hindu religious practices has its origin in various tribal rituals and practices. Hinduism has developed gradually out of the synbook of sacrificial cults brought into India by the Aryan invaders around 1500 B.C. with religion of various indigenous peoples.[354] Taking the various aspects of nature and believing the existence of God therein has been the benchmark of tribal religious practices. This trend has been followed in various mythological interpretations exclusive to Hindu religion. The distribution of Hinduism is widespread, throughout the length and the breadth of the country. Almost the entire country with the exception of the extreme North in North Western corner and the North Eastern corner shows that Hindus form over 80 per cent of the total population.[355]

Apart from Hindus, Muslims, Christians, Sikhs, Buddhists and Jains, Jews are present in adequate numbers in India. A total number of 183 other religions are there present in the country[356]under the head 'Other Religions and Persuasions'. A lot of tribal religious practices can be found within this category of religious practice. Most of these tribal religions have a common denominator, their attachment with nature. The tribals have a close affinity and attachment with nature and this can be noticed in their religious practiced and rituals that have been followed for centuries. Tribal religions can be seen concentrated on certain fears of destructive activities by nature for non compliance.

---

352 Marriage between two individuals who have at least one traceable common ancestor is said to be consanguineous marriage. Further more, the offspring of such marriages are inbred.

353 Bhasin and Nag (1994)

354 Supra note at 7. p 263

355 Ibid

356 Census of India, 1981

3.1.5.2 ISLAM AND TRIBALS

Islam began in Arabia in the beginning of the 7th century. The founder of this religion was Prophet Muhammad who was born in 570 A.D. in a distinguished family of Mecca. After Prophet Muhammad's death (A.D. 632) the leadership passed to Calipus or Khalifas who were both religious and political heads. Arabs spread Islam from the Atlantic to Sind within eighty years of Prophet's death.[357]

Muslims are divided into two major religious, endogamous sect—Shia and Sunni and several other minor groups *inter alia* Bohra, Momins, Domon, Moplahic and Khoja. Though Islam proclaimed the idea of equality, but in India it has been characterized by caste. The true Muslims are divided into four large families—Saiyad, Shaikh, Pathan and Moghul. Though they are referred as castes in India, they are neither castes nor tribes but are merely names given to groups of tribes supposed to be of similar blood. [358] The Muslims invaded India and in the process converted a large number of Indian including tribals and non tribals into Islam. Today, many of these converts preserve their ancestral religious and customary traits that they used to practice.

3.1.5.3 INFLUENCE OF CHRISTIANITY ON TRIBALS OF INDIA

Colonial invasions brought with it Christianity in the First Century AD by St. Thomas. The Catholic Church of Edessa confirmed the visit of St. Thomas at least twice to India to promote Christianity in India. This spreading of Christianity was seen amongst the tribals and tribal communities who found a lot of redress of their regular ailments and distress in the Christian Missionaries. A large scale conversion succeeded in rural and tribal belts of the country. Even today, this religion is found in great number in the Southern and North eastern regions of the country. Many tribal states like Nagaland, Meghalaya and Mizoram has predominant Christian population. Again about 60 percent of the country's Christian population is concentrated in Kerala, Tamil Nadu and Andhra Pradesh.

Thus it may be seen that the country has a vast Christian population amongst whom a lot of them are tribal communities. These communities are not only limited in certain coastal areas of the country but with the passage of time the religion flourished across the country. The church flourished even in remote parts of the country reflecting a large scale conversion to Christianity amongst the tribal peoples and more popularly to the lower caste of Hindu communities.

3.1.5.4 BUDDHISM AND TRIBES IN THE NORTHEAST

Kshatriya Prince Siddartha founded the religion as a revolt against the Vedic religion or Brahmanism in the 6th century BC. Buddhism is further divided into two sects:

(i) Hinayan (The Small Vehicle)[359] and (ii) Mahayanas (The Great Vehicle)[360]

Taking the country as a whole the largest number of Buddhists is found in Maharashtra. It is well known that the neo-Buddhist movement during the decade 1951-61 saw a large scale adoption of Buddhism particularly by the Scheduled Castes population in Maharashtra, though this tempo was not maintained in

---

357 Supra note 7

358 Blunt 1931: p. 189

359 Old followers of the old religion who believed in Buddha as a Guru or the Great Master

360 They raised Buddha to the position of a saviour god

196171; in fact the growth rate recorded appears to be less than even the natural growth rate. It is possible that certain converts from Scheduled Castes to Buddhism preferred to return their religion as "Hindu" finding that as Buddhists they were not entitled to certain concessions available to Scheduled Castes. In North Eastern states the Buddhists account for 28.71 per cent in Sikkim, 13.69 in Arunachal Pradesh and 8.19 per cent in Mizoram.[361]

1.1.1.5 OTHER RELIGIOUS ASPECTS OF TRIBALS

i.   Jainism:
     The sect that grew against Brahmanism along with Buddhism was Jainism. It was founded by another Kshatriya Prince Vardhaman. This religion emphasises on the act of good deeds. They are further divided into two sub sects
a)   Svetambara - clothed in white
b)   Digambara - clothed in atmosphere, because their Munis wear no clothes.

Mostly Jains are found in Gujarat, Rajasthan, Maharashtra, Madhya Pradesh, Karnataka and the Union Territory of Delhi. Jains are mostly urban dwellers and only a few of their followers reside in semi urban and rural areas. Only a handful of tribals are seen to be followers of Jainism.

ii. Parsis[362]: Some Iranian belonging to an endogamous group migrated to India and started their permanent settlement in West India. They were Zoroastrian fire worshippers, and came to India about 8th century A.D. to escape from forcible conversion to Islam. They show high frequency of inbreeding as well. Some of the tribal population in the North Indian states have been influenced by them and instances of conversion has been there but too few in numbers.

3.1.6 LINGUISTIC GROUPS IN INDIA AND TRIBAL LANGUAGES

Language is the mode of conduct between two individuals and also with the family to the outside world. It is an entity of social significance. Tribal groups in India have a high degree of diversity in their languages and dialect. At times there has been co existence o two or more languages which reflects the co ordination between two or more communities in furtherance of social and economic correlations. There has been a long history of heterogeneous ethnic groups drawn from the neighboring regions of Asia.

Development of a specific language initiates from a specific condition and place of isolation nd from there it develops to various other parts of nearing territory with which the said community develops various social and economic relationships. Language also signifies the various elements present and practices in the society. It explains the social identity of the region it has developed.

India has 179 languages and 544 dialects[363]. Of these languages 116 are small tribal speeches of the Tibeto-Chinese family; these are found only in the northern and north-eastern fringes of India and are present among less than 1per cent of the entire population of the country.[364] Nearly two dozen more are likewise insignificant speeches of other language groups; or they are languages not truly belonging to India[365].

---

361 Supra Note 7 at p 264

362 as their name suggests from Fars (Persia)

363 Grierson (1903-1928)

364 Supra note 7 at p 270

365 Census Centenary Monograph No.10, 1972; Gazetteer of India 1973

There were 187 languages spoken by different sections of our society[366]. Ninety four out of 187 languages are spoken by less than 10,000 persons each and that 23 languages together account for 97 per cent of the total population of the country.[367] Out of these 23 languages, 15[368] besides English have been specified in the Eighth Schedule of the Constitution of India. It shall be relevant in this regard to note that because of cultural insignificance, the Eighth Schedule does not recognize any of the languages belonging to the Austro-Asiatic and Tibeto Chinese families. But a majority of tribal communities of these regions vastly uses these languages. Hindi and English have been given the status of official language of the country. A study of these groups has been provided in chapter one of this research. However, a greater analysis of these families and groups are vitally important to understand the true origin of these communities and what lies behind their dreams and aspirations. These aspirations categorically formulate the socio economic and other practices which in turn become the law of the clan or the community with the passage of time. Thus in order to understand the true nature of social and economic rights of these people a broad analysis with a brief study of them becomes relevant.

3.1.6.1 CLASSIFICATION OF INDIAN LANGUAGES

India has almost all the languages and dialects of the following four language families.
1. The Austro-Asiatic Language Family (Nishada),
2. The Tibeto-Chinese Language Family (Kirata),
3. The Dravidian Language Family (Dravida), and
4. The Indo-European Language Family (Aryan).

According to the Gazetteer of India 1965,

> "It is not known how and when these language families moved into India. Before their advent, there was the language of the Negroid people, who pioneered into India from Africa along the Asian coastline probably before the 6th millennium B.C. But on the mainland of India nothing has remained of their language, the original Negroid people having been killed or absorbed by subsequent immigrants"

Irrespective of their sequence of creation the fact remains that all these three groups were in India when the Aryans came.[369]

It was reported that Indian sub-continent had experienced massive gene flow from at least two Neolithic episodes of migrations.[370] Firstly about 10-15 thousand years ago, when agriculture developed in the fertile crescent region, a part of an eastward wave of human migration entered India and brought Dravidian languages[371] mainly, Elamo-Dravidian languages[372], which may have originated in the Elam province (Zagros Mountains, South western Iran) and are confined to south eastern India and to some isolated groups in Pakistan and northern India. The next was the arrival of pastoral nomads from the central Asian steppes

---

366 According to the 1961 Census of India

367 Supra note 7

368 These are Assamese, Bengali, Gujarati, Hindi, Kannada, Kashmiri, Malayalam, Marathi, Oriya, Punjabi, Sanskrit, Sindhi, Tamil, Telugu and Urdu

369 Renfrew (1987, 1989) and Cavalli-Sforza *et al*

370 Ibid

371 Renfrew 1989

372 Ruhlen 1991

to the Iranian plateau about 4000 years before present, brought with it the Indo-European language family which eventually replaced Dravidian languages from most of Pakistan and northern India, perhaps by an elite-dominance process.[373] Out of these language families, the Aryan family is numerically and culturally the most important in India. According to 1961 Census of India over 73.3 per cent of the Indian people spoke languages belonging to the Aryan family. Dravidian came next representing 24.47 per cent. There are only 1.5 per cent for the Austric languages and still less for the Tibeto-Chinese languages (0.73 per cent).[374]

1. The Austro-Asiatic Language Family (Nishada)

According to Gazetteer of India 1965,

> *"Between the Austrics and Dravidians, the former possibly represent the earlier group. According to some scholars, the Austrics had their origin in Indo-China and South China; they spread east into India and south into Malaya, and then passed into the islands beyond another view, which is more recent is that the Austrics are a very old off-shoot of the Mediterranean people who came into India from the west, probably even before the Dravidians. Austric speech influenced Dravidian and Aryan. In the plains, Austric has been very largely suppressed by Dravidian and Aryan, but Austric languages survive in the less easily accessible hills and forests of Central and Eastern India. On the Himalayan slopes, Austric languages have deeply modified the Tibeto-Chinese dialects— these took over some Austric features. In Assam, one Austric language survived among the Khasis, who are largely Mongoloid in race but Austric in speech"*

This family is again classified into two sub groups, viz,
- (i) Mon-Khmer Branch (Mon-Khmer Group): this group is again divided into two sub groups, viz,
  - 1. Khasi group of languages of Assam and
  - 2. Nicobarese of the Nicobar Islands
- (ii) Munda Branch (Munda Group)

Munda Branch is represented by the speakers belonging to the Central and Eastern regions of India. This includes the people inhabiting mostly the hills and jungles of Bihar, Chota Nagpur, Orissa and Central India.[375] There are many speeches of this Austro Asiatic language group.[376]

It must be referred that the Mundari speakers are mostly concentrated in the tribal districts of Santal Parganas, Mayurbhanj, Ranchi, East Nimar, Betul and Baudh Khondmals.

2. The Tibeto-Chinese Language Family (Kirata)

According to the Gazetteer of India, 1965

> *"The original Sino-Tibetan speakers appear to have become characterized with their basic language at least 4000 years before Christ in the area to the west of China, between the sources of the Yangtze and*

---

373 Renfrew 1987, 1989, 1996, Cavalli-Sforza et al. 1988; Quintana-Murci et al. 2001

374 Supra note 7.

375 Ibid at p 266

376 The names of the speeches in the branch are: 1. Kherwari 2. Santali 3. Mundari 4. Bhumij 5. Birhor 6. Koda/Kora 7. Ho 8. Turi 9. Asuri 10. Agaria 11. Birjia/- Brigia/Binjhia 12. Korwa 13. Korku 14. Kharia 15. Juang 16. Savara 17. Gadaba and Munda - unspecified

the Hwang Rivers. There they developed a language which ultimately became the source of Chinese, Tibetan, Burmese and possibly also Thai, though the genetic connection of Thai with the Sino-Tibetan family is now being questioned. The Tibeto-Burman speaking Mongoloids with yellow complexion came to be known among the Vedic Aryans as the Kiratas. The Kirata influence in the amalgam of Aryo-Dravido-Austric culture, which is Indian culture or Hindu culture, was not very farreaching. The role of the Sino-Tibetan languages and their present position also are not very significant"

The speakers of this family of language belong to the Tibeto Chinese and are of Mongoloid origin. They have entered the territory of India much before the Indo-Aryan speakers. The language can be notices in the extreme north eastern places of Baltistan to the southern portions of Assam. There are two sub families of this language family, viz,

I. Siamese-Chinese Sub-Family and, II. Tibeto-Burman Sub-Family
I. Siamese-Chinese Sub-Family: It includes the Tai Group of languages which is distinct from Tibeto-Burman, and is represented only by one language i.e. Khamti.
II. Tibeto-Burman Sub-Family: The second sub-family of Tibeto-Chinese Family is divided into three branches—

(a) Tibeto-Himalayan Branch; (b) North-Assam Branch; and (c) Assam-Burmese Branch.

(a) Tibeto-Himalayan Branch: This branch consists of the following groups:
 (i) Bhotia Group (Tibetan Group)
 Bhotia Group[377]: This group is represented by a number of important numerically strong speeches within Indian borders, namely: Ladakhi, Lahuli, Sikkim Bhotia, Balti and a number of small communities combined under the common name of Bhotia. This group includes languages like Tibetan, Balti, Ladakhi, Lahauli, Spiti, Jad, Sherpa, Sikkim Bhotia, Bhutani, Kagate and Bhotia-Unspecified.
 (ii) Himalayan Group[378]: This group of speeches is spoken along the tracts to the south of the Himalayas from Himachal Pradesh in the west to the western borders of Bhutan in the east. These are further split into pronominalized and non-pronominalized groups of speeches. The pronominalized group of speeches has given evidence of Austro-Asiatic traits remaining in some of their member speeches. This group includes the following speeches:

Lahauli of Chamba; Kanashi; Kanauri; Jangali; Dhimal; Limbu; Khambu; Rai; Gurung; Tamang; Sunwar; Mangari; Newari; Lepcha; Kami; Toto.

(b) North-Assam Branch: A significant group of languages the Tibeto-Burman sub-family occupies the north-eastern frontier and may be named as 'North-East Frontier Group'.[379] North-East Frontier Group: This group consists of a number of languages like Aka/Hrusso, Dalfa, Abor, Adi, Miri and Mishmi.

(c) Assam-Burmese Branch: This branch of Tibeto-Burman sub-family consists of groups like Bodo, Naga, Kachin, Kuki-Chin and Burma.
 (i) Bodo Group (Bara or Bodo Group): This group includes the following languages:
 Bodo/Boro; Lalung; Dimasa; Garo; Koch; Rabha; Tripuri; Deori; Mikir.

---

377 Tibetan Group

378 (Pronominalized/ Non-pronominalized Himalayan Groups

379 Supra note 7 at p 268

(ii) Naga Group: This group consists of the following languages:

Angami, Sema; Rengma; Khezha; Ao; Lotha; Tableng; Chang-Naga; Kacha Naga; Zemi Naga; Kabui; Khoirao; Mao; Maram;Tangkhul; Maring; Konyak; Pochury; Phom; Yimchungre; Khiemnungam; Nocte; Wancho; Makware; Tangsa and Naga-Unspecified.

(iii) Kachin Group: This group includes the two languages:

1. Kawri 2. Singpho.

(iv) Kuki-Chin Group: It consists of the following speeches:

1. Manipuri/Meithei; Thodo; Ralte; Paite; Tlangtlang; Pawi; Lakher; Lushai/Mizo; Rangkhol; Halam; Langrong; Aimol; Chiru; Kom; Hmar; Lamgang; Chote; Purum; Anal; Gangte; Vaiphei; Khami; Khawathlang; Simte and Kuki Unspecified and Chin-Unspecified.

(v) Burma Group: This group includes the following speeches:

1. Mru and 2. Arkanese

The languages and the dialects belonging to the Sino-Tibetan family are spoken by tribal groups of north-east and of the Himalayan and sub-Himalayan regions of the North and NorthWest.[380] The speeches of the Tibeto-Himalayan branch are spoken in Ladakh and parts of Himachal Pradesh and Sikkim.[381] The Assam-Burmese Branch is concentrated in the states of North-east India along the Indo-Burmese border. Among these, Naga dialects are spoken in Nagaland; Lushai is concentrated in Mizo Hills, Garo in Garo Hills and Meithei in Manipur.[382]

1. The Dravidian Language Family (Dravida)

According to the Gazetteer of India 1965,

> *"The Dravidians are said to have come from Asia Minor and the Eastern Mediterranean. They were Mediterranean people, of the same stock as the people of Asia Minor and Crete, and the Pre-Hellenic people of Greece (The Aegean). The Dravidians of India were thus originally a branch of the same people as the Pre-Hellenic people of Greece and Asia Minor. The exact affiliation of Dravidian with the language of the Eastern Mediterranean has not yet been settled. But some common lexical elements are noticeable. Certain religious notions and ideas as well as cults and practices among the Dravidian people of India have strong West Asian and Mediterranean affinities. The city civilization of Sind and Punjab and other parts of India appears to be Dravidian, and therefore connected with West Asia. The Dravidian languages are now found in solid blocks in the Deccan and in South India, where they have their separate existence in spite of strong inroads upon them by the Aryan speech. There is an Austric element in the Dravidian languages, just as there is a strong Dravidiancum-Austric substratum in the Aryan speeches of India."*

The language families have been broadly grouped geographically and the relative position of particular language is discussed with reference to its situation in three broad group areas.

They are listed below:

(i) South Dravidian Group: It consists of the following speeches:

1. Tamil 2. Malayalam 3. Kannada 4. Coorgi/Kodagu 5. Tulu 6. Toda 7. Kota 8. Telugu.

(ii) Central Dravidian Group: It includes 1. Kui 2. Kolami 3. Gondi 4. Parji 5. Koya 6. Khond/ Kondh 7. Konda

---

380 Ibid

381 Ibid

382 Ibid

(iii) North Dravidian Group: It includes: 1. Kurukh/Oraon and 2. Malto

(iv) Unspecified Dravidian Tongues: A few (6742) persons belong to unspecified Dravidian Tongues, which are 1. Dravidian, 2. Madrasi, 3. Ladhadi and 4. Bharia

Languages of the Dravidian family are concentrated in the plateau region and the adjoining coastal plains. Telugu is spoken in Andhra, Tamil in Tamil Nadu, and Kannada in Karnataka and Malayalam in Kerala. The speeches of the Dravidian family are also spoken by a large number of tribal groups living in the eastern and the north-eastern parts of the peninsular plateau. These groups include the Gonds of Madhya Pradesh, Central India and the Oraons of Chota Nagpur Plateau.[383]

2. The Indo-European Language Family (Aryan)

According to the Gazetteer of India 1965,

"The Aryan speeches of India, beginning from Vedic Sanskrit, their oldest form, have been the great intellectual and cultural heritage of India. They form our mental and spiritual link with the European world, on the genetic side; and with the world of South-East Asia and East Asia, on the cultural side, through Buddhism and Brahmanism. The modern Indo-Aryan languages of India are near or distant cousins of the Indo European languages outside India, like Persian, Armenian, Russian and other Slav languages; Greek, Italian, French, Spanish and other Latin languages; German, English, Norwegian and other Teutonic languages; and Welsh and Irish among Celtic languages. The Indo-European speech family is today the most important in the world. With the exception of the various languages within the orbit of Chinese (the so-called dialects of Chinese or Han), Japanese, Indonesian or Malay, and Arabic, all the main languages of the world, and the most important culturally, are IndoEuropean. And all these languages are descended from a common source-speech, the "Primitive Indo-European", which flourished about 5000 years ago"

In India this great language family is represented by its sub-family of languages, which covers the widest area of the country and is spoken by the largest proportion of the Indian population.

I. Aryan Sub-Family

The Aryan sub-family is further divided into three branches—(a) Iranian Branch (b) Dardic (or Pisacha) Branch, and (c) Indo-Aryan Branch.

(a) Iranian Branch: It is represented by languages like Persian, Pashto and Balochi considered of foreign origin.

(b) Dardic (or Pisasha) Branch: It is represented by following groups of languages: (i) Kafir Group: Wai Ala (ii) Khowar Group: Khowar (iii) Dard Group: 1. Dardi 2. Shina 3. Kashmiri 4. Kohistani. Speakers of Kafir and Khowar groups do not come within the Indian boundaries.

(c) Indo-Aryan Branch: The coverage of the language of the Indo-Aryan Branch being much too wide, it will perhaps be convenient to restrict the brief description of the main languages and dialects of the branch through enumeration of broad groups of languages classified in their proper circles with reference to common characteristics and socio-linguistic tendencies, often not found in the other groups.[384] The Indo-Aryan Branch can be divided into two sub-branches as Outer Sub-Branch and Mediate Sub-Branch/Inner Sub-Branch

---

383 Ibid at p 269

384 Ibid at p 269

1. Outer Sub-Branch: This consists of the following (i) North-Western Group: This includes 1. Lahnda or Western Punjabi Dialects and 2. Sindhi. (ii) Southern Group: This group includes 1. Marathi; 2. Konkani. (iii) Eastern Group: This includes 1. Oriya; 2. Bihari with sub-groups- Bhojpuri, Maghi/ Magadhi, Maithili; 3. Bengali; 4. Assamese.

2. Mediate Sub-Branch/Inner Sub-Branch: This includes the groups—(i) Mediate Group/ Central Group and, (ii) Pahari Group. (i) Mediate Group/Central Group: This includes—1. Hindi; 2. Hindustani; 3. Urdu; 4. Punjabi; 5. Gujarati; 6. Bhili; 7. Khandeshi; 8. Rajasthani. (ii) Pahari Group: It is divided into—1. Eastern Pahari; 2. Central Pahari; and 3. Western Pahari Grierson adopted name 'Pahari Group' in the Indo-Aryan speeches spread along the Himalayan region from Bhadrawah in the west to Nepal in the east.

(1) Eastern Pahari: It consists of Nepali. (2) Central Pahari: It includes 1. Kumauni, 2. Garhwali. (3) Western Pahari: It includes 1. Jaunsari; 2. Sirmauri; 3. Baghati; 4. Kiunthali; 5. Handuri; 6. Siraji; 7. Soracholi; 8. Bashahri; 9. Siraji-InnerSiraji; 10. Sodochi; 11. Kului; 12. Mandi; 13. Mandeali; 14. Suketi; 15. Chameali; 16. Bharmauri/ Gaddi; 17. Churahi; 18. Pangwali; 19. Bhalesi; 20. Padari; 21. Pahari-Unspecified. The unspecified Indo-Aryan tongues, Old Middle-Indo-Aryan languages and Mother Tongue with unspecified family affiliation are listed below:

II. Unspecified Indo-Aryan Tongues: 1. Mahasu Pahari; 2. Tharu; 3. Kewati

III Old Middle-Indo-Aryan Languages: 1. Ardhamagadhi; 2. Pali; 3. Prakrit; 4. Sanskrit

IV. Mother Tongue with Unspecified Family Affiliation: 1. Kisan and 2. English

Languages of the Indo-Aryan family are concentrated in the plains of India.[385] The domain of Indo-Aryan languages, however, extends over the peninsular plateau also, reaching as far as the Konkan coast.[386] The central part of this region has Hindi as the principal language. It is spoken by the majority of people in India. Hindi is spoken in Uttar Pradesh, Madhya Pradesh, Bihar, Rajasthan, Haryana, Himachal Pradesh and the Union Territory of Delhi. Urdu is closely akin to Hindi and is widely distributed in this belt.[387] The speeches belonging to the north-western groups, such as Sindhi is mainly concentrated in Western India. Marathi is the most important language of the southern group of the Indo-Aryan family. The languages of the eastern group, such as Oriya, Bengali and Assamese are spoken in the Eastern India.[388] The languages of the central group are confined to Punjab, Rajasthan and Gujarat. The Himalayan and the sub-Himalayan areas are inhabited by the speakers of the various forms of Pahari speeches.[389]

3.1.6.2 LINGUISTIC REGIONS

The various languages and dialects formulate the basis of linguistic regions of India. It is however unfortunate to state that the tribal languages do not fit in this scheme of linguistic regions as the tribal groups are generally concentrated in areas like enclaves in central, eastern and north eastern parts of the country.

---

385 Ibid at p 270

386 Ibid

387 Ibid

388 Ibid

389 Ibid at p 270

This regional mosaic of the tribal languages is complex and does not tend itself to a simplified scheme of regions.[390] The tribal languages are so distributed that either they have their own small clusters or they overlap the regions of major languages.[391] In the north-east, however, the tribal speeches such as those of minor groups in Arunachal have almost knife-edged boundaries of their own.[392]

The twelve linguistic regions identified are as follows

1. Kashmiri, 2. Punjabi, 3. Hindi/Urdu, 4. Bengali, 5.Assamese, 6. Oriya, 7. Gujarati, 8. Marathi, 9. Kannada, 10. Telugu, 11. Tamil and 12. Malayalam.

These linguistic regions generally correspond with the states of Indian Union. But the state boundaries do not always correspond with the linguistic boundaries. In fact the linguistic boundary in itself is not a line, it is one of transition over which one language gradually loses its dominance and gives way to the other.[393]

3.1.7 LANGUAGES SPECIFIED IN SCHEDULE VIII TO THE CONSTITUTION OF INDIA

The Schedule VIII recognizes fifteen languages in India; there are 95.37 per cent speakers of these languages in the total Indian population (Part 'A'). The remaining 4.63 per cent is accounted for by ors (Part 'B'). The identifiable mother tongues at all India level have been grouped under the relevant language (s) (Census of India 1971) as given below: Part 'A' 1. Assamese 2. Bengali: Chakma; Haijong/Hajong; Malpaharia; Rajbansi 3. Gujarati: Saurashtra 4. Hindi: Awadhi, Baghelkhandi, BagriRajasthani; Banjari; Bhadrawahi; Bharmauri/ Gaddi; Bhojpuri; Braj Bhasha; Budelkhandi; Chambeali; Chattisgarhi; Churahi; Dhundhari; Garhwali; Gojri; Harauti; Haryanvi; Hindustani; Jaipuri; Jaunsari; Kangri; Khairari; Kortha/ Khatta; Kulvi; Kumauni; Kurmali; Thar; Lamani/ Lambadi; Lodhi; Madhesi; Magadhi/Maghi; Maithili, Malvi; Mandeali; Marwari; Mewari; Mewati; Nagpuria Nimadi; Pahari (It is a combination of various speeches spoken over long stretches of areas, where the speakers preferred to give a general name as Pahari); Panchpargania; Pawari/Powari; Rajasthani; Sadan/Sadri; Sirmauri; Sondwari; Surgujia. 5. Kannada: Badaga 6. Kashmiri: Kishtwari, Siraji 7. Malayalam: Yerava 8. Marathi: Karami 9. Oriya: Bhatri, Relli 10. Punjabi: Bagri, Bilaspuri/Kahluri 11. Sanskrit 12. Sindhi: Kachchhi 13. Tamil: Kaikadi; Yerukala/Yerukula 14. Telugu: Vadari 15. Urdu Part 'B' Adi: Adi Gallong/Gallong; Adi Minyong/ Minyong Angami: Chakra/ Chokri Bhili/Bhilodi Barel; Bhilai; Chodhari; Dhodia; Gamti/Gavit; Garasia; Kokna/Kokni/Kukna; Mawchi; Paradhi; Pawri; Tadavi; Vasava; Varli; Wagdi Bodo/Boro: Kachari; Mech Gondi: Dorli; Maria; Muria Khandeshi: Ahirani; Dangi; Gujari-Khandeshi Khasi: Pnar/Synteng; War Konda: Kodo Korku: Muwasi Lahnda: Multani, Punchhi Munda: Kol Naga: Zeliang Nissi/Dafla: Apatani; Bangni; Nishang; Tagin Paril: Dhurwa Santali: Karmali; Mahili Tripuri: Jamatia; Reang.[394]

Irrespective of these languages prevailing in Indian Constitution, many dialects can be seen to be practices in the territory of India especially amongst the tribals.

390 Ibid

391 Ibid

392 Ibid

393 Ibid

394 Ibid at p 271

3.2 NATURAL REGIONS OF INDIA AND SOCIO ECONOMIC POSITION OF TRIBALS

The socio economic condition of tribals and adivasis largely depends on the natural factors responsible to regulate their habitat and functioning. Various rights in respect of these natural elements are needed for the existence of the right to life and livelihood as guaranteed by the Constitution of India. A study of the natural regions of the country will establish the actual position of tribals amongst all other communities present in this huge country. Tribals and adivasis largely depend upon the geographical location they live in and have developed their way of life and profession in furtherance of these factors. These professions are so unique that they tend to exist only amongst these communities in the entire world and only to a few existing people of these tribal communities. These people also had special intellectual property rights which are mostly customary based and not of the Indian legal setup on various subject matter including medicinal values of various trees, plants, crops and fruits of the geographic region they live in. The concept of preservation of resources is alien to tribals and they vastly depend upon the regular consumption system. Thus any disruption in the enjoyment of these natural environment and resources may prove fatal to the existence of such primitive practices. Large scale displacement of tribals from their habitat has been the benchmark of the last century and this has led to a lot of extinction of tribal knowhow and indigenous practices. There has been a complete end to many tribal practices in India which once has been the symbol of economic and social prosperity of these people. Certain laws have been incorporated in the Indian legal system of late to preserve these areas and the conservation and management of these areas have been vested upon the tribas but a long gap after displacement has made the process of revival of tribal existence in certain areas irretrievable. The damage has already been done in most of the cases. The international obligation of the country has virtually forces the government to secure a lot of socio economic rights of the indigenous communities of India. In this backdrop the existing natural regions of the country plays the pivotal role in understanding the possibilities of revival of tribal economic and social system that has once been the identity of these tribal communities.

i. Natural regions: The Natural regions of the country can broadly be classified into:

  1. The Himalayan Mountain Complex; 2. The Indus-Ganga-Brahmaputra Plain;
  3. The Peninsular Plateau and 4. The Islands

These natural regions have some broad similarities such as relief, geomorphologic, history, drainage, climate, soil, natural vegetation and wild life. Tribal economy is vastly dependant on these factors. The tribes who are dependent on agriculture are dependent not on the irrigational facilities available in the remote areas they live in but the rainfall upon which their cultivation is solely dependent.

ii. Climatological Factors and Climatic Regions of India

The various climatological factors are rainfall, humidity and temperature. There are various natural regions in India which varied upon these factors. These climatic factors along with the soil type determines the nature of cultivation and along with that the type of economic and social condition these areas fall belonging to these varied natural regions.

Tribals live in almost all the climatic regions in India. Their economic conditions also depends upon the place they live in. Thus the tribals in India can be seen in all the economic stratification of the country.

A climatic region generally possesses a broad uniformity in climatic conditions produced by combined effects of climatic factors. India can be divided into the following climatic regions after Köppen's method, based on the monthly values of temperature and precipitation: (1) Tropical Savannah Type, (2) Monsoon Type with Short Dry Season, (3) Monsoon Type with Dry Season in High Sun Period, (4) Semiarid and Steppe Climate, (5) Hot Desert Type, (6) Monsoon Type with Dry Winters, (7) Cold Humid Winters Type with Shorter Summer, and (8) Polar Type.[395]

3.3. HISTORICAL ANALYSIS AND RACIAL CLASSIFICATION IN INDIA

3.3.1 PRE HISTORIC AND HISTORICAL ANALYSIS OF INDIA AND TRIBAL DEVELOPMENT

A systematic study of the pre historical and historical development of human habitants in India will serve the purpose of understanding the indigenous peoples and their existence in various part of India. The tribals throughout this phase have developed their culture and social norms and all these are visible in their modern day existence. The tribal population in India has been affected in various ways throughout the pre historic and historic period by a number of natural and man-made phenomenons. These factors along with their development shall help to identify the economic conditions of these communities and how much they are a part of sustained economic order.

India has witnessed throughout its past the existence of human beings in both historical and pre historical age. Evidence in the forms of tools discovered from excavations has a scientific explanation as to Indian human civilization in these ages.

Prehistoric age generally denotes a period of around 5,00,000 years ago. Discovery of stone tools in Indian Palaeolithic and caves have given a fair amount of certainty as to the existence of human in India in that age. A detailed diagram is annexed to identify the sites of discovery of these evidences. This explains that the indigenous population how so ever small it may be were not dependant on agriculture. Neither they had any domesticated animals nor they were enjoying a life non nomadic with human settlements. Evidence however shows that these inhabitants generally used caves etc temporarily to avoid natural calamities and seasonal distress. These communities were nomadic and semi nomadic in nature and had their sole reliability on natural produce and other animals to feed upon. Thus hunting and gathering communities[396] were present in this age. It shall be relevant in this point of time that in many parts of India today the tribals and adivasis still continues their nomadic and semi nomadic features where they depends upon the forest produce for their sustenance. The socio economic condition of those men and these of this century have a few things in common as well.

The concentration of these habitats was mostly by the side of major river valleys in India. The majority of discovery of these Stone Age tools are made in these locations.

Epiglacial phase (10,000 to 50,000 B.C.) following the end of Pleistocene to some extent made a coincidence with the transitional Mesolothic cultural dispersal in India. During this phase there has been a noticeable inclination towards natural resources like water bodies, resources within such water bodies, birds, fruits and plant produces. One of the presumable reasons for this change is the reduction in the availability of big game to feed the growing community of human habitats in various parts of India is the marked climatic change. These communities actually increased in numbers dramatically as they left their nomadic behaviour and relied more upon static natural resources. Thus concentration of human habitat was progressive by

---

395 Ibid at p 252

396 Piggot, 1952

the rivers of India. This phase witness the start of a new culture and socio-economic system departing the ancient habit of food gathering to food producing.

However their numbers are estimated to be in hundreds which is incidentally the number of certain primitive tribes in existence in India today. However, with the advent of non tribals in recent centuries, the tribals of India have fled to remotest areas of hills and forest and followed their ancient practice of food gathering and to some extent wherever possible food producing communities.

A study of the genetics of Indians suggests that

> "Both western and eastern Eurasian-specific mtDNA haplo types can be found in India together with strictly Indian-specific ones. However, in India the structure of the haplo groups shared either with western or eastern Eurasian populations is profoundly different. This indicates a local independent development over a very long time period. Minor overlaps with lineages in other Eurasian populations clearly demonstrate that recent immigrations have had very little impact on the innate structure of the maternal gene pool of Indians. Despite the variations found within India, these populations stem from a limited number of founder lineages. These lineages were most likely introduced to the Indian subcontinent during the Middle Palaeolithic, before the peopling of Europe and perhaps the Old World in general. Our demographic analysis reveals at least two major expansion phases that have influenced the wide assortment of the Indian mtDNA lineages. The more recent phase, which according to our estimation started around 20,000-30,000 years ago, seems to correspond to the transition from the Middle to the Upper Palaeolithic. The first expansion phase may reflect a demographic burst immediately after the initial peopling of India around 50-60 thousand years ago. This wave of expansion brought forward also those maternal lineages that can rightfully claim the name of "Eurasian Eves"* [397]

A similar study was conducted where DNA profiling was conducted on various ethnic groups of India. Members of different culture, linguist and geographical background participated in this research work. It was observed that Indian populations were founded by a small number of females, possibly arriving on one of the early waves of out-of-Africa migration of modern humans; ethnic differentiation occurred subsequently through demographic expansion and geographic dispersal. Further they have found that South-east Asia was peopled by two waves of migration, one originating in India and the other originating in Southern China.[398]

Neolithic Age is approximately dated from 6000 to 4000 B.C. In India, various communities started to develop the use of non metallic implements. Instances of domesticating animals were also notices during this phase in India. But the most fascinating of all the changes this period brings up is the advent of agriculture. A detailed figure is annexed hereto to reflect the sites where agriculture flourished in India. This knowhow has been the natural process of development in India or it being applied in these areas by people from outside is another subject of debate. The indigenous agricultural system is still found in some areas in India today amongst the tribals and adivasis.

Neolithic age witnessed the development of community habitat in forms of small villages and townships. India too witnessed the growth of human habitat and the formation of communities residing together in a more systematic manner. Various use of pottery was found in this era. However, it must be stated in this regard that there has no scientific proof that India made uniform step by step progress in various places

---

397 Kivisild et al. 2000 at p. 150

398 Roychoudhury et al. 2000

of the country as the age characterise. There are various places in India which remained static even in this dynamic era as has been the case of various tribal and indigenous communities being far off the river valleys. At this point of time, there is a bifurcation of development zones based on geographical and climatic factors. This bifurcation subsequently leads to the permanent division of economic and social conditions of tribals in India.

The ability to control production and storage of life's essentials encouraged the growth of larger permanent settlements and these in turn led to technical innovation, division of labour, the formation of social classes and ultimately the superimposition of a system of administrative controls. Biologically such developments meant an increase in the demographic dimensions of a limited number of populations (gene pools) these possessing the knowledge of food production at the expense of other who retained the earlier type of natural economy and who could not expand numerically beyond the limits set by nature.[399]

One of the remarkable instances of existence of indigenous peoples in this era was the existence of the civilization of Harappa and Mohenjodaro. The Indus Valley Civilization extended from the river basin at the foothills of Himalaya and the Gangatic watershed to coastal Gujarat. It also had an estuarine dock at Lothal and an outpost at Thane[400]. Some of the distinctive features of this civilization are uniform assemblages of tools, unique methods of water supply, drainage, hypocaust system for heating grand central bath. Apart for these sophisticated and unique settlement features, some remarkable individual achievements like ceramic techniques, the systems of weights and measures are seen. There has been differentiation between the citadel and slave quarters as well. All these features ultimately identifies and points out the existence of a complex society with social stratification and a uniform administrative mechanism. About the origin of the Harappan Civilization practically nothing definite is known. Different versions are put forward-right from Sumerian or a Semitic origin, to the Dravidian and Mundari are often mentioned. Even origins from Baluchistan and Iranian uplands were suggested[401].

At about 3000 B.C. Baluchistan which as less arid than now was inhabited by small groups of people from the Iranian uplands. These migrants brought with them the knowledge of agriculture and the organisation of small self-sufficient village communities. In the course of about 500 years, after they had settled in Baluchistan, they migrated in big or small group into the Indus valley.[402] But the sudden emergence of the urban civilization still baffles the interpreters of Harappan cultures. Some believe that urban civilization was superimposed on the people suddenly by strangers coming from outside at some time in the middle of the 3rd millennium B.C. It is quite impossible to say when Harappan civilization grew up'. The civilization is unique in a sense that it was almost a fully classified state as early as 3000 B.C. It is said that it may well have been evolved by the natives of the soil and foreign settlers induced new ideas which Harappans absorbed and evolved into a distinct mature culture. The Indus Valley Civilization has spread from it southern bases to the Himalayan foothills, up the valley of Kashmir, around 1800 B.C.[403]

---

399 Bowles (1977)

400 A place near Mumbai

401 Excavations at Harappa were resumed in 1986 under the direction of Dr. George F. Dales of the University of California, Berkeley, and are countinuing each year at that site. Some 100 skeletons have been removed from site (Mature Harappan cemetery of R-37) by Drs. Nancy C. Lovell, John R. Lukacs, Brain E. Hemphill and Kenneth A.R. Kennedy

402 Sastri and Srinivasachari (1980)

403 Bhasin 2006 at p 240

The Chalcolithic period is dated roughly from 4000 to 3000 B.C. this is the next culture according to chronological order. This nomenclature came from the fact that the main tool types representing this culture were made of copper along with stone. A detailed diagrammatical representation has been given of the sites in India where evidence of various aspects are excavated of this age. [404]

However no detailed evidence can actually show that there is any Bronze Age in India. However, there are various Bronze artifacts excavated at various sites. Historians argued that these might have been migrated into India.

It is proved that the valley of Kashmir was known earlier to the settled people and Mesolithic artifacts have been found. Excavations in Kashmir also give evidence of earlier proto-urban settlements. Apart from the above, Kashmir also yielded earlier Paleolithic artifacts which are more allied to those of North India, so it might be conjectured that the builders of Burzahom (Kashmir) crossed the Hindukush by 2000 B.C. or thereabouts.[405]

3.3.2 HISTORICAL ANALYSIS OF INDIA AND TRIBAL DEVELOPMENT.

The historical period starts from 4000 B.C. onwards for 2000 years. This phase has been marked by various penetrations of alien people of alien lands in the territory of India. The said movement of foreigners may be summed up *in seriatim*:
1. The Greek invasion
2. The invasion of Sakas
3. Invasion of Pahlavas
4. The Kushan invasion
5. Huns invasion
6. The influx of the Jews and Parsis
7. Invasion of the Arabian Muslims
8. Invasion of the Persian Muslims
9. Turk invasion and
10. The Afghan invasion of India
11. The Mughal invasion
12. The European invasions which can be classified into Portuguese b. Dutch c. French and d. British

Amongst the worst sufferers among all these invasions have been the indigenous inhabitants of India. The adivasis have been victims of these invasions and were literally running to various remotest corners of the country to save themselves and their family. The tribals' choice of these extreme areas in India for habitat was thus not a matter of choice but a matter of compulsion. Amongst all the invasions, the British colonial movement has witnessed the most adverse effects on these communities not only in India but also across the world. The British policy of drainage of wealth went to such an extent; even the remotest areas were not spared. Thus the systematic socio economic conditions of tribals have been damaged permanently. The tribals who were mostly dependant on the natural resources were deprived of their sacred places by the influx of non tribals. Their resistance didnot suffice to ward off the upcoming annihilation of Indian indigenous population, along with the extinction of a large number of floral and faunal species. There has been uninterrupted and systematic cutting of trees of immense value for the sake of so called development. Indian tribals lost a so much of land and natural resources in the 200 years of British colonialism that they

---

404 (for the sites see Fig. 3)

405 Bhasin

have not in the last 2000 years. The tribals have been declared the enemy of the forests. They have been barred to use the forest resources. Such great was the atrocity upon these people that millions of these poor and unarmed people have to leave their land which they have been enjoying for ages, and join the labour force of the country which is mostly unorganized. History witnessed the death of multiple ethnic systems prevalent in this country. With that comes the death of the culture, knowhow, and human rights. It is not the number game that matters, as India has witnessed gradual increase[406] in tribal population, but the death of their rich socio economic system which is the essence of tribal culture and social system.

3.3.2.1 RACIAL CLASSIFICATION AND THE POSITION OF TRIBALS IN INDIA.

There are two theories to determine the origin of man and major human races.
1. The Mono Centric Theory and
2. The Polycentric Theory

The mono centric theory as the name suggests considers modern man to have evolved in a single region and when human groups spread geographically and started to reside in various definite territories, the various racial types evolved.[407] Darwin was one of the advocates of this theory as he ventured to predict more than a century ago that one day it would be found that man had originated in Africa.

On the other hand, the polycentric theory claims that modern man evolved in several regions relatively independent of one another and that the people people developed at different rates.[408] This theory claims that the modern man evolved from the 'oldest' and 'old' people in each region and that this gave rise to the formation of major races.

Position in India

A list of various classification has been made by various authors, Indian and foreign and all tend to have some sense. However, the racial migration in India as has been discussed and reported by Guha and ors eminent scholars.

1. Negrito Element

Negritos generally represents the oldest surviving type of man and it has been argued that they may have preceded the Neanderthal man. It is presumed that it is by the Neanderthals displaced and disposed the Negritos.[409] The Negritos may be safely stated to be the first inhabitants of South East Asia. Negritos traces are noticed in some of the forest tribes of the higher hills of the south of India and similar traces can be noticed in various inaccessible areas of Bengal, Assam and Burma.

2. Proto-Australoid Element

The earliest stratum of Indian populations was a long-headed, dark skinned, broad nosed people. Their physical features are closely akin to modern aborigines of Chota Nagpur, Central India and the primitive

---

406 9.6% of the Total Population. Census Report 2011

407 Henri Victor Vallois and G Oliver of France and other scientists of various countries advocating this theory

408 Franz Weidenrich, U.S.A

409 Grifth-Taylor

tribes of South India.[410] They are original inhabitants, the so called 'Adi-basis' of India. In the hymns of Rig-Veda the oldest sacred texts of the Hindus, they are mainly addressed as 'Dasa' (Barbarians) or 'Dasyu' (ugly, sub-human) described as 'Anas' ('a-nas' = nose less or 'an-as' = without a mouth), Krishnagarba (Dark skinned), 'Mridhravak' (Hostile speech) not worshiping Vedic gods with whom Aryan speaking tribes fought during their advent into India from Transcapia.

3. Mongoloid Element

The Mongoloids are present in the northern and north eastern zones of the Himalayan ranges, valleys and eastern frontiers. It is an interesting fact that one of the Mohenjo-Daro skulls as well as a terracotta figurine has been identified as definitely Mongoloid with features like the typical sloping narrow eyes of caricatures.

A SUM UP

Social and economic rights arise out of a number of variables that varies from one sect to another; one clan to the other. A basic anthropological analysis can ultimately bring out the origin of the said distinctive clan and tribe and their aspiration in life. Such aspirations bring out the goals they want to achieve. This leads to the creation of certain inalienable rights that these communities must enjoy and the state must protect and continue to provide. It must be understood that social and economic aspirations are the outcome of the historical and cultural heritage of the society a person resides in. The geographical and environmental conditions are directly linked with the economic aspects of the member of the society. Thus the chapter analyzes the anthropological and other allied aspects that are inalienable to the people belonging to tribal and indigenous communities. These aspects form the basis of the socio economic aspirations of the people concerned. These aspirations are the basis of rights they think they deserve for proper functioning of their life. Their culture, education, habitat all depends upon their anthropological background. The social and economic aspirations of the tribals in India largely depend upon their historical development, geographical positioning and certain other factors. It is these factors that contribute towards the process of law making for these communities. Even the Constitution of India acknowledges these factors and certain aspirations have been considered to the part of the mother law of the country. The following chapter makes an elaborate study of those provisions along with other enactments providing key to the socio economic rights of tribals in India.

---

410 Supra note 7 at p 249

CHAPTER 4

ROLE OF STATE LEGISLATIVE ORGANS IN THE PROTECTION OF CIVIL AND ECONOMIC RIGHTS OF TRIBALS IN INDIA

AN OVERVIEW

India is the largest democracy of the world and to cater the various needs of the people various laws have been enacted. The most significant of them all is legislation or 'the law properly so called' as has been propagated by Jeremy Bentham while defining law. Even when there are various limitations and criticism attached with the philosophy of codified laws, the need of codified laws have been best felt in a society which is earmarked with huge population and great diversity.

India, in furtherance of the protection of the basic rights of the people belonging to indigenous and tribal communities has enacted a plethora of legislation. This chapter analyses some relevant legislations along with their relationship with the tribals in India.

4.1. CONSTITUTIONAL GUARANTEES FOR TRIBES AND TRIBAL PEOPLES

The Constitution of India is the supreme law of India. It lays down the framework defining fundamental political principles, establishes the structure, procedures, powers, and duties of government institutions, and sets out fundamental rights, directive principles, and the duties of citizens.[411] It is the longest written Constitution of any sovereign country in the world, containing 450 articles in 22 parts, 12 schedules and 94 amendments, for a total of 117,369 words in the English language version.[412]

When the United Nations was founded in 1945, some 750 million people, which is nearly a third of the world's population, lived in territories that were dependent on colonial powers.[413] Today, fewer than two million people live under colonial rule. Since the creation of the United Nations, 80 former colonies have gained their independence, 16 of them were countries in Asia and Africa who gained their independence from the United Kingdom and, while remaining in the British Commonwealth of nations, gave unto themselves their Constitutions of Independence.[414] Since then, while Constitutions have come and gone at an astonishing rate, only one of those 16 Afro-Asian countries, India still has its Independence Constitution in place some 65 years later.[415]

The Constitution was drafted and adopted[416] by the 308 member Constituent Assembly, which was elected by the elected members of the provincial assemblies. The Constituent Assembly was a highly representative body with significant representation and participation of women, minorities and scheduled caste members.[417]

---

411 Indian Constitutional Law, Available at, http://jabalpuradvocate.com/ (Accessed on December 5, 2015)

412 Prof. Dias, "The Indian Constitution: the Vast done; the Little as Yet Left Undone" unpublished

413 Decolonization, Available at, http://www.un.org/en/globalissues/decolonization/ (Accessed on December 5, 2015)

414 Ibid

415 Ibid

416 over a period 12 days short of 3 years

417 Jawaharlal Nehru, C. Rajagopalachari, Rajendra Prasad, Sardar Vallabhbhai Patel, Sandipkumar Patel, Dr Ambedkar, Maulana Abul Kalam Azad, Shyama Prasad Mukherjee, Nalini Ranjan Ghosh, and Balwant Singh Mehta were some important figures in the Assembly. There were more than 30 members of the scheduled classes, as well as representatives of the Anglo-Indian community, the Parsis, the Christians other than Anglo-Indians and the Gorkha Community. Prominent jurists such as Alladi Krishnaswamy Iyer, B. R. Ambedkar, Benegal Narsing Rau and K. M. Munshi, Ganesh Mavlankar were also members of the Assembly. Sarojini Naidu, Hansa Mehta, Durgabai Deshmukh, Rajkumari Amrit Kaur and Vijayalakshmi Pandit were important women members.

There are a few basic features of the Constitution of our country that establishes and tends toward a more human rights friendly Constitution and also in the process safeguards the rights of the tribes in India. These features may be summarized as under:

- It enumerates a legally enforceable set of fundamental rights and freedoms in Part III of the Constitution. It also enumerates a set of "Directive Principles of State Policy" (containing human rights which are to be progressively realized) which while non-legally enforceable are nonetheless to be "fundamental in the governance of the country".
- It provides for effective remedies (by way of the so-called high prerogative writs) for infringement of fundamental rights with original jurisdiction vested in the Supreme Court and the High Courts.
- It provides for extensive powers of judicial review of laws; as well as over administrative actions; with power to strike them down if inconsistent with the fundamental rights contained in Part III of the Constitution.
- Although it provides the State with extensive powers to deal with external and internal emergencies, including the power to temporarily suspend certain fundamental rights; it makes certain key fundamental rights "non-derogable" even in times of emergency and also makes them "non-waivable" even by the beneficiaries of the rights.[418]

The Constitution of India has provided certain very important provisions to protect the rights of the tribes and tribal communities in India. The provision categorically incorporates the various rights that are essential for the sustenance and development of these communities. It shall be relevant in this regard to state that the provision incorporated in the Constitution of India has got its source from a plethora of other Constitutions. It must also be acknowledged that the United Nations Organisation has also played a very important role in providing rights to tribal and indigenous peoples of India. The Universal Declaration of Human Rights has been a key document that has many similarities to the rights granted to the people of India including the tribal peoples of the country.

The Constitution of India from time and again has played a significant role in protecting various rights of the tribals. As a matter of fact, it is the Constitution that provides a working definition of the term Scheduled Tribes. It also provides the procedural safeguards as to their creation and abolition through public notification. The process of determination of a tribe or a tribal area still remains within the closed doors of the discretion of the President of India. However, this discretion is not arbitrary, it is still ambiguous as to the fact that a considerable number of people claim themselves within the purview of tribes and still they have not been given the status of scheduled tribes under the Constitution and are considered by many as political victims. The debate of declaring a tribe as scheduled tribe has been the subject matter of discussion in both national and international forum, where in the matter has been considered more of politics than of law. Again there has been instances of incorporating certain classes within the purview of Scheduled caste and Scheduled Tribe and has subsequent been rejected by the Honourable Supreme Court of India. The role of the Governor of respective states also call for a reasonable attention as the Constitutional provision also points out the need of the President to consult with the respective Governor of the state before declaring any group of part of any group as tribes.

The Constitution of India has provided certain very important provisions to protect the rights of the tribes and tribal communities in India. The provision categorically incorporates the various rights that are essential for the sustenance and development of these communities.

The position of the tribes in India as to their respective rights have been formally dealt with by various other provisions of the Constitution including that of Part III which deals with Fundamental Rights. In

---

418   Supra Dias

this regard a thorough study of the provisos and exceptions of the respective provisions calls for significant consideration. The Directive Principles of State policy also attracts special attentions while discussing the various provisions of the rights of tribes and tribal peoples in India. It must also be stated that a specialised agency in the form of National Commission of Scheduled Tribes for monitoring the rights of the tribal peoples plays a dominant role in protection of various rights of these subaltern groups and communities.

The term Scheduled Tribes have been formally taken up by Article 366 of the Constitution. [419] The importance and dominance of the President of India is explicit in the provision. It is the President who has been empowered to specify the tribes or tribal communities or parts of or groups within tribes or tribal communities which shall for the purposes of this Constitution be deemed to be Scheduled Tribes by notification. It shall be relevant to state in this regard that the Governor of respective states also plays an important role as the President is to consult with respective Governors before declaring a tribe in that state as notified.[420]

Land refers to heritage to tribals and this heritage is the primary source of livelihood to them. Land plays the most dominant role in their sustenance. As a matter of practice the land belonging to them is the basis of their social, economic, political and cultural platform. Alienating tribals from their land is at par with infringing their rights as granted by Article 19(1)(g) of the Constitution of India and not merely the violation of Article 19(1)(f) and Article 31(as it was then before the amendment of the Constitution deleting the said provisions).

The provisions inter alia in Part III, IV, X calls for special attention to the protection of Tribes and tribal areas. Schedule V and VI were specifically created for the Scheduled Tribes in India.

It is worth mentioning that the Executive and the Legislative power of the State to transfer Land under Article 298 and Article 245 respectively are subject to the provisions of Fifth Schedule. A host of Articles in The Directive Principles of State Policy also refers to the responsibility of the state to protect and promote the welfare of the tribes in India.

The tribal population in India may be classified into the following four divisions on the basis of habitation and assimilation.[421]
1.   Tribals or adivasis who confine themselves to original forst habitats and are still distinctive in their pattern of life. They may be termed as tribal communities;

---

419 In this Constitution, unless the context otherwise requires, the following expressions have the meanings hereby respectively assigned to them, that is to say-

(23) "Schedule" means a Schedule to this Constitution.

(25) "Scheduled Tribes" means such tribes or tribal communities or parts or groups within such tribes or tribal communities as are deemed under article 342 to be Scheduled Tribes for the purposes of this Constitution.

420 Scheduled Tribes— as has been stated in Article 342 is as follows.

(1) The President [may with respect to any State [or Union territory], and where it is a State, after consultation with the Governor thereof,] by public notification, specify the tribes or tribal communities or parts of or groups within tribes or tribal communities which shall for the purposes of this Constitution be deemed to be Scheduled Tribes in relation to that State [or Union territory, as the case may be].

(2) Parliament may by law include in or exclude from the list of Scheduled Tribes specified in a notification issued under clause (1) any tribe or tribal community or part of or group within any tribe or tribal community, but save as aforesaid a notification issued under the said clause shall not be varied by any subsequent notification.

421 Mahendra Mohan Verma, 'Tribal Development in India: Programmes and Perspectives' Mittal Publication, 2008 p 19.

2. Tribals who have more or less settled down I rural areas, taking to agriculture and other allied occupations. This category of people may be termed as semi-tibal communities.
3. Tribals who have migrated to urban or semi urban and rural areas and are engaged in civilized occupations in industries and other vocations and who have, with discrimination, adopted trails and culture of other population of the country. These may be classified as semi assimilated tribal communities; and
4. Totally assimilated tribals.

The Indian Constitution has vested the power to notify any community as schedule tribe upon the President of India which he does, with the consultation of the Governor of the respective states.[422] This notification may involve the entire community or parts or groups within the tribes or tribal communities, as Scheduled Tribes through the notification. Further, the parliament may include or exclude tribes specified in the notification by passing any law. But it must be mentioned that the economic and social condition of many tribes have not been addressed as many of them have not been provided with the status of Scheduled tribe to get the Constitutional benefits and the protection of various other statutes.

4.1.1. EQUALITY AND NON-DISCRIMINATION

One of the interesting approaches of the makers of the Constitution in providing equality to the un-equals is by incorporating Article 15.[423] This article is of the prominent fundamental rights provided for the protection of tribals is in Article 15 of the Constitution of India. This article is one of the most important and significant Fundamental Rights providing direction to protect the interest of tribal and indigenous peoples of India. Fundamental rights are justiciable and binding upon the state.

It prohibits any discrimination on grounds of religion, race, caste, sex or place of birth. It further protects all citizens from any disability, liability restriction or condition like access to shops, public restaurants, hotels and places of public entertainment; or the use of wells, tanks, bathing ghats, roads and places of public resort maintained wholly or partly out of State funds or dedicated to the use of general public on grounds relating to religion.

In this provision there has been an incorporation of special provision for the advancement of any socially and educationally backward classes of citizens or for the Scheduled Castes and the Scheduled Tribes. This application of *generalia specialibus non derogant* is very important for not only the protection of tribal and certain specified class of people but also their social upliftment.[424]

---

422 Article 342 in Part XVI of the Constitution of India

423 Article 15: Prohibition of discrimination on grounds of religion, race, caste, sex or place of birth— (1) The State shall not discriminate against any citizen on grounds only of religion, race, caste, sex, place of birth or any of them,.. (2) No citizen shall, on grounds only of religion, race, caste, sex, place of birth or any of them, be subject to any disability, liability, restriction or condition with regard to— (a) access to shops, public restaurants, hotels and places of public entertainment; or (b) the use of wells, tanks, bathing ghats, roads and places of public resort maintained wholly or partly out of State funds or dedicated to the use of general public.
(3) Nothing in this article shall prevent the State from making any special provision for women and children. 1[(4) Nothing in this article or in clause (2) of article 29 shall prevent the State from making any special provision for the advancement of any socially and educationally backward classes of citizens or for the Scheduled Castes and the Scheduled Tribes]

424 Ibid

4.1.2. EQUALITY AND OPPORTUNITY IN PUBLIC EMPLOYMENT

Another important right granted by the Constitution is the right to equality of opportunity in matters of public employment. Equality of opportunity is needed for those who have been deprived of it for decades. In order to address the problem, Article 16[425] of the Constitution has been incorporated.

4.1.3. PROTECTION AGAINST UNTOUCHABILITY

One of the fascinating creations of Hindu religion is the caste system and with it the creation of certain categories of people vested with certain specific derogatory functioning. It must be stated in this regard that the constituent assembly always wanted to put this discriminatory practice to an end. This led to the incorporation of Article 17 to the Constitution of India. "Untouchability" is abolished and its practice in any form is forbidden. The enforcement of any disability arising out of "Untouchability" shall be an offence punishable in accordance with law. Article 17 of Indian Constitution seeks to abolish 'untouchability' and to forbid all such inhuman and derogatory practices. It is basically a "statement of principle" that needs to be made operational with the ostensible objective to remove humiliation and multifaceted harassments meted to the Dalits and to ensure their fundamental and socio-economic, political, and cultural rights.[426]

Discrimination has been the customary practice of the upper caste people of India over the lower class people. Prohibition from entering certain places, using certain water resources, using certain passage even for walking, for religious or other cause are some of the few instances of discriminating behaviour that the lower caste people have been facing for centuries. The caste system in India has some inherent vices in it. Untouchability in various forms is some of them.

The people falling in the lower caste system of Hindu religious have been vested with certain jobs of lower profile like cleaning, scavenging etc; Mahatma Gandhi called these people as Harijans which means child of God.

---

425 Article 16: Equality of opportunity in matters of public employment— (1) There shall be equality of opportunity for all citizens in matters relating to employment or appointment to any office under the State. (2) No citizen shall, on grounds only of religion, race, caste, sex, descent, place of birth, residence or any of them, be ineligible for, or discriminated against in respect of, any employment or office under the State. (3) Nothing in this article shall prevent Parliament from making any law prescribing, in regard to class or classes of employment or appointment to an office 2[under the Government of, or any local or other authority within, a State or Union territory, any requirement as to residence within that State or Union territory] prior to such employment or appointment. (4) Nothing in this article shall prevent the State from making any provision for the reservation of appointments or posts in favour of any backward class of citizens which, in the opinion of the State, is not adequately represented in the services under the State

[4(A) Nothing in this article shall prevent the State from making any provision for reservation in matters of promotion to any class or classes of posts in the services under the State in favor of the Scheduled Castes and the Scheduled Tribes which in the opinion of the States, are not adequately represented in the services under the State].

[4(B) Nothing in this article shall prevent the State from considering any unfilled vacancies of a year which are reserved for being filled up in that year in accordance with any provision for reservation made under clause (4) or Clause (4A) as a separate class of vacancies to be filled up in any succeeding year or years and such class of vacancies shall not be considered together with the vacancies of the year in which they are being filled up for determining the ceiling of fifty per cent reservation on total number of vacancies of that year.] (5) Nothing in this article shall affect the operation of any law which provides that the incumbent of an office in connection with the affairs of any religious or denominational institution or any member of the governing body thereof shall be a person professing a particular religion or belonging to a particular denomination.

426 This has been the standing of the Supreme Court of India.

4.1.4 OTHER FUNDAMENTAL RIGHTS

One of the major reasons for formation of a written Constitution is to provide a set of written rights for the citizens of the country. Part III of the Indian Constitution, under Article 17 prohibits all forms of practices relating to untouchability. Abolition of the customary practice of untouchability confers relief and liberty of the people who once belonged to the untouchable categories. Apart from the Constitutional guarantees, various other enactments have been passed by the Indian parliament to prohibit any practice of untouchability including making such practice an offence.[427]

4.1.5. DIRECTIVE PRINCIPLES OF STATE POLICY AND RIGHTS OF TRIBALS

The objective of Article 39(b) provides "to minimise the inequality in income" and also "to eliminate inequalities in status, facilities and opportunities" among people in different areas.

Thus the government must look after the economic interest of those who are weaker in the society. Tribals are weaker economically. Although not by choice but by compulsion.

A lot of acts coupled together with the massive so called developmental projects have let to this irretrievable breakdown of tribal economy in various parts of the country. The major so called developmental projects like mining and construction of dams on big rivers have created a lot of economic imbalance amongst the tribals and adivasis who are solely dependent upon their natural resources of their land which they have been holding from time immemorial. Along with their economy a lot of their culture are also involved which are also in the verge of extinction. The practice of carrying on the family tradition in various professions amongst the tribes has been discontinued for the sake of sustenance of life and livelihood. Because of such uncalculated acts and risks taken by state has done things opposed to the directives of the Constitution of India and the time has come to control such un necessary creation of inequality in the status of the life of the people of adivasis and tribals in India. And parallel to this, the state in under direct direction of the Constitution, to minimise the inequality in income and in the process, provide parallel income opportunities to the tribals and indigenous population of the country. The compulsive creation of in equality in status, facilities and opportunities are basic aspects of state created development consequences. Thus the state has also the moral obligation of protecting and preventing the inequality amongst the tribals in respect of status, facilities and opportunities. Other essential directive principles that have been incorporated in the Directive Principles of State Policy apart from Article 39 are Article 41, Article 42, Article 43, Article 46 and Article 47 of the Indian Constitution.

In order to protect the economic and educational interest of the SC/ST and weaker section of the society, Article 46 of the Indian Constitution plays a significant role. The provision directs the State to promote with special care the educational and economic interests of the weaker sections of the people, and in particular, of the Scheduled Castes and the Scheduled Tribes. The provision also directs the state to protect these vulnerable classes from social injustice and all forms of exploitation. The article particularly emphasises the responsibility of the state to promote special case towards the education and economic interest of the weaker section of the people particularly of scheduled castes and scheduled tribes. This provision in the Indian Constitution also promotes various educational and vocational schemes to protect education to these communities. However special care must be taken to protect their indigenous educational technique which is based on practical experience and exposure rather than through books.[428]

---

427 The Protection of Civil Rights Act 1955 is one such Act which came with the primary objective to make any practice of untouchablity an offence under that act.

428 It must be referred that the tribal knowhow must be preserved along with their language and folklore.

4.1.6. CONSTITUTIONAL PROTECTION AS TO THE ADMINISTRATION AND CONTROL OF SCHEDULES AREAS AND SCHEDULED TRIBES.

The Constitution of India has provided for special provisions for the administration and control of Scheduled areas and scheduled tribes. The Fifth and Sixth Schedules of the Constitution have been incorporated to deal with the administration of tribal areas in India.

The term 'Scheduled Areas' specified in the Constitution of India identifies the tribal regions to which either the Fifth Schedule[429] or the Sixth Schedule applies.[430] These two Schedules have separate and unique mechanisms for governance.

The Fifth Schedule was an entirely centralized system where the tribal communities were directed in their affairs by provincial governors.[431] The Schedule actually allowed the states to extend their executive power to these Scheduled Areas,[432] which has a vast tribal population. The provision further granted necessary power and authority to the Governor of each state to make regulations for the peace and good governance of any area in a State which is for the time being a Scheduled Area.[433] The Governor was thus the sole legislature for the Scheduled Areas and the Scheduled Tribes,[434] competent to make laws on all subjects enumerated in the Constitution's Union, State, and Concurrent[435] Lists.[436] This view appears to be incongruous with the colonial policy of allowing the Governor to act in his or her discretion only in Excluded Areas (present day Sixth Schedule areas). The term Scheduled Tribes" refers to those tribes designated as such through a process of identification based on the procedures and provisions made in Article 342 the Constitution of India." In designating a tribe as a Scheduled Tribe, the government would consider their traits, distinctive culture, geographical isolation, level of contact with communities beyond their own and general social and educational development. Religion is not a consideration.[437] The inclusion of a tribe in the list of Scheduled Tribes permits the government to take 'Affirmative Action' in favour of such tribes.[438] This approach of

---

429 The Fifth Schedule covers tribal areas in nine peninsular states, namely, Andhra Pradesh, Orissa, Jharkhand, Chhattisgarh, Madhya Pradesh, Maharashtra, Gujarat, Rajasthan and Himachal Pradesh. The Sixth Schedule includes in its purview the tribal areas in the north-eastern states of Assam, Meghalaya, Tripura and Mizoram and is excluded from the purview of the Fifth Schedule.

430 The Fifth and Sixth Schedules are made applicable to their respective jurisdictions by Article 244 of the Constitution.

431 PESA was incorporated in the Indian legal system and changed the existing setup of administration in the scheduled areas.

432 Constitution of India, 1950, Sch. V

433 Ibid, Sch. V, 5(2)

434 Edwingson Bareh v. State of Assam, A.I.R. [1966] S.C. 1220 p 47 (Justice Hidayatullah dissenting). See also Constitution of India, 1950, Sch. V 5(1).

435 Tribal law and customs in India, Available at, http://www.legalservicesindia.com/article/article/tribal laws & customs-in-india-847-1.html, (Accessed on December 5, 2015)

436 See Justice Y.V. Chandrachud, V.R. Manohar & Justice Bhagwati Prosad Banerjee, eds., Durga Das Basu: Shorter Constitution of India, 13th ed. (Nagpur: Wadhwa, 2002) at 1709 [Durga Das Basu] (citing Chhaturam v. Commr. of I.T., [1947] F.L.J. 92).

437 Meenakshi Hooja, Policies and Strategies for Tribal Development: Focus on the Central Tribal Belt (New Delhi: Rawat Publications, 2004) at pp 19-20.

438 Apoorv Kurup, 'Tribal Law in India: How Decentralized Administration Is Extinguishing Tribal Rights and Why Autonomous Tribal Governments Are Better', Indigenous Law Journal, Volume 7 Issue 1/2008 p 94

Affirmative Action contiunues till date and has also been reflected in the UPR report submitted by India in January 2017.

The Governor could also preclude the application of any federal or state law in the Fifth Schedule areas.[439] Gubernatorial authority was "of a very wide nature[440] and subject to only two restrictions:[441] (i) that the Governor would consult a Tribes Advisory Council "before making any regulation;[442] and, (ii) that all regulations would receive Presidential assent before taking effect.[443]

The Sixth Schedule, unlike the Fifth Schedule has always given the tribes considerable autonomy. This Schedule divides the tribal areas in India's north-eastern states into autonomous" regions, each allocated to a particular tribe.[444] The elected councils in the Sixth Schedule areas are vested with administrative authority,[445] make laws with respect to a variety of subjects,[446] and even exercise judicial authority through traditional legal systems[447] embedded with certain features of federal law.[448] The councils are also financially independent and do not labour under the executive authority of the states.[449] Though the Sixth Schedule's scheme renders all exercise of executive and legislative authority by the councils subject to the approval of the provincial Governor, the superior courts have interpreted the Governor's authority to be considerably restricted.[450] [451]

---

439   See Constitution of India, 1950, Sch. V. 5(1)

440   The Governor's law-making powers permit even retrospective legislation. See Ram Kripal Bhagat v. State of Bihar, A.I.R. [1970] S.C. 951 at 958, and V.S.S. Sastry v. State of Andhra Pradesh, A.I.R. [1967] S.C. 71 at 74.

441   Edwingson Bareh v. State of Assam, A.I.R. [1966] S.C. 1220 at para. 45.

442   Constitution of India, 1950, Sch. V 4.

443   The Governor's authority remains unchanged even after PESA. The most reasonable interpretation would therefore be that the Governor can continue to make laws for the Fifth Schedule areas, subject to the powers of self-government guaranteed by PESA.

444   Constitution of India, 1950, Sch. VI 1.

445   Ibid, Sch. V 2(4).

446   See Ibid, 1950, Sch. VI 3(1) (laws can be made to regulate social customs, land use, forest management, and cultivation; or to appoint Chiefs or Headmen, and administer villages or towns. These laws become enforceable after the assent of the Governor of the state is received.).

447   Supra Note 22.

448   The Councils are authorized to establish their own justice dispensation system with tribal courts that adjudicate disputes "between the parties all of whom belong to Scheduled Tribes." See Ibid, Sch. VI clause 4(1) and (2). See also State of Meghalaya v. Richard Lyngdoh, [2006] 2 G.L.R. 328 at para. 17.

449   Paragraph 7 of the Sixth Schedule enables provincial Governors to establish District and Regional Funds. The District and Regional Councils also have the power to "assess and collect land revenue and to impose taxes" [para. 8]. Paragraph 9 authorizes the Councils to collect the royalties accruing each year from mineral licenses or leases granted by the state governments in respect of any area within an autonomous district.

450   For instance, in Cajee v. Siem the Indian Supreme Court held that "the administration of an autonomous district shall vest in the District Council and this in our opinion [is] comprehensive enough to include all such executive powers as are necessary to be exercised for the purposes of the administration of the district." See T. Cajee v. U. Jormanik Siem, A.I.R. [1961] S.C. 276.

451   Supra Note 22.

The Supreme Court of India decided in Pu Myllai Hlychho[452] clarified that even though the Sixth Schedule is not a self-contained code[453] or a Constitution within the Constitution,[454] the courts must nevertheless refer to the legislative, administrative and judicial independence that the Schedule grants District and Regional Councils.[455] There were two reasons for the different treatment that the tribes received.[456] First, the tribes in Fifth Schedule areas were considered incapable of self-government.[457] Second, unlike the Sixth Schedule areas, some tribal communities in peninsular India coexisted with a minority non-tribal population, and autonomy for the tribes in such a case seemed impractical. These were considerations that had been settled well before independence,[458] so that by voting on the inclusion of the Fifth Schedule in the Constitution the founding fathers were, in a sense, continuing the colonial typecast that the tribes contentment depended not so much on rapid political advance as on experienced and sympathetic handling, and on protection from economic subjugation by the [non-tribal] neighbours.[459] Even the Supreme Court of India later endorsed this paternalist justification when it said that the tribals need to be taken care of by the protective arm of the law, so that they may prosper and by an evolutionary process join the mainstream of the society.[460] This view was however rejected by ILO 169 and being consistent with now rejected ILO 107.

---

452 Pu Myllai Hlychho v. State of Mizoram, [2005] 2 S.C.C. 92.

453 Contra Edwingson Bareh v. State of Assam, A.I.R. [1966] S.C. 1220 at para. 11 ("the scheme of the Sixth Schedule … purport[s] to provide for a self-contained code for the governance of the tribal areas").

454 See Pu Myllai Hlychho v. State of Mizoram, [2005] 2 S.C.C. 92 at para. 21 ("The Sixth Schedule to the Constitution is a part of the Constitution and cannot be interpreted by forgetting the other provisions in the Constitution.").

455 But see District Council of the Jowai Autonomous District v. Dwet Singh Rymbai, [1986] 4 S.C.C. 38 at para. 11 (The powers enjoyed by these District Councils cannot be equated with the plenary powers enjoyed by a legislature. Their powers to make laws are limited by the provisions of the Sixth Schedule).

456 Supra at 20 p 94.

457 Modern sociology has however extra-legally compelled a review of the "colonial theories and practices" that categorized the primitive and the civilized based on "modes of subsistence", "transformation of the physical environment", "literacy" and the presence of "codified laws regulating society". See Ajay Skaria, "Shades of Wildness Tribe, Caste, and Gender in Western India" (1997) 56 J. Asian Stud. 726 at 730-731.

458 The Government of India Act 1935, which introduced special measures for the protection of the tribes in India, had earlier reclassified the tribal regions of the country into "Excluded' and 'Partially Excluded Areas' based on the preponderance of tribal communities and the feasibility of introducing civil administration in those regions. See Indian Statutory Commission, Report of the Indian Statutory Commission (London: Her Majesty's Stationary Office, 1930). Thus, "where there was an enclave or a definite tract of country inhabited by a compact tribal population, [the area] was classified as an Excluded Area," while regions with a substantial tribal population, but a minority non-tribal population, were declared Partially Excluded Areas. J.K. Das, Human Rights and Indigenous peoples (Delhi: A.P.H., 2001) at 135 (both regions "were excluded from the competence of the Provincial and Federal Legislatures," but "the administration of Excluded Areas was vested in the Governor acting in his discretion" and that of the Partially Excluded Areas "was vested in the Council of Ministers subject … to the Governor exercising his individual judgment"). After independence, the drafters of the Indian Constitution adopted the distinction between Partially Excluded and Excluded Areas and renamed them with minor modifications as the Fifth and Sixth Schedules respectively. See B. Shiva Rao, Supra note 13 at 681-782.

459 See Amit Prakash, Supra note 10 at 122. See also Indian Statutory Commission, Report of the Indian Statutory Commission, vol. 2 (London: Her Majesty's Stationary Office, 1930).

460 Amrendra Pratap Singh v. Tej Bahadur Prajapati, [2004] 10 S.C.C. 65 at para 15 It was observed that the situation bears a striking resemblance to the United States' belief that the Native American tribes "were the 'wards' of the government in need of protection." See Joseph William Singer, "Lone Wolf, or How to Take Property by Calling It a Mere Change in the Form of Investment" (2002) 38 Tulsa L. Rev. 37 at 39

4.1.7. RIGHT TO REPRESENTATION IN THE LEGISLATIVE AND OTHER BODIES

There are certain political safeguards provided in the Constitution of India for the tribal and indigenous peoples of India. These special provisions have been laid down in Article 330[461] in respect of reservation of

---

461 Article 330 Reservation of seats for Scheduled Castes and Scheduled Tribes in the House of the People-

1. Seats shall be reserved in the House of the People for - a. the Scheduled Castes; b. the Scheduled Tribes except the Scheduled Tribes in the autonomous districts of Assam; and c. the Scheduled Tribes in the autonomous districts of Assam.

2. The number of seats reserved in any State or Union territory for the Scheduled Castes or the Scheduled Tribes under clause (1) shall bear, as nearly as may be, the same proportion to the total number of seats allotted to that State or Union territory in the House of the People as the population of the Scheduled Castes in the State or Union territory or of the Scheduled Tribes in the State or Union territory or part of the State or Union territory, as the case may be, in respect of which seats are so reserved, bears to the total population of the State or Union territory.

3. Notwithstanding anything contained in Clause (2), the number of seats reserved in the House of the People for the Scheduled Tribes in the autonomous districts of Assam shall bear to the total number of seats allotted to that State a proportion not less than the population of the Scheduled Tribe in the said autonomous district bears to the total population of the State.

seats in the Lok Sabha and Article 332[462] in respect of State Legislative Assemblies. The House of the People is the primary law making body of the parliament including the Rajya Sabha and the President. Reservation of seats in the House of the People is of special significance as it permanently allows tribal representation in the Parliament of the country. Not only do the tribals[463] of the country get the benefits of this provision, the scheduled castes[464] also get their numbers present in the elite legislative body. The provisions also take care of the proportional equation relevant in the representation of tribals and scheduled castes.

---

462 Article 332 Reservation of seats for Scheduled Castes and Scheduled Tribes in the Legislative Assemblies of the States

1. Seats shall be reserved for the Scheduled Castes and the Scheduled Tribes, except the Scheduled Tribes in the autonomous districts of Assam, in the Legislative Assembly of every State

2. Seats shall be reserved also for the autonomous districts in the Legislative Assemble of the State of Assam

3. The number of seats reserved for the Scheduled Castes or the Scheduled Tribes in the Legislative Assembly of any State under clause (1) shall bear, as nearly as may be, the same proportion to the total number of seats in the Assembly as the population of the Scheduled Castes in the State or of the Scheduled Tribes in the State or part of the State, as the case may be, in respect of which seats are so reserved bears to the total population of the State

[(3A) Notwithstanding anything contained in clause (3), until the taking effect, under article 170, of the readjustment, on the basis of the first census after the year [2026], of the number of seats in the Legislative Assemblies of the States of Arunachal Pradesh, Meghalaya, Mizoram and Nagaland, the seats which shall be reserved for the Scheduled Tribes in the Legislative Assembly of any such State shall be,—

(a) if all the seats in the Legislative Assembly of such State in existence on the date of coming into force of the Constitution (Fifty-seventh Amendment) Act, 1987 (hereafter in this clause referred to as the existing Assembly) are held by members of the Scheduled Tribes, all the seats except one;

(b) in any other case, such number of seats as bears to the total number of seats, a proportion not less than the number (as on the said date) of members belonging to the Scheduled Tribes in the existing Assembly bears to the total number of seats in the existing Assembly.]

[(3B) Notwithstanding anything contained in clause (3), until the re-adjustment, under article 170, takes effect on the basis of the first census after the year [2026] of the number of seats in the Legislative Assembly of the State of Tripura, the seats which shall be reserved for the Scheduled Tribes in the Legislative Assembly, shall be, such number of seats as bears to the total number of seats, a proportion not less than the number, as on the date of coming into force of the Constitution (Seventy second Amendment) Act, 1992, of members belonging to the Scheduled Tribes in the Legislative Assembly in existence on the said date bears to the total number of seats in that Assembly.]

(4) The number of seats reserved for an autonomous district in the Legislative Assembly of the State of Assam shall bear to the total number of seats in that Assembly a proportion not less than the population of the district bears to the total population of the State.

(5) The constituencies for the seats reserved for any autonomous district of Assam shall not comprise any area outside that district.

(6) No person who is not a member of a Scheduled Tribe of any autonomous district of the State of Assam shall be eligible for election to the Legislative Assembly of the State from any constituency of that district:

[Provided that for elections to the Legislative Assembly of the State of Assam, the representation of the Scheduled Tribes and non-Scheduled Tribes in the constituencies included in the Bodoland Territorial Areas District, so notified, and existing prior to the Constitution of the Bodoland Territorial Areas District, shall be maintained.

463 Supra at 43 Article 330 clause 1(b) and (c)

464 Ibid at clause 1(a)

Special provision has also been incorporated in the Constitution for reservation of seats in the Panchayats.[465] Article 243D was accompanied by Article 243T to extend the reservation of seats in the Municipalities as well. Similar to the provisions of reservation in the House of the People and the State Legislative Assemblies, Panchayats and Municipalities also secures the seats for the Scheduled Castes.[466]

4.1.8. AGENCY FOR MONITORING SAFEGUARDS

Article 338A of the Constitution of India established the much needed and much awaited monitoring agency in the form of National Commission for Scheduled Tribes. The monitoring agency has been vested with certain powers[467] including the powers of a civil court[468] and functions with certain Constitutional duties[469]. The commission has been vested with the power to regulate its own procedure.[470]

Another interesting move on the part of this incorporation of the National Commission for Scheduled Tribes is to provide necessary consultations[471] to the Union and the State Governments on all major policy matters affecting the Scheduled Tribes.

---

465 Article 243D deals with Reservation of seats

1. Seats shall be reserved for- a. the Scheduled Castes; and b. the Scheduled Tribes, in every Panchayat and the number of seats so reserved shall bear, as nearly as may be, the same proportion to the total number of seats to be filled by direct election in that Panchayat as the population of the Scheduled Castes in that Panchayat area or of the Scheduled Tribes in that Panchayat area bears to the total population of that area and such seats may be allotted by rotation to different constituencies in a Panchayat.

2. Not less than one-third of the total number of seats reserved under clause (1) shall be reserved for women belonging to the Scheduled Castes or, as the case may be, the Scheduled Tribes.

3. Not less than one-third (including the number of seats reserved for women belonging to the Scheduled Castes and the Scheduled Tribes) of the total number of seats to be filled by direct election in every Panchayat shall be reserved for women and such seats may be allotted by rotation to different constituencies in a Panchayat.

4. The offices of the Chairpersons in the Panchayats at the village or any other level shall be reserved for the Scheduled Castes, the Scheduled Tribes and women in such manner as the Legislature of a State may, by law, provide:

Provided that the number of offices of Chairpersons reserved for the Scheduled Castes and the Scheduled Tribes in the Panchayats at each level in any State shall bear, as nearly as may be, the same proportion to the total number of such offices in the Panchayats at each level as the population of the Scheduled Castes in the State or of the Scheduled Tribes in the State bears to the total population of the State:

Provided further that not less than one-third of the total number of offices of Chairpersons in the Panchayats at each level shall be reserved for women:

Provided also that the number of offices reserved under this clause shall be allotted by rotation to different Panchayats at each level

5. The reservation of seats under clauses (1) and (2) and the reservation of offices of Chairpersons (other than the reservation for women) under clause (4) shall cease to have effect on the expiration of the period specified in article 334. 6. Nothing in this Part shall prevent the Legislature of a State from making any provision for reservation of seats in any Panchayat or offices of Chairpersons in the Panchayats at any level in favour of backward class of citizens.

466 Article 243D clause 1(a) and Article 243T clause 1

467 Article 338A clause (8) *inter alia*

468 Ibid at Clause (8)

469 Ibid at Clause (5)

470 Ibid at Clause (3)

471 Ibid at Clause (9)

4.2. MAJOR ENACTMENTS PASSED IN INDIA TO PROTECT CIVIL AND ECONOMIC RIGHTS OF TRIBALS

The majority of statutes made for the tribals in India are in furtherance of the protection of their civil and economic rights. This has been a sharp contrast to the laws that was passed by the British colonial rulers. It is the advent of human rights that prompts the creation of these laws to provide basic protection of their life and liberty as has been guaranteed by the Constitution of India.

Various enactments were passed by both the centre and the state to prevent large scale alienation of the lands of the tribals to non tribals.[472] Some of these *inter alia* are worth mentioning; The West Bengal Land Reforms Act, 1955, Abolition of Zamindari Act, 1950, and various tenancy legislation.

The Transfer of Property Act, 1882, The Scheduled Castes and The Scheduled Tribes (Prevention of Atrocities) Act, 1989, The Orissa Gram Panchayat (Amendment) Act, 1997, Tripura Land Revenue and Land Reforms Act, 1960 *inter alia* have made their mark in the pages of Indian judicial system for being pro active for the protection of tribal peoples all across the country.

Some of these enactments are worth a discussion to identify the process by which the legislations are protecting these vulnerable groups and communities. The researcher has identified four major enactments intended to protect the civil and economic rights of tribals in India. As the study of various relevant provision of these enactments are done we must have a note on the various principal difference that exist between the Colonial legislation and its various trends that continued after India's independence and the later enactment which got their influence from international convention and the application of the 'specific adoption theory' in practice. The aforesaid enactments are discussed below *in seriatim*:

4.2.1. THE SCHEDULES CASTE AND SCHEDULED TRIBES (PREVENTION OF ATROCITIES) ACT, 1989[473]

4.2.1.1. OVERVIEW

The Schedules Caste and Scheduled Tribes (Prevention of Atrocities) Act, 1989 came up to protect the scheduled tribes and scheduled castes from various atrocities defined in the Act. The Act provides a territorial jurisdiction to the whole of India except the state of Jammu and Kashmir.

The enactment was passed by the Indian Parliament in 1989 on 11th of September as Act no. 33.The Act is divided in five chapters comprising of 23 sections. Chapter 1 is preliminary and comprises of section 1 and 2, where section 2. Defines various words used in the Act. The second chapter incorporates section 3 to section 9 and is headed as offences of Atrocities. This chapter comprises of six sections and describes various acts considered to be offences and the corresponding punishments. An amendment to this Act was passed on 26th January 2016.

Chapter 3 deals with the provisions relating to externment and includes within it section 10 to section 12. Chapter 4 of the Act provides the provision relating to the establishment of Special Courts which will deal with cases of Atrocities involved in this Act. Section 14 and 15 laid down the provisions there of. Chapter 5 of the Act provides for miscellaneous provisions within Sections 16-23.

---

472 Attempts to subvert 'Samatha' judgement, Available at, http://www.pucl.org/reports/National/2001/samatha.htm, (Accessed on December 5, 2015)

473 The Schedules Caste and Scheduled Tribes (Prevention of Atrocities) Act, 1989 (Act 33 of 1989)

4.2.1.2. BACKDROP AND OBJECT OF THE ACT

Tribals in India have been subjected to lot of deprivation for centuries. The process of urbanization has further forced these people to choose the remotest corner of human habitat at extreme weather conditions and to sustain a very hard life. Over and above this there has been a continuous influx of non tribal peoples in these regions as well for further exploitation of tribals and adivasis in India like in many other parts of the world. The growth of intolerance and torture on the tribals and the absence of legal and other safeguards have even made their life miserable.

Most places in India have witnessed growing intolerance and violence upon the weak and marginalised tribal peoples during the post independence period and that has substantially influenced the incorporation of laws to protect these people of their basic rights guaranteed by the Constitution of our country.

The Constitutional safeguards have been further supplemented with various enactments passed by the parliament of India. Apart from the Constitutional promises, international obligation of India has been another promising reason for developing laws to protect various human rights of the indigenous and tribal peoples. India has been a member of the United Nations Organization and has also been a member nation to be a signatory of ILO Convention No. 107. It shall be relevant in this regard to specify that all the member states are obliged to submit a periodic review of the protection of human rights of their respective countries every four years known as the Universal Periodic Review. This UPR started from 2008 and is ready to submit its third report on the first quarter of 2016.

In the year 1989 a very important enactment was passed by the parliament for the protection of certain basic rights of the scheduled tribes and scheduled class in the form of The Schedules Caste and Scheduled Tribes (Prevention of Atrocities) Act, 1989. The Act came up with the sole objective of protecting the SCs and STs from various unlawful acts including acts done by a non tribal in public office.

This act opens up the nude picture of the Indian behaviour with tribals and schedule castes. Moreover it shall be relevant to state in this regard that it is emotionally disturbing to read and study the nature of atrocities these vulnerable people faces everyday in their lived from the non tribals. The growth of intolerance and atrocities has been rightfully addressed by this Act to some extent.

The object of the Act is the prevention of commission of offence of atrocity upon the members of the SCs and STs.

The Act also provides for special courts for the trial of such offences of atrocities and to provide for the relief of SC/STs. The Act also provides necessary provision for the rehabilitation of the victims of such offences.

The Act also addresses necessary matters connected therewith and incidental thereto. The act extends to the whole of India except the state of Jammu and Kashmir.[474]

---

474 Object, The Schedules Caste and Scheduled Tribes (Prevention of Atrocities) Act, 1989

4.2.1.3. MEANING OF ATROCITY

Atrocities have been defined in section 2(a)[475] of the Act. Various offences as provided in section 3 of this act are considered to be atrocities in this act. The definition also states that the offences as laid down in the act are punishable. Thus atrocities are both offences and punishable in nature.

A brief study of the provisions stated in section 3[476] clearly identifies the various acts committed upon the indigenous and tribal peoples as gross violation of human rights. The various acts of atrocities may broadly be classified as follows:
1. Infringement of right to life and personal liberty
2. Infringement of the right to property
3. Exploitation of the tribal peoples

---

475 (a) "atrocity" means an offence punishable under section 3 of the The Schedules Caste and Scheduled Tribes (Prevention of Atrocities) Act, 1989

476 3. (1) whoever not being a member of a Scheduled Caste or a Scheduled for offences of Tribe, atrocities. (i) forces a member of a Scheduled Caste or a Scheduled Tribe to drink or eat any inedible or obnoxious substance;

(ii) acts with intent to cause injury, insult or annoyance to any member of a Scheduled Caste, or a Scheduled Tribe by dumping excreta, waste matter, carcasses or any other obnoxious substance in his premises or neighbourhood; (iii) forcibly removes clothes from the person of a member of a Scheduled Caste or a Scheduled Tribe or parades him naked or with painted face or body or commits any similar act which is derogatory to human dignity; (iv) wrongfully occupies or cultivates any land owned by, or allotted to, or notified by any competent authority to be allotted to, a member of a Scheduled Caste or a Scheduled Tribe or gets the land allotted to him transferred; (v) wrongfully dispossesses a member of a Scheduled Caste or a Scheduled Tribe from his land or premises or interferes with the enjoyment of his rights over any land, premises or water; (vi) compels or entices a member of a Scheduled Caste or a Scheduled Tribe to do 'begar' or other similar forms of forced or bonded labour other than any compulsory service for public purposes imposed by Government; (vii) forces or intimidates a member of a Scheduled Caste or a Scheduled Tribe not to vote or to vote to a particular candidate or to vote in a manner other than that provided by law; (viii) institutes false, malicious or vexatious suit or criminal or other legal proceedings against a member of a Scheduled Caste or a Scheduled Tribe.

(ix) gives any false or frivolous information to any public servant and thereby causes such public servant to use his lawful power to the injury or annoyance of a member of a Scheduled Caste or a Scheduled Tribe;

(x) intentionally insults or intimidates with intent to humiliate a member of a Scheduled Caste or a Scheduled Tribe in any place within public view;

(xi) assaults or uses force to any woman belonging to a Scheduled Caste or a Scheduled Tribe with intent to dishonour or outrage her modesty;

(xii) being in a position to dominate the will of a woman belonging to a Scheduled Caste or a Scheduled Tribe and uses that position to exploit her sexually to which she would not have otherwise agreed;

(xiii) corrupts or fouls the water of any spring, reservoir or any other source ordinarily used by members of the Scheduled Castes or a Scheduled Tribes so as to render it less fit for the purpose for which it is ordinarily used;

(xiv) denies a member of a Scheduled Caste or a Scheduled Tribe any customary right of passage to a place of public resort or obstructs such member so as to prevent him from using or having access to a place of public resort to which other members of public or any section thereof have a right to use or access to;

(xv) forces or causes a member of a Scheduled Caste or a Scheduled Tribe to leave his house, village or other place of residence, shall be punishable with imprisonment for a term which shall not be less than six months but which may extend to five years and with fine.

4.2.1.4. RIGHTS GUARANTEED UNDER THE ACT

Right to life and personal liberty has been one of the most significant fundamental rights protected under the Constitution of India. The act makes a similar effort in some of the prominent sections in it to uphold the right to life and personal liberty of the members of the scheduled tribes. A thorough reading of the provisions laid down in section 3 puts forward the following rights:

4.2.1.4.1. RIGHT TO CAST VOTE AND ACCESS TO CUSTOMARY RIGHT OF PASSAGE AND CLEAN WATER

1.   Universal adult suffrage is the benchmark of any democracy and India is no different. The act categorically provides the right to cast vote[477] to the members of the scheduled tribes in scheduled areas declared under the schedule of the Constitution of India. This right to choose their representative in the parliament and state legislations is in furtherance of the rights to enjoy life in the proper sense of the term.

2.   Another right that has been provided under this provision of this act is the right to clean water, access to springs, reservoirs[478]. This provision is very important for the sustenance of life. Without water and access to water bodies, no person can live their respective life in the simplest of ways. The law prohibits anybody who tries to infringe this right of tribals. The penal provision has done a commendable job where these people have been forced out of their respective resources.

3.   The tribals have been denied their conventional ways and passages [479] by the non tribals in recent past. This hardship has led to a lot of conflict between the tribals and the non tribals and also against the administration. This conflict has witnessed bloodshed of many innocent tribals as well as non tribals including destruction of public property. There have been terrible instances of 'tribal-state' and 'tribal–non-tribal' conflicts due to the continuous exploitation of the tribals by the State as well as the non-tribals with Government showing blind eyes to the legitimate pleas of the tribals. The police firing on adivasis at Muthanga in Wayanad District of Kerela lead to the death of adivasis and policemen, and with hundreds of adivasis including women and children getting injured. The incident occurred when over 2000 adivasis occupied the protected forest land and were there in temporary huts and tents for 45 days with the demand which the then Chief Minister has made to them two years ago in Trivandrum. When the police came to evict them, the activists captured one policeman and one forest guard and keep them in custody. A massive police force was subsequently diploid which unleashed a brutal attack on the innocent adivasis and opened fire resulting in the death of two adivasis.[480]

This right to access to various roads, passage etc, has provided new ray of hope for these people. Those who obstruct such rights are considered to be offenders under this act and penal provisions have been created to punish the wrongdoer. This provision is very apt to the fact that untouchability has been a very inhuman practice.

---

477 Section 3 (1) (vii) of the The Scheduled Castes and Scheduled Tribes (Prevention of Atrocities) Act, 1989

478 Ibid at Section 3 (1) (xii)

479 Ibid at Section 3 (1) (xiv)

480 Mathew Aerthayil, 'Muthanga Police Firing in Kerala: Tribal Reaction to Exploitation and Alienation of their Land', Mainstream, July 19, 2003 at p 28.

4.2.1.4.2. RIGHT AGAINST EXPLOITATION

Some of the provisions created under section 3[481] of the act are in furtherance of protecting the tribals against exploitation by the non tribals. The tribals who were generally very simple minded and un-complicated were easy prey to the crooked non tribals. The growing loss of land of the tribals and adivasis has affected their economic conditions adversely. Adivasi live a life of economic sustenance which is very much dependable upon their land. The term sustainable with its various dimensions became an institution by itself.

However, very little has been thought about those who originated the concept and practiced it in the true sense of the term. The indigenous communities across the globe had a sustainable way of life. Whether it is their economy or attitude towards life, it is the term sustainable that perhaps suits them the best.

The forest has been the breeding ground of the tribal and it is this forest which teaches them the essential lessons of life and death. The customary practices and usages form an integral process of the education system of the tribals. The elderly from a very early stage teaches their toddlers, the usages of various plants in the forests and with that different method to protect and preserve them.

It has been evident amongst the tribal communities the medicinal use of various plants and shrubs of the forest. The origin of aurvedic medicine and unani that has gained much popularity in the modern urban communities restores its source in the indigenous way of healing. The various form of indigenous healing have continued and evolved through centuries and are still in practice in various tribal areas of India.

Because of the growing loss of land and other resources the tribals have been left with little ways of economic sustenance. The biggest number of displaced people in India is the tribal peoples and they have been affected mostly by the so called developmental projects in the form of Dams and barrages to generate electricity. Research suggests that only one project on the river Narmada has been the reason for displacement of populace as big as that of Australia.[482] Such displacement has been the root cause of destruction of not only the tribal communities but also with them their entire culture, knowledge and education.[483]

This mass displacement of tribals from their homeland has led to their involvement in the unskilled labor force of the country. Today, India is witnessing a large number of tribal peoples in various forms of labor including bonded labor. Section 3 of the act addressed this issue of labor exploitation and provides for penal measures against the practice of penal measures.[484]

India has witnessed large scare violence against women and children and tribal women and children are not an exception to this inhuman practice. Some of the instances of such sexual violence upon tribal women by non tribal men have been provided in chapter 5[485] of this book. Section 354 of the Indian Penal Code, 1860 has categorically provided punishment for any person outraging the modesty of women. This enactment is also in tune with IPC and has incorporated this heinous act of males over females.[486]

---

481 Section 3 of The Scheduled Castes and Scheduled Tribes (Prevention of Atrocities) Act, 1989.

482 Shambhu Prasad Chakrabarty, 'Tribals And Adivasis: Bearing The Light For A Brighter Future In Sustaining The Forests, Protection Of Health And Education: A Socio-Legal Reflection' JCC Law Review, 2014

483 Ibid at pg

484 Section 3(vi) of The Scheduled Castes and Scheduled Tribes (Prevention of Atrocities) Act, 1989.

485 Chapter 5 of this book is titled 'Role of Judiciary in Protecting the Civil and Economic Rights of Tribals in India'

486 Section 3(xi) of The Scheduled Castes and Scheduled Tribes (Prevention of Atrocities) Act, 1989

There have been innumerable instances of physical violence by non tribals upon tribal peoples and in certain cases the entire non tribal community upon a tribal community. In order to prevent such act of violence like a penal provision has been incorporated to protect the right of tribal peoples against physical assaults.

The section also protects the tribals from any false harassment or false suits made against them with the object of exploitation. This act of non tribals has been addressed in the act[487]rightfully in the said provision along with sub section 2 of section 3 of this Act.[488]

4.2.1.4.3. RIGHT TO PROPERTY

The most significant rights of tribal and indigenous communities are their land and resources in the said property. Land is at the heart of tribal life. More than a thing of value, land to him is mother earth, which satisfies both his material and spiritual needs. Hence depriving him of his land is to snap his continuation as a self respecting member of society. In fact, the root cause of all human right violations perpetuated on them can be traced to land alienation, since the tribals depend on land for their identity, existence, security and livelihood. [489]

The importance of forest land to the tribes and tribal communities can be aptly compared as life to a human body. Without it the life of the tribes are mere body without *animus*. They consider their land as heritage. Forest is their habitat and the source of life. It is not only the source of fodder and food; it provides the fuel to make life easier for them. As a matter of fact, everything concentrates on forest and its produce when it comes to tribal life.[490]

Tribes are ever dependant on the forest and its rich natural resources. It was because of these resources the tribes choose their habitat in the forest. The tribes gather their food and fuel from the forest. As a matter of practice the women in these communities spent a considerably long time to gather these from the forest. The economic system of these tribes is also forest centric. The product of the forest is being sold in the market either directly or with various modifications. The tools for convenient collection of forest produce are generally collected by the tribals out of these economic activities. The economy is greatly self-sustained.

Apart from the materials collected and created by these communities for their own use, they also use them for commercial gain even when it is very negligible.

All international instruments dealing with indigenous and tribal peoples have equivocally recognized this and so did this act. It is beyond any doubt that the tribals and their economy have largely been dependent upon their resources in their land. The large scale displacement has left most of the adivasis in no man's land and bereft of their indigenous economic and other practices. The act rightly protects this right to their land and property against the non tribal land grabbing vultures by making an act in furtherance of the same as an offence.[491]

---

487 Section 3(viii) of The Scheduled Castes and Scheduled Tribes (Prevention of Atrocities) Act, 1989

488 Section 3(ii) of The Scheduled Castes and Scheduled Tribes (Prevention of Atrocities) Act, 1989

489 Lingappa Pochanna Appelwar v. State of Maharashtra (1985) 1 SCC 481

490 Shambhu Prasad Chakrabarty and Dr Rathin Bandhyaadhyay 'Alienation of Tribals from Land and Forest Vis-À-Vis Tribal Retaliation in India: An Analysis Through the Lens of Human Rights Jurisprudence.' KIIT Law Review, 2014

491 Section 3(v) of The Scheduled Castes and Scheduled Tribes (Prevention of Atrocities) Act, 1989

The provision of the act aptly makes an act which infringes the rightful use and enjoyment of land and various resources thereof as a crime punishable with penal consequences. Hence an act which forcibly dispossesses a tribal from his house or village or other place of residence and habitation has been prohibited by the act.[492]

4.2.1.5. EFFICACY OF THE RIGHTS GUARANTEED UNDER THIS ACT

The beneficial changes that this act has brought are aplenty. Many instances of protection of tribals against atrocities of the non tribals upon the tribals have been addressed after incorporation of this enactment. The tribals can now after the incorporation and effectiveness of this act have a proper forum to redress their grievances as to the violation of their basic rights guaranteed by the Constitution. Such variety of socio economic exploitation has been left unabated prior to the incorporation of this act that has caused a lot of social and economic distress to the tribal and indigenous peoples of India. The Act addressed the problem of a tribal in person as well as a community as separate provisions have been laid down in this act to deal with these two situations separately.

The efficacies of this act lie in its object to prevent atrocities committed by the non tribal peoples upon the vulnerable tribals. This positive and commendable step taken by the parliament must be appreciated as this enactment has made such offences cognizable in nature. The act has by itself provides both substantive and procedural aspects to protect the tribals.

After the incorporation of this act there has been a constant growth in the sense of security of the tribals as it can be a handy weapon to ward off the inhuman practice of various atrocities which are coupled with violence in most of the cases.

The efficacy of the act has further been enhanced with the recent amendment made to the act. On 26th January, 2016 the Amendment Act came into force with the accent of the President of India. Certain new offences have been incorporated in the act. Addition of certain offences in IPC is now accepted as offences falling under this Act as well.

Another interesting incorporation is the establishment of Special Executive Courts to exclusively try cases under this Act. This would definitely enhance the importance of offences under this Act.

The existence of presumption on the part of the offender with regard to the status of the victim is a very interesting move. This will certainly put the burden of proof on the part of the offender and relieve the victim from proving his case which is at times practically very difficult. This addition is a positive step in furtherance of the protection of these people from the acts of atrocities which is really a matter of disgrace not only for the society but overall the image of the nation in the international forum.

These set of amendments *inter alia* have truly made this act a very effective step on the part of the Legislature to address the plight of tribal rights in India. However it must be stated in this regard that the rights of tribals must be protected as far as possible.

---

492 Ibid

4.2.2. THE PROTECTION OF CIVIL RIGHTS ACT, 1955

4.2.2.1. OVERVIEW:

The Protection of Civil Rights Act, 1955 came up to protect the scheduled tribes and scheduled castes from various inhuman practices relating to untouchability elaborated under the Act. The Act provides a territorial jurisdiction to the whole of India.

The enactment was passed in 1955 on 8th of May as Act no. 22.

The Act is divided into 17 sections and one schedule. The schedule incorporates the list of 21 various state acts with the objective to repeal them to the extent to which they are or any of the provisions contained therein correspond or are repugnant to this act or to any of the provisions contained herein this enactment.

In the year 1977, a subordinate legislation came up in the form of protection of Civil Rights Rules, which consists of five sections and was objected in furtherance of the exercise of the powers conferred by section 16B of the Protection of Civil Rights Act, 1955.

The enactment provides punishment for enforcing religious disabilities in section 3[493] due to untouchablity. The act also provides for provisions prohibiting social disability. It provides for punishment for enforcing social disability in section 4[494] of the Act.

The Act makes specific provisions for punishing those who prevents or refuses a person to be admitted in hospital because of the practice of untouchability.[495]

The Act provides and propagates social justice as well as economic justice to the member of any tribes or untouchables. The act specifically punishes those who exercise discrimination in certain trade practices due to untouchability. This statute also prohibits certain acts committed in furtherance of untouchability as offences punishable with penal consequences including compulsory labour[496], molestation, physical violence and injury, annoyance or boycotting a person belonging to so called lower untouchable class.[497]

The Act makes an interesting move in section 8 by providing the provision of cancellation or suspension of licences in certain cases of conviction. The act also takes the bold step of protecting the community rights of tribals and other vulnerable classes being victims of untouchability. The Act also provides the power upon the respective state governments to impose collective fine if the act done is by a community as a whole.

It shall be relevant to note in this regard that the offences incorporated in this Act are cognizable and triable summarily.

Apart from the penal measures the Act also provides the power and duty on respective state governments to ensure that the rights may be conferred upon the tribals and other so called untouchable classes who are

---

493 The Protection of Civil Rights Act, 1955

494 Ibid

495 Ibid at Section 5

496 Ibid at Section 7A

497 Ibid at Section 7(1) (b)

victims of untouchability like legal aid etc.[498] This incorporation has been done through an amendment Act.[499]

4.2.2.2. BACKDROP AND OBJECT OF THE ACT

Tribals in India have been subjected to lot of deprivation for centuries. Over and above this there has been a continuous influx of non tribal peoples in these regions as well for further exploitation of tribals and adivasis in India like in many other parts of the world. The growth of intolerance and torture and practices like untouchability on the tribals and the absence of legal and other safeguards have even made their life miserable. At this juncture of time, the Protection of Civil Rights Act, 1955 came up.

In almost all places in India the practice of untouchablity has been growing since the British era. The weak and marginalised tribal peoples have been victims of various inhuman practices of the non tribals. It is during the post independence period that substantial influenced steps have been taken to incorporate laws to protect these people of their basic rights guaranteed by the Constitution of our country.

The Constitutional safeguards against untouchability have been further supplemented with various provisions of the Protection of Civil Rights Act, 1955 which was rightfully passed by the parliament of India. Apart from the Constitutional promises, international obligation of India has been another promising reason for developing laws to protect various human rights of the indigenous and tribal peoples including the abolition of the inhuman practice of untouchability. India has been a member of the United Nations Organization and has also been a member nation to be a signatory of ILO Convention No. 107.

It shall be relevant in this regard to specify that all the member states are obliged to eliminate untouchability in all forms against the indigenous and tribal peoples of the country.

With the growing international commitment and the objective of protecting human rights, the Protection of Civil Rights Act, 1955 came up. The primary objective of the Act as stated earlier is the abolition of untouchability.

The object of the Act is to prescribe punishment for the preaching and practice of untouchability for the enforcement of any disability arising there from for matters connected therewith.[500]

The preamble of the Act reiterates the object of the Act in very clear words by prohibiting untouchability and declaring any such practices as punishable with penal consequences. The Act also addresses necessary matters connected therewith and incidental thereto.

The Act extends to the whole of India including the state of Jammu and Kashmir[501]and tries to extend the protection to almost everyone within the territorial limits of the country.

---

498 Ibid at section 15A

499 Act 106 of 1976 w.e.f. 19/11/1976

500 Ibid at the Preamble

501 Ibid

4.2.2.3. MEANING OF UNTOUCHABILITY

Untouchability is basically the inhuman practice of ostracising a group by segregating them from the main stream by social customs or legal mandates. It may be considered to be the direct product of the caste system in India. The major causes of untouchability in India are racial discrimination, religious causes and social stigma.

Under Article 17 of the Constitution of India, untouchability in all forms has been abolished. The primary objective of prohibiting this practice is to control the malpractice involved in caste system for ages. The higher castes have been practicing this by showing some reasons as aforementioned and exercise discriminatory practice to the people and the community as a whole.

The Protection of Civil Rights Act, 1955 has not specifically defined the term untouchability but addresses the civil and religious rights which a person shall be entitled to enjoy and exercise because of the abolition of this practice. The act also makes any effort made by members of the higher castes to carry on this derogatory practice as an offence punishable with penal consequences.

4.2.2.4. THE PROTECTION OF CIVIL RIGHTS ACT, 1955

4.2.2.4.1. RIGHT AGAINST RELIGIOUS DISABILITIES

One of the primary causes of untouchability is religion. It has been the Hindu religious practices and customs that certain classes of people are supposed to perform certain specific functioning of lower strata or those related to unclean environment like sweeping, scavenging etc, which makes them untouchable. Because of the stigma attached to them, they were not allowed to enter places involving purity and cleanliness like that of the place of worship. Thus these peoples are barred from entering temples and are considered to be outcastes.

The Act provides punishment for enforcing religious disability due to untouchability. The rights granted to these people after the abolition of untouchability is to consider them to be at par with any other person who was not having such disabilities before the passing of this act. The rights conferred not only includes entering any place of public worship but also extends to worshipping or offering prayers or performing any religious service, or bathing in a sacred lake etc.

The Act categorically provides the punishment to the person who imposes such religious disability upon the peoples belonging to such tribes or castes.

The punishment as laid down in section 3 of the Act for such breach is that of imprisonment for a term of not less than one month and not more than six months and also with fine which shall not be less than one hundred rupees and not more than five hundred rupees.

4.2.2.4.2. RIGHT AGAINST SOCIAL DISABILITIES

The other dominant cause of untouchability is social in nature. In furtherance to address this cause section 4 has been incorporated in this Act, providing social rights to these people who have been subjected to social disabilities and discrimination for ages.

The list of social disability was aplenty and a handful has been incorporated in the provisions of this Act. Some of them are as follows:

a. Right to use and access or enjoy: this right includes the right to access to any shop, restaurant[502] etc or to use any service or goods[503] therein. It also incorporates the use and access of any place of charitable nature[504] or public conveyance[505]. The use of any river or stream[506] etc. This right also encompasses within itself the right to observe any social or religious custom or usage or ceremony[507] or the use of any jewellery[508] etc.

b. Right to freedom of residence and to profess any business or trade: this right allows any person to construct, acquire, or occupy for residential purpose or to practice any profession or business or trade.

c. Right to medical aid: the act specifically incorporates the right of all to have the benefit of medical aid in hospitals. Section 5 of the act specifically incorporates the penal provision upon anyone who refuses admission to any person on the ground of exercising untouchability. The right also extends to admission to any dispensary, educational institution or any hostel established or maintained for the benefit of general public.[509]

4.2.2.5. EFFICACY OF THE RIGHTS GUARANTEED UNDER THIS ACT

The beneficial changes that this act has brought are aplenty. Many instances of protection of tribals against atrocities of the non tribals upon the tribals have been addressed after incorporation of this enactment. The tribals can now after the incorporation and effectiveness of this act have a proper forum to redress their grievances as to the violation of their basic rights guaranteed by the Constitution.

Such variety of socio economic exploitation has been left unabated prior to the incorporation of this act that has caused a lot of social and economic distress to the tribal and indigenous peoples of India. The act addressed the problem of a tribal in person as well as a community as separate provisions have been laid down in this act to deal with these two situations separately.

The efficacies of this act lie in its object to prevent atrocities committed by the non tribal peoples upon the vulnerable tribals. This positive and commendable step taken by the parliament must be appreciated as this enactment has made such offences cognizable in nature. The act has by itself provides both substantive and procedural aspects to protect the tribals.

After the incorporation of this act there has been a constant growth in the sense of security of the tribals as it can be a handy weapon to ward off the inhuman practice of various atrocities which are coupled with violence in most of the times.

---

502 The Protection of Civil Rights Act, 1955 at Section 4 (i)

503 Ibid at Section 4(ii)

504 Ibid at Section 4(v)

505 Ibid at Section 4(vii)

506 Ibid at Section 4(iv)

507 Ibid at Section 4(x)

508 Ibid at Section 4(xi)

509 Ibid at Section 5(a)

4.2.3. THE PROVISIONS OF THE PANCHAYATS (EXTENSION TO THE SCHEDULED AREAS) ACT, 1996 (PESA)

4.2.3.1. OVERVIEW

The Bhuria Committee Report submitted before PESA was introduced brought within the scope of village governance control over its surrounding natural resources like water, forests, land etc which is basically stressing upon the concept of participatory democracy. The concept of tribal community management was first thought of to settle village conflicts and also to administer law and order in these areas. The report also stressed upon the object of planning and implementation of development programmes along with accountability of bureaucracy to the tribal community. In short, the report provided the tribal peoples a chance to govern their own lives and shape their destiny.on this backdrop, PESA was enacted by Parliament in the Forty-seventh Year of the Republic of India as Act No. 40 of 1996. The main object of the Act has been incorporated in the preamble of the Act. The preamble specifically states that this act is to provide for the extension of the provisions of Part IX of the Constitution relating to the Panchayats to the Scheduled Areas. This step specifically extended the jurisdiction of the Part IX to the Scheduled areas.

The Act defines the term Scheduled Area in Section 2 of this Act. It states that in this Act, unless the context otherwise requires, "Scheduled Areas" means the Scheduled Areas as referred to in Clause (1) of Article 244 of the Constitution.

4.2.3.2. BACKDROP AND OBJECT

The main object that is the extension of the Part IX of the Constitution of India has been specified in Section 3 of this Act. The section categorically states that the provision of Part IX of the Constitution relating to Panchayats is extended to the Scheduled Areas subject to such exceptions and modifications as are provided in section 4.

The relevance of PESA lie in the fact that this enactment to a great extent literally prohibits and limits the various powers of the government and its agencies in respect to the matters encompassing the rural and tribal life.[510]

4.2.3.3. VARIOUS RIGHTS GUARANTEED UNDER THE ACT

The Act prohibited the state legislative bodies to make any laws which may be construed against the customary practices of such area. This is the first of its law since the colonial rulers took over and sealed the fate of tribals and their customary practices. With this came a lot of positive things or these people as well, like the right to religious practices and also the management rights over community practices. This is the first of its kind in independent India and truly brought with it the hope of millions of tribals of the country to regain their social freedom after five decades of political independence.[511] Thus, the legislation firmly upheld the importance of customary law, the social and religious practices and traditional management practices of community resources which were the most important aspect of tribal life and society. It shall

---

510 As stated in section 3, there are certain exceptions and modifications which have been stated in section 4 of this Act. The said exceptions and modifications are mentioned through a non obstante clause. It states that notwithstanding anything contained under Part IX of the Constitution, the legislature of a State shall not make any law under that Part which is inconsistent with many things laid down in the act.

511 Section 4(a) of PESA 1996

be relevant in this regard to note that the international law in relation to tribal and indigenous peoples is also in tune to respecting the customary law and religious practices and traditional management practices of community resources.[512]

The law further vests the right to manage its own deliberations in the community they are in. The law states that a village shall ordinarily consist of a habitation or a group of habitations or a hamlet or a group of hamlets comprising a community and managing its affairs in accordance with traditions and customs;[513] The power of planning and management over minor water bodies has been the subject matter in clause 'j' of section 4 of this Act. It states that planning and management of minor water bodies in the Scheduled Areas shall be entrusted to Panchayats at the appropriate level; [514]

The need of having a Gram Sabha[515]got its recognition in the act as well. It states that every village shall have a Gram Sabha consisting of persons whose names are included in the electoral rolls for the Panchayat at the village level.[516]Apart from constituting the Gram Sabha the law further empowers it like never before and makes every Gram Sabha competent to safeguard and preserve the traditions and customs of the tribal peoples, their cultural identity, community resources and the customary mode of dispute resolution; thus this provision identifies four basic aspects namely, their

    i.   Traditions and customs,
    ii. Cultural identity
    iii. Community resources and
    iv. Customary mode of dispute resolution.[517]

Gram Sabha is empowered by this Act to approve the plans, programmes and projects for social and economic development before such plans, programmes and projects are taken up for implementation by the Panchayat at the village level and also be responsible for the identification or selection of persons as beneficiaries under the poverty alleviation and other programmes; [518] In this way enormous powers have been vested upon the Gram Sabha and parallel limitation to the existing autocratic power of the state was invoked by this act. The right to economic liberty has also been achieved by this Act as the law categorically states that the economic aspect of the tribals in relation to utilization of funds etc and directs every Panchayat at the village level to required to obtain from the Gram Sabha a certification of utilisation of funds by that Panchayat for the plans, programmes and projects referred to in clause(e); [519] The prior recommendation of the Gram Sabha or the Panchayats at the appropriate level have been made mandatory for grant of concession for the exploitation of minor minerals by auction as well. [520]

---

512 ILO Convention No. 107

513 Section 4(b) of PESA 1996

514 Section 4(j) of PESA 1996

515 Gram sabha includes all adult citizens of the village. It is empowered to elect the gram panchayat. It can even modify certain decisions of the panchayats in case of ambiguity and inherent weakness in them if any.

516 Section 4(c) of PESA 1996

517 Section 4(d) of PESA 1996 interestingly these objectives have already been founded and incorporated in ILO 107 where India was a signatory

518 Section 4(e) of PESA 1996

519 Section 4(f) of PESA 1996

520 Section 4(l) of PESA 1996

The Act also uplifts the intention of the Constitution as it states that the reservation of seats in the Scheduled Areas at every Panchayat shall be in proportion to the population of the communities in that Panchayat for whom reservation is sought to be given under Part IX of the Constitution; [521]

The right to consultation with the natives to deal with the aspects of the natives was again the first of its kind after the colonial ruler left India. The act has not made this right of consultation an option to the government but has made it mandatory especially before any acquisition of land. The act states that the Gram Sabha or the Panchayats at the appropriate level shall be consulted before making the acquisition of land in the Scheduled Areas for development projects and before re-settling or rehabilitating persons affected by such projects in the Scheduled Areas; the actual planning and implementation of the projects in the Scheduled Areas shall be coordinated at the State level;[522] Not only consultation but also implementation of the recommendations of the Gram Sabha or the Panchayats at the appropriate level has been made mandatory prior to grant of prospecting licence or mining lease for minor minerals in the Scheduled Areas; [523] the Panchayats were empowered with powers and authority as may be necessary to enable them to function as institutions of self-government shall contain safeguards to ensure that Panchayats at the higher level do not assume the powers and authority of any Panchayat at the lower level or of the Gram Sabha.[524]

In furtherance of the rights vested upon the tribal peoples of India the act also makes necessary procedural changes to actually implement the provisions of this act. The act empowered the Panchayats in the Scheduled Areas with such powers and authority as may be necessary to enable them to function as institutions of self-government, a State Legislature shall ensure that the Panchayats at the appropriate level and the Gram Sabha are endowed specifically with-

(i)   The power to enforce prohibition or to regulate or restrict the sale and consumption of any intoxicant;
(ii) The ownership of minor forest produce;
(iii) The power to prevent alienation of land in the Scheduled Areas and to take appropriate action to restore any unlawfully alienated land of a Scheduled Tribe;
(iv) The power to manage village markets by whatever name called;
(v)   The power to exercise control over money lending to the Scheduled Tribes;
(vi) The power to exercise control over institutions and functionaries in all social sectors;
(vii) The power to control over local plans and resources for such plans including tribal sub-plans; [525]

It can be noticed from the provisions of the Act that the Parliament exercised the reserved legislative authority to extend the provisions of Part IX of the Constitution exclusively to the 5th Schedule areas.[526] This resulted in limited self governance to any habitation or hamlet which comprised a community and managing its affairs in accordance with customary laws.[527]

---

521 In Section 4(g) of PESA 1996 there have been two provisos. The first proviso states that the reservation for the Scheduled Tribes shall not be less than one-half of the total number of seats; and the second proviso states that all seats of Chairpersons of Panchayats at all levels shall be reserved for the Scheduled Tribes;

522 Section 4(i) of PESA 1996

523 Section 4(k) of PESA 1996

524 Section 4(n) of PESA 1996

525 Section 4(m) of PESA 1996

526 Article 243 M(3A) (b) of the Constitution of India, 1950

527 Section 4(b) of PESA 1996

Post enactment, the communities of the 5th Schedule areas were directed to follow democratic process of election. In other words, to conform to the hierarchical Panchayat system stipulated in Part IX. In other words, this was objected to enable them to function as institutions of self governance. However, these powers were subjected to various exceptions and modifications.[528]

As the power in certain cases devolved upon the local communities, the State were to ensure certain legal directions prescribed in Section 4 of the Act.

Thus PESE may be considered as a logical extension of the 5th Schedule on one hand and part IX of the Constitution on the other.[529] But as innocuous as it may seem, this top down model has in the last 10 years progressively denied tribal communities, self governance and rights to their natural resources.[530]

4.2.3.4. EFFICACY OF THE ACT

The said enactment has got within its fold a lot of success in furtherance of its applicable extensions. But, there have been a lot of criticisms of this Act. The most important of which is the intention of the administrators to actually let the power transfer to the Gram Sabha and the Panchayat as intended by the act. In the absence of such will of these officials, the act remained a piece of legislation with very little change in the actual position of India at the grass root level. The lack of awareness also contributed to the non-fulfilling of the objectives of the Act.

The government was however unaware at the time of passing of this act that it may be a cause of distress in subsequent vesting of tribal land. When in certain cases the Gram Sabha went against the approach of the government, the state had no other option but to question the Constitutionality of this Act. The Supreme Court of India however made the situation worse for the government by upholding the act as Constitutional. This left the state to amend the provision of the Act which the government actually did in 2012.

Still, the Act has made its mark in its short span of its life so far in protecting the civil and economic rights of the tribals in various parts of the country.

4.2.4. THE SCHEDULED TRIBES AND OTHER FOREST DWELLERS (RECOGNITION OF FOREST RIGHTS) ACT, 2006

4.2.4.1. OVERVIEW

The Forest Conservation Act 1980 prohibits all the encroachments of the forest which dramatically affected the adivasis and tribal communities all across India. This enactment actually highlighted the tribals as the biggest enemy of the forest. It was a gross violation of justice to the tribal life and economy. Mass agitation followed with international pressure led to the 42nd Constitutional Amendment Act which shifted 'forest'

---

528 Article 243 G of the Constitution of India, 1950

529 See India, Planning Commission, Planning at the Grassroots Level: An Action Programme for the Eleventh Five Year Plan (New Delhi: Planning Commission of India, 2006) at 84, online: Planning Commission, Government of India <http://planningcommission.nic.in/plans/ stateplan/sp_scy2stat.pdf>. The Government of India Ministry of Tribal Affairs believes that "PESA ... clearly supports the fifth schedule and the rights of the Gram Sabhas in the scheduled areas." See, India, Ministry of Tribal Affairs, Fifth Schedule and Other Related Laws, online: Ministry of Tribal Affairs <http://tribal.nic.in/fifthschedule.html>

530 APOORV KURUP, Tribal Law in India: How Decentralized Administration Is Extinguishing Tribal Rights and Why Autonomous Tribal Governments Are Better, Indigenous Law Journal/Volume 7/Issue 1/2008 p

from the State list to the concurrent list of the Seventh Schedule. Sustainable forest management through participatory approach was introduced for the very first time with due regard to the traditional rights of the tribal peoples on forest land, which did more injustice than remedying them.

This mass agitation and outcry from all corners ultimately led to a new enactment commonly known as the Forest rights Act.

The Scheduled Tribes and Other Forest Dwellers (Recognition of Forest Rights) Act, 2006 came up to empower and strengthen local self governance.

It is objected to address the challenges of livelihood security of the tribal peoples with the intention to alleviate poverty and pro poor growth and protect the tribes both individually and collectively from various economic deprivations. The Act provides a territorial jurisdiction to the whole of India.

The enactment was passed on 29th December 2006 as Act no. 2 of 2007. It commenced from 31st December 2007. The Act went through an amendment in the year 2012.

4.2.4.2. BACKDROP AND OBJECT OF THE ACT

Tribals in India have been subjected to lot of deprivation for centuries and more recently over their own natural resources. This deprivation has basically imbalanced the tribal economy to a great extent as they primarily rely upon the various forest produce for their sustenance. Research shows that the tribal use of forest produce has been sustainable and it's the colonial use and annihilation of forest produce that has led to the extinction of thousand varieties of flora and fauna in India.

The act was objected to empower and strengthen the local self governance.

Another reason for the enforcement of the act is to address the issue of conservation and management of natural resources and conservation governance of India. The act also addresses the growing concern of poverty alleviation amongst the tribals and adivasis in India. To address the question of livelihood security is also one of the key objectives of this act.

However there has been a set of recognized developmental activities that can be made on traditional tribal areas, namely, building of schools, hospitals, anganwadis, fair price shops, tanks drinking water pipe lines, minor canals and roads.

However, there are two conditions that have to be complied with in order to implement the aforesaid developmental measures.
1. The land diverted is less than one hectare in each case and
2. Clearance of such development projects that is, the same is recommended by the Gram Sabha.

4.2.4.3. THE FOREST RIGHTS ACT AND THE RIGHTS OF TRIBAL PEOPLES

4.2.4.3.1. TITLE RIGHTS

The act set out a host of significant rights to the adivasis in India. The primary and most significant of them all is title rights. This right has been subsequently classified in the following rights:

a. Right to hold and live: this right is given to both the tribal individually and the community or clan collectively. This right may be for habituation as well as for cultivation and in furtherance of livelihood. The community right in the name of nistar[531] or any other name so called is also provided by the act. It must be mentioned that these nistar produce are for the use of the tribas and cannot be used for sale or barter.

b. Right to ownership, access to collect use dispose of certain minor forest produce which are collected traditionally within or outside village boundaries are provided expressly in the act.

c. Right in and over disputed lands under any nomenclature in any state where the claims are disputed have been vested upon the tribals. This is another title right which has been the cause of many disputes and conflict between the tribals and the non tribals and the tribals and the state authorities.

d. Conversion rights of pattas or leases or grants issued by any local authority or state government on forest lands or titles have been conferred upon the tribals through this act.

4.2.4.3.2. RIGHT TO USE

a. The Act extensively provides the right to use a large area of tribal land and resources to the tribals. Community rights have also been one of the benchmark of this act and this right of use and exploit is also available to the community as a whole. Certain basic resources like fishing, grazing and traditional seasonal resources like fruits, flowers and access to and by nomadic and pastoral communities have been specified by this act.

b. b. Community rights of tenures of habitat and habituation for primitive tribal groups and pre historical communities is yet another new development of this Act. Recognition of such right to use is a boon for the tribals whose entire economy stands upon tese practices which they have been continuing from centuries.

c. c. Right to access to biodiversity is another integral right of the tribes. This right has been vested on the tribals by this act very specifically. Right to access to biodiversity or community rights to intellectual property and traditional knowledge related to biodiversity and cultural diversity has been vested equivocally upon the tribals. It must be prudent in this regard to refer to the various international instruments which India has been a signatory has recognised this right.[532]

d. D Another important inclusion is the residuary rights upon the tribals. The Act specifically includes the provision that reiterates that the tribals are vested with the rights which are traditionally and customarily been enjoyed by the forest dwelling Scheduled Tribes or other traditional forest dwellers, as the case may be whether or not those have been specified in clause 1 to 11 of the Act. The Act however makes an exception to certain practices like hunting or trapping or extracting a part of the body of the species of wild animals.

4.2.4.3.3. MANAGEMENT RIGHTS

The right to manage, the entire habitat have been vested upon the tribals collectively. The rights to settlement and conservation of the same are some significant measures that the act takes to involve the tribes in their own welfare measures. They are in charge of all forest villages including old habitation, which may include unsurveyed villages as well. It is imperative to mention in this regard that this right includes all the villages whether recorded or not, whether notified or not into revenue villages. The act also provides the right to protect, regenerate, conserve manage any

---

531 Nistar rights include produce of the forest like bamboo, timber of specific class, timber poles, firewood etc.

532 ILO Convention No. 107 and No 169

community forest resources which the tribals have been traditionally protecting and conserving for sustainable use.

4.2.4.4. EFFICACY OF THE RIGHTS GUARANTEED UNDER THIS ACT

This Act has been the subject matter of many debates and discussions from the time of its enactment. Even a case on the Constitutionality of this act has been evaluated by the Supreme Court of India in the affirmative. Many critics have suggested this act to be repealed as it is a bad law passed by the UPA Government.

The journey from its inception as to its implementation has been patchy and dependent upon the initiative of the individual district administrator.

The Act provides rights over use and management of land, forest and minor forest resources upon the individual and the community as a whole. However, the tribals have been facing stern opposition in enjoying such rights by the state bureaucrats in almost every level as they are not interested in transferring their authority and power upon the tribals.

One of the significant achievements of this act is the recognition of the habitat and there are 75 such groups including the Jarawas, Onges of Andaman and Nicober islands.

According to Jual Oram, the Minister of Tribal Affairs, Govt of India, the country is big and knowledge of people living in interior forest area is limited and the state bureaucracy which is responsible for raising awareness is very slow. These are the main problems why Forest Rights Act is not implemented.[533]

Some of the critics have identified a few lacunae of the Act. They criticize the move of moving from the concept of individual rights and individual freedom to the concept of community trumping over individual. The power upon the Gram Sabha or Panchayat has been a cause of great discomfort for the Government as it has lost its autonomy because of the Act.

In the process of any specified development schemes, the decision of Gram Sabha must be taken to some extent uplifted the panchayati raj. One of the primary objectives of the act was the upliftment of livelihood security. Such efforts of poverty alleviation could have done in an alternative and more effective way like that of implementing schemes like NREGA.[534]

The Act has again been criticised as an encroachment over the jurisdiction of other enactments like the issue of Conservation and management being the subject matter of Forest Conservation Act, the Wildlife Protection Act and the Biological Diversity Act, amongst others.[535] Thus this Act has been criticised to be more patronisation than protection.

Another critical view states that by enacting a separate and special law for tribals may essentially imply that:
  i.   They are not amongst us and
  ii. Tribals are endangered species. Taking the second proposition, it must be relevant to state that tribal population in India has increased from 9.2 percent in 2001 to 9.6 percent in 2011.[536]

---

533 Diptesh Narayanan, Economic Times Bureau 1ˢᵗ October, 2015.

534 R Jagannathan 'Forest Right Act need to go: Tribals aren't part of Tiger Reserve', Economic Times, September 12, 2014.

535 Ibid

536 Ibid

It must be relevant in this regard that the question of Constitutionality of the act has been challenged and the said was decided by the Hon'ble Supreme Court of India to be Constitutional.

India has a long history of local government. The term 'Panchayat', is now used to describe the democratic bodies which govern local areas, officially made part of the Indian Constitution in the 1990s in an effort to include small tribal communities in the democratic process of government. However, the word literally translates as 'council of five persons' (Mathew, 2003) and used to mean the small groups of elders that governed small towns and villages according to the ancient caste system, which still holds a lot of influence in parts of India. The new system of local government was designed to ease poverty in more remote regions and improve access to education and healthcare. Unfortunately, the clash of cultures has caused tension in tribal regions, particularly in those communities that have more contact with 'modernized' urban India.[537]The government approach has created widespread disaffection and several protests in the state. The kind of development government intends has created a feeling that it only means evicting tribals to make way for multi-nationals and big companies to exploit their land. Widespread impression is, the compensation offered in return for displacement is grossly paltry, transient and only to a few actual sufferers. The past experience of rehabilitation and resettlement does not inspire any confidence in them: particularly since, Gladson says, the government that lost no time in declaring its industrial policy has not yet formulated a policy for resettlement and rehabilitation of persons displaced due to mining or other projects.[538]

4.3. MINOR ENACTMENTS AND EXECUTIVE FUNCTIONING AND CIVIL AND ECONOMIC RIGHTS OF TRIBAL PEOPLES

4.3.1. AN OVERVIEW

Apart from the major enactments protecting the basic socio economic rights of tribals in India, there are certain minor enactments which have come up with similar objectives. In furtherance of such enactments being passed by the legislature, various executive orders and published to secure various civil and economic rights of tribals. The primary object of providing certain civil rights like right to life, safety, ethnicity, right to religion, integrity to all the people of the country has been fulfilled by making various laws and the necessary executive orders in this regard. With the existence of the major tribal legislation like the PESA, there has been an immediate need to amend certain provision of the minor legislations affecting tribals and adivasis.

In terms of the PESA 1996, the Gram Sabha or the Panchayats at the appropriate level are required to be consulted before making any acquisition of land and before making any arrangements for resettlement and rehabilitation of displaced persons. No such provision exists in the Land Acquisition Act, 1894, which is a colonial hangover. This is a provision, which necessitates suitable amendments in the Land Acquisition Act, 1894. On similar lines, suitable amendments are also required to be made in the Indian Forest Act, 1927 to make it consistent with the provisions of the PESA Act. For instance, the PESA Act confers ownership of minor forest produce on the Gram Sabha and Panchayats.

On the contrary, the Indian Forest Act, 1927 does not make any distinction between major and minor forest produce and vests the ownership of the entire range of forest produce on the State, meaning thereby the Forest Department. Hence, this Commission is of the view that there is an urgent need for necessary

---

537 Mathew, G. (2003) 'Panchayati Raj Institutions and Human Rights in India' *Economic & Political Weekly v.38:no.2(pp.155-162)*

538 By Rajesh Sinha, 'Trampling Tribal Rights Tribals protest in Orissa' *Samay Live*, June 8, 2010

amendments in the Land Acquisition Act, 1894 and the Indian Forest Act, 1927 to bring them in conformity with the provisions of the PESA Act to enable the effective functioning of the Gram Sabhas and Panchayats in terms of the PESA Act.[539]

4.3.2. ECONOMIC RIGHTS

There have been a few schemes made in furtherance of protection of economic rights of the tribals in India. Some of these schemes are:

4.3.2.1. NODAL AGENCY FACILITATING TRIBAL ECONOMIC ACTIVITIES

The National Scheduled Tribes Finance and Development Corporation (NSTFDC) were established through the bifurcation of the National Scheduled Castes and Scheduled Tribes Finance and Development Corporation in 2001-02. The Corporation was set up as a company under Section 25 of the Companies Act, 1956 for providing financial assistance to schemes/projects launched with the aim of economically developing Scheduled Tribes. As such the Corporation has the following broad objectives:

(a) Identification of economic activities of importance to the Scheduled Tribes so as to generate employment and raise their level of income;

(b) Upgradation of skills and processes used by the Scheduled Tribes through providing both institutional and on the job training;

(c) To make existing state/union territory Scheduled Tribes Finance and Development Corporations, that are nominated as State Channelising Agencies (SCAs) for the purpose of availing assistance from NSTFDC and other developmental agencies engaged in the economic development of Scheduled Tribes, more effective;

(d) To assist SCAs in project formulation, implementation of NSTFDC assisted Schemes and in imparting necessary training to their staff;

(e) To provide financial support for meeting the working capital requirement of Central/State government owned agencies, for undertaking procurement and marketing of minor forest produce, agricultural produce, and other products grown/made or collected by the Scheduled Tribes; and

(f) To innovate, experiment and promote rather than replicate the work of the existing agencies. The NSTFDC finances viable income generating schemes/projects that cost upto Rs10 lakhs through SCAs. They also assist SCAs through grants to set up training programmes for skill and entrepreneurial development of eligible Scheduled Tribes.[540]

4.3.2.2. GOVERNMENT SCHEMES FACILITATING TRIBAL ECONOMIC RIGHTS

The Scheduled Tribes and Other Traditional Forest Dwellers (Recognition of Forest Rights) Act, 2006 was enacted to make restitution for historical injustice enacted upon Scheduled Tribes and traditional forest dwellers from colonial times onwards through the appropriation of their traditional land use and community rights on forest land. The key objectives of granting Scheduled Tribes and Other Traditional Forest Dwellers forest rights that secure them individual or community tenure or both on all forest lands, such as

(a) The right to hold and live on forest land under individual/common occupation for habitation/self-cultivation,

(b) Community rights that were formerly granted customarily,

---

539 National Commission for Scheduled Tribes

540 NSTFDC (Source: http://nstfdc.nic.in, the section on "objectives of organization')

(c) The right of ownership, access to collect, use and dispose off minor forest produce which was traditionally collected within or outside village boundaries,

(d) Other community rights of uses or entitlements to water bodies, pastures, etc.,

(e) Right of protection/regeneration/ conservation/management of any community forest resource that they had traditionally adopted,

(f) Right to *in situ* rehabilitation including alternative land in cases where they had been illegally evicted or displaced from forest land without receiving their legal entitlement to rehabilitation prior to 13 December 2005, and related rights. Such rights will be conferred subject to the condition that the beneficiaries had occupied forest land before the 13 December. Any displacement of rights holders for purposes of wildlife conservation until facilities and land allocation for resettlement have been provided and the permission of the Gram Sabha have been taken in writing. The gram sabha is the authority responsible for initiating the process of determining the nature and extent of individual and community forest rights or both of claimants under their jurisdiction. All registration of land titles will be in the names of both husband and wife. Further, it is the intention of the Act to involve beneficiaries in conservation of biodiversity and forest management.

4.3.2.3. NATIONAL RURAL EMPLOYMENT GUARANTEE ACT, 2005

The Act, commonly referred to as NREGA, was enacted with the objective of enhancing livelihood security in rural areas by providing at least 100 days of guaranteed wage employment in a financial year to every household whose adult members volunteer to do unskilled manual work. The NREGA currently covers the entire country with the exception of districts that have a hundred per cent urban population. While Scheduled Tribes are important beneficiaries under the Act, importantly one of the works permissible under the Programme is the provision of irrigation facility to lands owned by households belonging to Scheduled Tribes.[541]

4.3.2.4. DISTRIBUTION OF CEILING SURPLUS LAND

Land ceiling legislation introduced land ceilings in 19 states and 3 union territories from 1972 onwards. The national guidelines recommended ceiling limits of 10–18 acres for irrigated land with two crops, 27 acres for irrigated land with one crop and 54 acres for dry land.

The surplus ceiling land is then distributed to Scheduled Tribes (among other specified beneficiaries). According to the Department of Land Resources, under the Ministry of Rural Development, that is the administering authority of the Scheme, the beneficiaries also include the Scheduled Tribes.

4.3.2.5. LEGISLATIONS PROTECTING AGAINST LAND ALIENATION

A key reason for the continued poverty and vulnerability of Scheduled Tribes is usurious money lending and land alienation. Several states have enacted laws to protect them from land alienation – some of the examples are the Karnataka Scheduled Castes and Scheduled Tribes (Prohibition of Transfer of Certain Lands) (Amendment) Act, 1984, Andhra Pradesh (Scheduled Areas) Land Transfer Regulation, 1959, the Himachal Pradesh Transfer of Land (Regulation) Act, 1968, the Orissa Scheduled Areas Transfer of Immovable Property (Scheduled Tribes Regulation) 1956, etc. For instance, in the Karnataka Scheduled Castes and Scheduled Tribes (Prohibition of Transfer of Certain Lands) (Amendment) Act, 1984, the Statement of Objects and Reasons states that this Act is meant to protect Schedule Tribes from exploitation

---

541 Among other specified beneficiaries

by 'affluent and powerful sections' who obtain sales or mortgages of land granted to Scheduled Tribes by the government for their upliftment either for a nominal consideration or for no consideration at all.

To fulfil the purposes of the grant, the Act aims to restore alienated land to the original grantee or his heirs. Section 4 renders null and void any transfer of granted land made either before or after the commencement of this Act and Section 5 provides for their resumption and restitution to the grantee or his heirs. Section 8 penalises any person acquiring granted land with imprisonment up to six months and/or fine up to Rs.2000.

This law has also been included in the Ninth Schedule of the Constitution. Article 31B protects all laws in the Ninth Schedule from being struck down as violative or as abridging of any other right guaranteed in Part III. Other states have enacted similar laws.

4.3.2.6. NATIONAL MINERAL POLICY, 1993 AND THE TRIBES NATIONAL MINERAL POLICY, 1993

Certain economic aspects of the tribes have led to constitute the essentials of National Mineral Policy which has evolved over the years. The policy also emphasises certain new aspects and elements like mineral exploration in the sea-bed, development of proper inventory, proper linkage between exploitation of minerals and development of mineral industry, preference to members of the Scheduled Tribes for development of small deposits in Scheduled Areas, protection of forest, environment and ecology from the adverse effects of mining, enforcement of mining plan for adoption of proper mining methods and optimum utilisation of minerals, export of minerals in value added form and recycling of metallic scrap and mineral waste. Infrastructural Facilities & Regional Development Mineral deposits generally occur in remote and backward areas with poor infrastructural facilities which often inhibit their optimum development. Mineral bearing areas are also often inhabited by tribal population and exploitation of mineral resources has not always contributed adequately to their economic development. Contribution of mineral development to overall regional development has also not always been commensurate with the huge investment in large mining projects. A major thrust needs to be given for development of infrastructural facilities in mineral bearing areas following an integrated approach for mineral development, regional development and also social and economic upliftment of the local population including tribal population. Small Deposits Small and isolated deposits of minerals are scattered all over the country. These often lend themselves to economic exploitation through small scale mining. With modest demand on capital expenditure and short lead-time, they also provide employment opportunities for the local population. Efforts will be made to promote small scale mining of small deposits in a scientific and efficient manner while safeguarding vital environmental and ecological imperatives. In grant of mineral concessions for small deposits in Scheduled Areas, preference shall be given to the Scheduled Tribes.[542]

4.3.2.7. NATIONAL POLICY ON RESETTLEMENT AND REHABILITATION, 2003

The National Policy on Resettlement and Rehabilitation, 2003, is in the form of broad guidelines applicable only to projects that displace 500 families or more en masse in plain areas and 250 families *en masse* in hilly areas; the guidelines also cover areas mentioned in Schedules V and VI and Desert Development Blocks. The first barrier of exclusion in this policy is the clause which says that only 100 percent of their lands will be eligible for compensation. Secondly, criterion of displacement of 500 families and 250 families en masse in plain areas and hilly areas respectively excludes the families who have been displaced, yet do not conform to this clause. Thirdly, the policy also makes allotment of land 'conditional to availability', thus,

---

542 http://mines.nic.in/nmp.html (Visited on November 28, 2015).

putting no burden on the government to find land.[543] It has to be understood that the policy has been one of its type meant for the people who have been suffering because of displacement and other various factors.

4.3.2.8. SCHEME FOR PRIMITIVE TRIBAL GROUPS, 2008

The Scheme of Development of Primitive Tribal Groups (PTGs) came into effect from April 1, 2008. The name of these groups has been changed and a more effective term Particularly Vulnerable Tribal Groups (PVTG) has replaced it. The Scheme defines PTGs/PVTGs as the section of tribal communities among Scheduled Tribes who have declining or stagnant population, low level of literacy, pre-agricultural level of technology and are economically backward. PTGs are considered the most vulnerable among the Scheduled Tribes and the Scheme therefore seeks to prioritise their protection and development. It identifies 75 such groups in 17 states and 1 (Andaman and Nicobar Islands) union territory. The Scheme seeks to adopt a holistic approach to the socio-economic development of PTGs and gives state governments flexibility in planning initiatives that are geared towards the specific socio-cultural imperatives of the specific groups at hand. Activities may thus include housing, land distribution, land development, agricultural development, cattle development, construction of link roads, installation of nonconventional sources of energy, social security, etc. Funds are available only for activities essential for the survival, protection and development of PTGs and not already funded by any other Scheme of the central/state governments. Each state and the Andaman and Nicobar Islands' administration is required to prepare a long term conservation-cum-development (CCD) plan valid for a period of five years for each PTG within its territory outlining the initiatives it will undertake, financial planning for the same and the agencies charged with the responsibility of undertaking the same. The CCD Plan has to be approved by an Expert Committee appointed by the Ministry of Tribal Affairs. The Scheme is funded entirely by the Central government.[544]

4.3.2.9. THE WEST BENGAL LAND REFORMS ACT 1955

An entire chapter of this state act deals with Scheduled Tribes. Chapter IIA of this act comprising of Sections 14A to 14I specifically relates to tribal areas. It shall be relevant to mention in this regard that this chapter has an overriding effect over other provisions of this Act. Chapter II of the act is named as "Restrictions on Alienation of land by Scheduled Tribes". As stated earlier this act shall have an overriding effect has been specified in Section 14 A. This section vests the power to override any other provisions of this Act.

The act came up to prevent and restricts alienation of land by scheduled tribes.[545] This provision is in consonance with international standards of land rights of the tribal peoples. However in reality, this provision has been the subject of great debate and discussion for last few decades as the critics have identified the great number of lands that has been transferred from the tribals to the non tribals. Apart from making the said prohibition the Act lays down the various modes by which land may be transferred by a member of the scheduled tribe in the schedule area[546]exclusively through a registered instrument.[547]

---

543 Rich Lands Poor People: Is 'Sustainable' Mining Possible?, Centre for Science and Development, New Delhi, 2008

544 Supra Note 127

545 West Bengal Land Reforms Act, 1955, (Act No. X of 1956) at Section 14B.

546 Ibid at Section 14C.

547 Ibid at Section 14D.

The act prohibits any transfer made in contravention of the provision of the Act and also vests powers on the Revenue Officer to set aside improper transfer by raiyat.[548] The act also prohibits Benami transaction [549]which was a common practice in Bengal for centuries. Section 14HH of the act vests the power upon the court to set aside any sale of land of a raiyat belonging to a schedule tribe.

Thus it can be seen from the aforesaid provisions of the west Bengal Land reforms act that the rights of the tribals are safeguarded to a great extent by this piece of legislation and along with this the economic rights are also protected.

4.3.3. CIVIL RIGHTS

Certain civil rights of the tribal peoples have been adversely affected by various enactments. Civil rights mean those rights which protect the right to freedom of individuals. Right to live and to live freely as a free man is the primary purpose to this right. Certain economic rights must also be addressed of the tribal at an urgent basis. For this a study of certain minor legislations and policies of the government have to be taken in the context of this chapter.

4.3.3.1. CRIMINAL TRIBES ACT

The 1871 Act came into force, on 12 October 1871 with the assent of the Governor-General of India. Under the act, ethnic or social communities in India which were defined as "addicted to the systematic commission of non-bailable offences" such as thefts, were systematically registered by the government. Since they were described as 'habitually criminal', restrictions on their movements were also imposed; adult male members of such groups were forced to report weekly to the local police.[550]

However with the passage of time after the independence from the colonial rule, these tribes have been de notified. But the way by which they have been treated for decades have not changed. A mere change in name has not changed the fate of these 313 Nomadic Tribes and 198 Denotified tribes (DNT) in India. The legacy of the past continues to haunt the majority of 60 million people belonging to these tribes. This alienation has put these people under tremendous hardship both economically and socially. By and large DNTs have not been given land titles, neither agricultural nor homestead forcing them to continue their unsettled life. This has serious negative implications for their children's education, health status of the community in general, protection of family, adequate standard of living, etc.[551]

4.3.3.2. HEALTH

Health of tribals suffers as the tribal children and women health indicators reflect. Further, the tribals suffer from the diseases specific to typical living conditions. It is widely accepted that malnutrition among tribals is widespread, which is largely attributable to poverty, illiteracy, environmental conditions, difficult terrain, traditional beliefs and customs and, above all, the non-availability of basic health services. The ill-nourished tribals live in an environment, which has been degraded, and, as a result, diseases such as malaria,

---

548 Ibid at Section 14E.

549 Ibid at Section 14FF.

550 Bates, Crispin, "Race, Caste and Tribe in Central India: the Early Origins of Indian anthropometry" and in Robb, Peter's "The Concept of Race in South Asia." Delhi: Oxford University Press. 227 (1995)

551 ActionAid Thematic Group on Indigenous peoples and their Rights, Report: Economic, Social and Cultural Exclusion of Tribals/Indigenous peoples, 2008

filaria, tuberculosis, and goitre are endemic in most of the tribal areas. The issues of tribal health are also intricately intertwined with tribal social conduct and issues of 'Inbreeding' and 'Genetic Disorders' like sickle cell anemia, etc. In many cases the tribal population is decreasing, and some tribes are on the verge of extinction. Infant Mortality Rate for Scheduled Tribes was 62 while it was 49 for the general population in 2001. Besides the mean body mass index for SCs, STs, and OBCs is 5–10% below that for the general population.[552]

One of the example of a scheme launched by the Government was Janani Suraksha Yojana.The Janani Suraksha Yojana is a safe motherhood intervention under the National Rural Health Mission, the objective of which is the reduction of maternal and neo-natal mortality among poor pregnant women. The funds are entirely sponsored by the Central government and the programme integrates cash assistance with delivery/post-delivery care. Scheduled Tribe women (among other specified beneficiaries) are entitled to assistance under this scheme.[553]

4.3.3.3. EDUCATIONAL SCHEMES FOR THE BENEFIT OF SCHEDULED TRIBE STUDENTS

There are numerous Scholarship Schemes that the Central Government through the Ministry of Tribal Affairs has notified in the educational interests of Scheduled Tribe students. They are:

(i) Scheme of up-gradation of Merit for Scheduled Tribe Students – This Scheme aims at upgrading merit of Scheduled Tribe students by providing them remedial coaching (to enable students to master their curriculum) and special coaching (for competitive examinations to medical and engineering colleges) in classes IX to XII. The Scheme provides 100% assistance to State governments and Union Territory administrations and each student is given a package grant of Rs.19,500 per student per year. Of the total beneficiaries covered under this Scheme, 30% preference is given to Scheduled Tribe girls and 2% preference to disabled students. This Scheme is funded by the Ministry of Tribal Affairs and administered by the concerned state/UT government.

(ii) Scheme of Post-Matric Scholarships to Students Belonging to Scheduled Tribes for Studies in India – This Scheme aims at providing financial assistance to Scheduled Tribe students enrolled within India in post-matriculation or post secondary courses at recognised institutions to enable them to complete their education. Those Scheduled Tribe students whose parents' annual income does not exceed Rs100000 per annum are eligible under this Scheme. The Scheme is a programme of the Ministry of Tribal Affairs and is implemented by state governments and union territory administrations.[554]

(iii) Central Sector Scholarship Scheme of Top Class Education for Scheduled Tribe Students – The objective of the Scheme is to encourage qualitative education for Scheduled Tribe students through the provision of full financial assistance for studies beyond Standard XII in 127 institutes of excellence spread out through the country, including IIMs, IITs, NITs, commercial pilot training institutes, medical and law colleges of repute and ors. Scheduled Tribe students whose total family income is up to Rs. 2 lakhs per annum are eligible for the scholarship which covers tuition fees, living expenses, books and stationery, and a computer. The Scheme is implemented by the Ministry of Tribal Affairs and the monies are released directly to the Institute concerned by the Ministry.[555]

---

552 Eleventh Five Year Plan 2007-2012, Vol.III, Planning Commission, Government of India, New Delhi, 2008, pp-82.

553 Supra Note 129 at p 41

554 Ibid at p 44.

555 Ibid at Pp 44-45.

A SUM UP

Perhaps, it is too late today to bring the tribes back to the land and the environment they used to enjoy for hundred of years. One of such effort was made in Kerala in furtherance of the Constitution.

Schedule V of the Article 244 of the Constitution of India make the State to ensure suitable legislation, total prohibition of transfer of tribal land to the non tribals. The Debar Commission appointed under Article 399 of the Indian Constitution, recommended that all tribal land alienated since 1950 should be returned to the tribals. But the Government of Kerala miserably failed to pass the necessary laws to protect tribal land. It passed the legislation in the year 1975.[556] But the rules needed to make it effective and operational was not passed. It took approximately 10 years to pass the Kerala Scheduled Tribes Restriction on Transfer of Lands and Restoration of Alienated Lands Act in 1986 providing the relevant provisions for restoration of tribal lands to the tribals who have been alienated from their land and forest dwellings. However, there has been no implementation of the act for a long span of time. This futile effort on the part of the executive and the legislation is yet another proof of tribal human rights violation.

According to Kurup,

> "India's population includes nearly one hundred million tribal peoples. These numbers are matched only by the remarkable diversity of India's tribes. The two main regions of tribal settlement are the country's northeastern states bordering China and Burma, and the highlands and plains of its central and southern regions. The latter is home to more than 80 per cent of the tribes, which differ from the northeastern tribes in ethnicity...There are also differences in the extent to which the tribes interact with non-tribal communities. While the northeastern tribes are usually isolated communities, the tribes in peninsular India may at times coexist with non tribal peoples." [557]

Thus, the tribals face an uphill task in the light of the various socio economic distress that the last few centuries have brought to them it is a small ray of hope today that has again given the hope to the tribals of India to survive.

Thus new legislative intervention must also be needed to provide adequate relief to these communities who have suffered unilaterally and consistently for centuries.

---

556 While piloting the Bill in the House, Sir Baby John observed: "In a state which claims to be progressive, it is for us to think whether there is real progress or whether the so called progress is a fallacy. When one such segment of the population is suffering from and is in slavery, what is the point in boasting that we are progressing! It is on realization of all these facts that the said bill is introduced intending to prevent assignment of such land and to scrutinize and assignments already affected."

557 Kurup, A. 'Tribal Law In India: How Decentralized Administration Is Extinguishing Tribal Rights And Why Autonomous Tribal Governments Are Better' *Indigenous Law Journal at the University of Toronto v.7:no. 87-88 2008/9*

CHAPTER 5

ROLE OF JUDICIARY IN PROTECTING THE CIVIL AND ECONOMIC RIGHTS OF TRIBALS IN INDIA

AN OVERVIEW

Today there are two sets of laws in practice almost all across the world. One the colonial legal system and its existing structures incorporating substantive and procedural laws which have been in existence ever since the colonial rulers took over the major part of the world through the doctrine of discovery[558]. The other is Humanitarian Law or the law most commonly known as Human Rights. Laws meant for the people by the people and accepted by the people world over without any prejudice. This has been propagated by the United Nations Organization (UNO) and its various organs with the people who have been facing the hardships during the last few hundred centuries. The United Nations (UN) has been playing a very important role since its inception after the fall of League of Nations. Lately the various principles developed by this international organization have been the guidelines for the majority of the people living in various socio economic conditions. The standard of research and quality of assessment has made this Organization the most favoured amongst many communities mostly vulnerable to various modern and colonial conditions of law and justice.

These two set of laws are practically poles apart in a number of aspects including the upliftment of the condition of living of the vulnerable section of the society. But it must be admitted that both these two sets of laws are indispensable in the modern legal system even when neither of their applicability is possible *stricto sensu* in the absence of the other.

It must be understood that no radical view of the existence of either of these legal setup is practically possible in today's world. It is a fact that all the existing courts[559] cannot be eliminated and a new set of courts be established which will hold key the principle of Human Rights to the utmost benefit of mankind. Neither the existing colonial legal principles be abandoned to embrace the principles of Human Rights because of the sheer legal philosophy and acceptance of most of the countries in their legal frame work. On the other hand the infrastructures needed for the implementation of Human Rights in most countries are very volatile. Till date many countries have not adhered to the policy and principles laid down in the Universal Declaration of Human Rights 1948. In its absence, the courts can do very little to protect the vulnerable population of the society from being further affected adversely by the state activities. Such is the condition of the majority of indigenous and tribal peoples of the world.

As it is not possible today to have an elimination of one to the existence of the other, the only thing that comes up is the need of a harmony between the two (the colonial principles and the human rights principles). In the perception of Dugait the Social Solidarity theory is what is needed today. And in furtherance of

---

558 Sir Robert Miller identified 10 features that he has perceived through the case of Johnson and Graham's Lessee v. McIntosh 21 U.S. (8 Wheat.) 543, 5 L. Ed. 681 (1823). The 10 elements are:

First Discovery

Actual Occupancy

Pre-emption European Title

Native Title

Sovereign and commercial rights

Contiguity

Terra nullius

Conquest

Christianity and

Civilization

559 Which is the outcome of the colonial legal system based on common law principles

this endeavour, the apex court of a country through judicial activism has tried to bring various important principles propagated by the UN in the domestic arena. This judicial activism has been the characteristics of the supreme court of the country. This incorporation of international human rights laws in the domestic forum has been commendable. Whether in uplifting the issues of vulnerable section of the society or the rights of the environment to be protected from adverse approach from human beings, court has played a commendable role for bringing international laws in the fore.

At the time when the Constitution of India came up, the Constituent Assembly firmly affirmed the idea of Parliamentary Supremacy. However, the Parliamentarians themselves failed to live up to the expectation the Constituent Assembly vested upon them. In the turn of events, the inefficiency and inefficacy merged with personal satisfaction and greed for power and money has left the national interest on the back foot. This has to a considerable extent obliterated the faith of common man over our Parliamentarians (as well as the executives) and overturned the concept of Parliamentary Supremacy. To put it another way - and give but one example, examine this National Law: "Tribal Lands are not to be sold or leased to non-tribal peoples"... 'Officially' ... sounds pretty straight forward. But rampant corruption and bribery (not to mention 'legal loopholes') that has infected all aspects of Indian Civil Service - to the point where it has become a 'National Malaise' and this consequently; results in this law (and many ors) being circumvented and openly flouted daily all across India.[560] Today this lost faith upon democracy has been restored to a great extent by the Judiciary and has to a considerable extent made India in tune of 'Judicial Supremacy'.

The Indian Judiciary in the 20th century has tried to come out of the shackles of the colonial prowess through Judicial Activism. Upliftment of Human Rights in the modern world structure has been one of the promising roles played by the judiciary today. Not only India but the world is witnessing today the role of judiciary in many commonwealth countries and also the European and American counterpart as to how the human rights of the people can be uplifted and protected. More importantly to those who have been deprived through ages and for centuries together in the realm of darkness and discrimination. The judiciary has felt this need to provide justice and equality to those who have not got justice throughout. These vulnerable classes have to a considerable extent been recognized by the judiciary as being a part of the bigger society[561] and also their right to get justice like any other person of the society.

Indigenous and tribal peoples are one of such categories that have been pushed to dark by the advent of colonial empowerment in most of the countries. Continuous pushing of these people from their original habitat has led to a complete imbalance in their socio economic conditions. The colonial system of oppression has been carried out by the post colonial era. As these people are in the minority in the literal sense of the term, little could they do to prevent their conditions from turning from bad to worse and ultimately to the verge of extinction. It is at this junction when the judiciary has taken up the challenge to protect these people from being further deteriorated and also to understand the international obligation of the nations to provide justice to these people.

Indigenous and tribal peoples have got their long waited recognition of being subject to disrespect and unequal treatment. This recognition of being the deprived one has brought them to the fore, where justice shall prevail.

---

560 Damon Gerard Corrie, "The India You Do Not Know' People Land Truth", Intercontinental Cry, 24 (2012).

561 This assimilistic approach was taken from the ILO Convention No 107 which India ratified. However the ILO Convention No 169 has corrected the limitations of the earlier convention but still many countries including India has not yet ratified this altered aspect of the international community.

The diversity and the plethora of practical rules and procedure have also reflected these people vulnerability in the society. The ways by which they are cheated, discriminated and tortured by their non tribal brors and the state is stunning in many respects. This tyranny to say the least had overwhelming impact over the miserable life of these people both short term and long.

The people of these communities lost their land, resources and livelihood to the non tribal and largely to the European settlers who being outsiders to these people decided how these people would live their life, earn their livelihood and the profession they would take. Through the doctrine of discovery,[562] the colonial settlers established their legal right over their newly discovered land. This doctrine of discovery was more of religion than of law. Pope Nicholas V issued to King Alfanso V of Portugal the bull Romanus Pontifex, declaring war against all non-Christian nations and their territories.[563] The non Christian states or people were declared by the Catholic to be enemies. These non Christians were considered as less than humans. Pope Alexander VI in an Inter Cetera document stated the desire that the 'Discovered' people be subjugated and brought to the faith itself.[564] Thus when Columbus sailed west across the Sea of Darkness in 1492-with the express understanding that he was authorized to 'take possession' of any land he 'discovered' that were not under the dominion of any Christian Rulers- he and the Spanish of Aragon and Castile were following an already well established tradition of discovery and conquest.[565] They imposed their legal right over the land and the existing inhabitants were provided with the secondary right, as trustees[566]. Not only did these Europeans impose their vested rights over the property of ors by force and in most cases only by deemed force, they even decided upon the international relations of these indigenous peoples. With whom they would trade in, with whom they would not was also decided by these colonial rulers. This was a very brutal step in furtherance of the socio economic conditions of these people[567]. The only thing that was thought about by this intruding fleet was about their own development at the cost of ors. The consistent economic empowerment of some places like England and France was evident at the cost of colony states. This view of earth as a place where resources are in abundance and is meant for the enjoyment of the masses is exclusively European and absolute opposite to that of these inhabitants. With this view of their superiority in terms of technology and science, they wasted a sea of knowledge that the indigenous communities has been carried along through centuries. Ignoring these treasures of indigenous knowledge has a price of its own. Global warming, population explosion, various incurable diseases are to name a few.

The new world has a lot of questions to ask and too far and few were answered. The concept of civilization was challenged in various international forums. A lot of debates took place over the concept of development as well. The European model of development which was followed by the post colonial governments was also a very volatile issue which is yet to be addressed. The very basis of taking a religion as superior than the other is another aspect that has to be addressed in the ongoing debate between indigenous and tribal peoples on one hand and the settlers on the other. Adherence of these colonial and pre colonial principles by the modern judiciary has raised yet another debate as it did with the judgement of Johnson Macintosh. [568]

---

562 Supra note 1

563 Steve Newcomb, "Five Hundred Years of Injustice: The Legacy of Fifteenth Century Religious Prejudice", Fall, Shaman's Drum 19 (1992)

564 Davenport:61

565 Thacher:96

566 Campbell, Kenneth, "Legal Rights", *The Stanford Encyclopedia of Philosophy* (Fall 2013 Edition), Edward N. Zalta (ed.), available at, http://plato.stanford.edu/archives/fall2013/entries/legal-rights/ (Accessed on December 4, 2015)

567 Ibid

568 Johnson and Graham's Lessee v. McIntosh 21 U.S. (8 Wheat.) 543, 5 L. Ed. 681 (1823)

One of the telling example of the attachment of indigenous peoples are the refusal of accepting an amount as huge as $400 million as compensation in lieu of the famous Black Hills of South Dakota, USA.

The growing movement of these people in the modern world has got its momentum from the judiciary itself. For instance the famous Australian case of Queensland where the Australian supreme court rightfully restored the entire area back to the aboriginal people of Australia. The Indian counterpart to this is the case of Samatha where the Hon'ble Supreme Court of India acknowledges the right to land and natural resources of the tribal peoples in India. In a very recent development in England where the Queen's Bench in 2012 has accepted the rights of Kenyan people and provided them monetary compensation.

It is true that there has been a lot of discrimination and abuse that did engulfed the tribals and indigenous peoples across the globe for centuries by the colonial settlers and the post colonial non tribal regime. The ways by which these people have been subjected to cruelty has also a very significant place in the ongoing debate. The acceptability of the truth over the pre existing notions and philosophy created and imposed by the colonial rulers have been subjected to open debate in international and national judicial forums to decide. This remarkable development has brought forward the actual position of these people and the need to protect them in every possible way to provide them with the minimal relief possible.

Indian courts have pressed hard to redeem this position in a number of cases but the intention of the legislature and the executive to provide relief has been far from satisfactory. The directions given by the High Court and the Supreme Court of our country has not been adhered in a number of cases and the lack of persuasion by the tribal communities due to the lack of modern education and financial capacity has left them with the continuing degradable conditions. The number game in Indian political scenario is another contributory factor as the total number of tribal population in India is around 8% amongst whom a majority does not participate in the Electoral College. The tribals believe in self determination and self governance. Their absence or minimalistic presence in the modern election system has its adverse effects as well. In such a situation the responsibility again vests upon the judiciary to protect these people from being subject of abuse and exploitation.

5.1. THE PRINCIPLES OF COMMON LAW

By the mid-20th century it was a generally held view that Native title was not part of the common law.[569] This view was further confirmed by Cooper v. Stuart[570] even when the subject matter did not directly concern the issue of Native title. In this famous case the English law heritage of the English Common Law did not always accept that native title should be acknowledged, in this 1889 Privy Council case the court considered that in 1788 on settlement by Europeans there were 'no settled inhabitants or settled law' in Australia. This provided the basis to ignore native title in subsequent authorities. This view was confirmed, when the issue was raised directly in yet another landmark case of Milirrpum v. Nabalco Ply Ltd.[571] The subject matter of the case was an action by a group of Australian Aborigines who claimed native title in regard to land on the Gove Peninsula in the Northern Territory. Mr Justice Blackburn held against the Aboriginal plaintiffs on the basis of his view that for a communal native title to be acknowledged by the common law it would be necessary for the native title to demonstrate that it constituted a proprietary interest. This would necessitate that interest to demonstrate the outward indicia of proprietary interests such as the right to use and enjoy

---

569 Attorney-General NSW v. Brown [1847]

570 [1889] 14 App Cas 286

571 [1971] 17 FLR 141

land, the right to exclude ors and the right to alienate. In his view the plaintiff's claim did not demonstrate those attributes existed in that case. In addition, based upon the Privy Council decision in Cooper v Stuart, he considered that the common law of Australia did not acknowledge the concept of native title. Mr Justice Blackburn stated that even if communal native title did exist, then in the circumstances of that case these rights had been extinguished.[572]

Justice Blackburn while providing this historic judgment categorically stated ''the doctrine of [Native title] does not form, and never has formed, part of the law of any part of Australia''.[573] He also went on to re-state what was accepted as established law when he said "(O)n the foundation of New South Wales... every square inch of territory in the colony became the property of the Crown"[574]. Despite the fact that, according to Blackburn J, ''the evidence showed a subtle and elaborate system highly adapted to the country in which the people led their lives, which provided a stable order of society and was remarkably free from the vagaries of personal whim or influence"[575] and despite the fact that J Blackburn thought that "if ever a system could be called 'a government of laws, and not of men', it [was] that shown in the evidence before [him]... "He was unable to conclude that the Yolngu people from Yirrkala on the Gove Peninsula of the Northern Territory held proprietary rights. According to Blackburn J, the claims of the Yolngu did not sufficiently resemble recognised understandings of property for those claims to be so categorised.[576]

Thus, the first major decision relevant to Aboriginal land rights prior to the Mabo decision in Australia, was the decision of Mr Justice Blackburn of the Federal Court in Milirrpum & Ors' v Nabalco Pry Ltd. This decision of Justice Blackburn has been criticised in many cases including the Canadian case of Calder et al. v. Attorney-General for British Columbia.[577] The court in this case declared that some of Blackburn J's propositions were ''wholly wrong"[578]. Under this situation the Honourable High Court was willing to review the law on the existence of Native title.[579] This case originated in 1969, when one Frank Arthur Calder and the Nisgaʼa Nation Tribal Council brought an action against the British Columbia government for a declaration that aboriginal title to certain lands in the province had never been lawfully extinguished. During the trial of this case and also during the appeal, the court was of opinion that if there ever was aboriginal title in the land, it was surely extinguished. The judgement during these stages was in tune of the famous Cooper judgement given by Justice Blackburn. When the matter was referred to the Supreme Court, it was found that there was indeed an aboriginal title to the land which was in existence at the time of the Royal Proclamation, 1763.

However, the Court was split 3 to 3 on whether the claim to land was valid. One group claimed that though title existed it had been extinguished by virtue of the government's exercise of control over the lands, while

---

572 Weir, Michael, "The Story of Native Title," Vol. 8: Issue. 1, The National Legal Eagle 1 (2002)

573 Ibid at 244-245

574 Ibid at 198

575 Ibid

576 Janice Gray, "The Mabo Case: A Radical Decision?", XVII, The Canadian Journal of Native Studies 36 (1997).

577 This historic case was brought by the Nisga'a Indians of British Columbia, Canada. The argument was based on the possession of land rights to their traditional territory since time immemorial. And that such right had never been surrendered or lost. In their verdict, the judges of the Supreme Court of Canada recognized the existence of Aboriginal rights to land for the first time.

578 [1977] SCR 313; [1973] 34 3DLR [3rd] 145

579 Administration of Papua v. Dera Guba ([1973] 130 CLR 353:397), Coe v. Commonwealth ([1979] 53 ALJR 403)

the other group stated that mere exercise of control over the land is not sufficient and something more was needed in furtherance of the mere exercise of control. It is at this point the judgement of Justice Blackburn was criticised.

The question was again raised in the famous Australian case of Gerhardy v. Brown.[580] Gerhardy v. Brown was the first opportunity for the Court to pronounce on the validity of active, positive measures aimed at the protection of Aboriginals, and the Court gave an affirmative answer to the question about the validity of such measures.[581] It is encouraging because the Court gave its unanimous "go ahead" (though some Justices were less enthusiastic than ors) to a measure aimed at the protection and advancement of the most disadvantaged and most unfortunate group in a generally affluent and prosperous society: to Australia's original inhabitants.[582]

The right of the tribal and indigenous peoples has again got recognition in a recent case in Canada.[583]In this case, which was brought by the Gitxsan and Wet'suwet'en tribes of British Columbia, Canada, the Supreme Court stated that native people have a Constitutional right to own their ancestral lands and to use them almost entirely as they wish. The Court also confirmed the continuation of the ownership of the indigenous peoples continued to own their lands unless the government had explicitly 'extinguished' their ownership. The court emphasised on the importance of oral history as evidence of indigenous peoples long ownership of their territories.

In a similar case in Malaysia in 2005[584], the court gave verdict in favour of the tribal peoples. The Temuan people of Bukit Tampoi village in Malaysia fought a ten-year battle to stop their land being used for the construction of a road link to a new airport. The authorities had claimed that the Temuans and other 'Orang Asli' or 'first people' were merely tenants on state land and therefore not entitled to any compensation. Malaysia's Court of Appeal affirmed the Temuans' rights to ownership of their land, and ordered a developer, the Malaysian government and a government agency to pay the tribe substantial compensation.

The position in South Africa is not much different as the country's apex court has acknowledged the long deplorable condition of tribal and indigenous peoples of the country. In this case[585] 3,000 Nama people[586] took the South African government to court after they were evicted from their diamond-rich land in the 1950s. This case had a close resemblance to the famous case of the Botswana Bushmen.

The country's highest court, the Constitutional Court, ruled that the Nama people had both communal land ownership and mineral rights over their territory. Furthermore, the failure to respect indigenous peoples' land ownership under their traditional law, even if it is unwritten, amounts to 'racial discrimination'.[587]

---

580 In this case, Justice Deane stated that Australia was not yet in the same position as America where there had been a "retreat from injustice" brought about by the acknowledgment and recognition of Native title ([1985] 57 ALR 472,532).

581 Wojczech Sadurskz, 'Gerhardy V. Brown V, "The Concept Of Discrimination: Reflections On The Landmark Case That Wasn't" 1 Sydney Law Review 6 (1986).

582 Ibid at p.5

583 'Delgamuukw', Canada, 1997

584 'Bukit Tampoi', Malaysia, 2005

585 Richtersveld', South Africa, 2003

586 An indigenous group related to the Bushmen.

587 Supra Richtersveld

In a fascinating change of events in Nicaragua in 2001, the tribes of Awas Tingni village filed a case in the Inter-American Court of Human Rights when a Korean company was granted a logging concession over their traditional lands. The Sumu Indians of the village of Awas Tingni contended that their right to their ancestral land has been compromised by the arbitrary act of the government. In this case the court upheld the existence of indigenous peoples' collective rights to their land, resources, and environment, and also declared that the community's rights were violated by the government granting the concession without either consulting with the community or obtaining its consent.[588]

The situation in India was not much different as being a colony of England, India inherited all the common law principles till the Constitution of India was framed and even thereafter. Tribes in India were in a deplorable condition as these people are guided by their customary rules and regulations. As a matter of practice criminal justice system amongst the tribes and non tribals were completely different. In case of a dispute between tribals, the tribal customary laws were the guiding principles. But when the offender is a non tribal, the situation was completely different to deal with. Because of their presence in the rural belts and the hills, the British administrative and judicial system was far away from these people. The non tribals were in a deciding position and continued their torture over these poor people. Study of some basic cases during this phase would make the situation very clear.

Case 1: Physical Assault and Outraging Modesty of a Tribal Woman by caste men in drunken state

A female daily wage labourer belonged to Kandh Community in the district of Phulbani. Two men belonging to general caste were residents of the same village at a little distance from the victims' house. On 27th June, 1984, at around 1:30 am, the two men belonging to generl caste being severely drunk came and kicked the door of the tribal girl. They were abusing her with slangs. But the girl didn't open the doors out of fear. One relative opened the door to enquire about the noise made by the two drunken men. Suddenly both the men attacked her and dragged her to the middle of the village by pulling off her sari and paraded her nude. They, apart from their verbal assault, slapped the girl. When the husband of the girl tried to intervene he was warned with dire consequences. When the drunken men left the spot, the girl with her husband went to the police station to file a complaint. However, the police didn't take any complaint and asked them to come the next morning. The next day on the basis of the complaint an FIR was drawn. The girl was advised by many persons not to go for medical examination as this would complicate the case and would force her into unnecessary harassment by the police and the court. Even at the time of investigation no adverse statements were recorded against the culprits.

The final judgement was as follows[589]:

> *"On basis of the above facts and circumstances and after taking all other incidents into consideration it was held that the accused persons were not to be considered as guilty under section 341/294/354/34 IPC and to be acquitted under Section 255 Code of Criminal Procedure 1979[590], for the benefit of doubt."*

Thus the case was proved to be a misrepresentation of facts and the accused were left scot free.[591]

---

588 Awas Tingni', Nicaragua, 2001

589 S.Mohanty, N.Mishra et. al., "Violence Against Tribal Women: A Sociological Analysis of some selected cases in Phulbani District, Orissa", 4 ICFS 17-18 (1993)

590 Act No. 15 of 1979

591 Supra note 587

Case 2: The Rape of a Tribal School Girl by Non Tribal Teacher.

In this case a non tribal teacher with the help of a cook raped the school girl who was studying in class three. However, the cook helped to burn the blood stained clothes of the victim and also asked ors not to speak about the incident to protect the chastity of the young girl. And no police report was made. However, the entire incident took a political turn after six months and a case was opened. However due to the delay and loss of vital evidence the non tribal teacher was not convicted under Section 376 IPC.[592]

Thus from the above two cases depicted and many more like this, a clear picture can be drawn to portrait the miserable situation of tribal peoples in most of the tribal localities in India.

5.2. CONSTITUTIONAL GUARANTEES AND JUDICIAL REMEDIES

The Constitution of India has borrowed Part III from the Bill of Rights of the American Constitution[593] which provides for basic fundamental rights. The provisions *inter alia* in Part III, IV, X calls for special attention to the protection of Tribes and tribal areas. Schedule V and VI were specifically created for the Scheduled Tribes in India.

It is worth mentioning that the Executive and the Legislative power of the State to transfer Land under Article 298 and Article 245 respectively are subject to the provisions of Fifth Schedule. A host of Articles in The Directive Principles of State Policy also refers to the responsibility of the state to protect and promote the welfare of the tribes in India.

5.2.1. PRE COMMENCEMENT PERIOD

Prior to the commencement of the Constitution, the need was felt to have a separate administrative setup for these areas for their uniqueness and distinctiveness from the rest of the country. The Government of India Act 1935 has made special provisions for these areas. The Governor was vested with special powers and responsibilities for their administration of justice. The areas were designated as 'Excluded Areas or Partially Excluded Areas'. The uniqueness of these areas was that no federal laws or the provincial legislation was applicable in these areas without the direction of the Governor. The power to administer these areas was solely the responsibility of the Governor and they are to act not under the advice of the ministers but on his own discretion.

The Constituent Assembly had also set up various sub committees and on the basis of the report of these sub committees provided the essential reservations for these areas for justice administration system.

5.2.2. THE CONSTITUTIONAL PROVISIONS

The Indian Constitution has taken up the idea of equality and justice both in the social and political fields. In furtherance of the aforesaid principles, there has been abolition of any sort of discrimination to any class of persons on the ground of religion, race or place of birth. The Constitution of India has specifically adopted certain provisions for the upliftment of tribals and to protect them from oppression caused by the other section of the society. The protective rights granted may be summed up as under:

---

592 Ibid at p 16-17

593 America was also once a colony of England and the common law principles was very much a part of their jurisprudence.

1. Educational And Cultural Rights
2. Social Rights
3. Economic Rights
4. Political Rights
5. Employment Rights

Apart from the aforesaid rights envisaged in various Articles, the Fifth and Sixth Schedule was completely dedicated for the tribals. In addition to these two schedules through the 89th Constitutional Amendment Act 2003, there has been the establishment of National Commission for Scheduled Tribes. The commission consists of a Chairman, Vice-chairman and three other members all of which shall be appointed by the President of India.

The notion of scheduled[594] and scheduled tribe[595] was established long before its nomenclature. Tribe was defined to identify people who among other things sang, danced and drink together. More formally, these groups have a distinct culture, fairly isolated and generally backward.

Irrespective of identifying these traits among a group of people scattered all around the country, the term scheduled tribe has not been defined in the Constitution of India. The term tribe has a typical notion and specific indices[596] attached to it. There are two parameters that is mostly taken into consideration to identify a tribe first, the relative isolation and second, backwardness. At times the notion of territoriality has also been taken into consideration in identifying a tribal community.

The Indian Constitution has vested with the power to notify any community as schedule tribe upon the President of India which he does with the consultation of the Governor of the respective states.[597] This notification may involve the entire community or parts or groups within the tribes or tribal communities, as Scheduled Tribes through the notification. Further, the parliament may include or exclude tribes specified in the notification by passing any law. It shall be relevant to put up the case of Amrendra Pratap Singh v. Tej Bahadur Prajapati[598]. The Supreme Court in this case observed that the situation bears a striking resemblance to the United States' belief that the Native American tribes "were the 'wards' of the government in need of protection."

The right to livelihood of the tribals as a Constitutional right has been acknowledged by the Supreme Court in the famous case of Banwasi Seva Ashram vs State of Uttar Pradesh.[599] In this case the Supreme Court accepted a letter written by Banwasi Seva Ashram, an NGO working for the protection of the rights of the tribal peoples, to the court. The primary issues raised by the NGO were questioning the acquisition proceeding initiated by the State of U.P. to locate a thermal Power Plant of National Thermal Power Corporation (NTPC). Consequently, the adivasis and the tribal peoples who have been habituating there for ages have to be displaces from their motherland, which was their only source of survival and livelihood. It was alleged that the forest officials, being the authority responsible for the protection of the people are

---

594 "Schedule" means a Schedule to this Constitution.

595 "Scheduled Tribes" means such tribes or tribal communities or parts or groups within such tribes or tribal communities as are deemed under Article 342 to be Scheduled Tribes for the purposes of the Constitution of India.

596 Indices like their place of abode, economic and social development etc

597 Article 342 in Part XVI of the Constitution of India

598 (2004) 10 SCC 65

599 (1987) 3 SCC 304

involved in encroaching upon the land and obstructing the free movement of tribal peoples in their own motherland.

The Public Interest Litigation was taken up by the Supreme Court and observed that,

> *"Forests are much wanted national assets. On account of the depletion thereof ecology has been disrupted; climate has undergone a major change and rains have become scanty. These have long term adverse effects on the national economy and also on the living process. Further, it is common knowledge that the adivasis and other backward people living within the jungle used the forest area as their habitat.... for generations they have been using the jungles for collecting the requirement for their livelihood-fruits, vegetables, fodder, flowers, timbers, animals and fuel wood."*[600]

The court however accepted and recognised the need for industrial growth and the need of energy to deal with future need of electricity. However, the Supreme Court passed the order to protect and safeguard the tribals and their habitat. The interest of the adivasis were protected so as their right to livelihood. In its direction the Supreme Court permitted the acquisition subject to certain condition to be met by NTPC. The conditions included rehabilitation, monetary compensation for crops and land and legal aid to the ousted forest dwellers.[601]

The problem of tribals not being able to raise their voice in the courts directly have been addressed by invoking the concept of PIL and the same has been referred to in the famous case of S P Gupta Vs. Union of India.[602] Thus it will be possible for any member of public, a social activist, an anthropologist, an economist to institute legal proceedings on behalf of the tribals. The Supreme Court also observed that through the instrumentality of Public Interest Litigation, it is possible to bring all parties together and discuss the problem face to face under the direct supervision of court of law. Thus Judiciary may become a forum for addressing and ventilating the problems of distributional equality with respect to tribals.[603] This aforesaid case of Banwasi Seva Ashram v. The State of U.P. is a solution and a positive outcome of such *locus standi* related problem.

A similar situation relating to mines related dispute was reflected by Jacqueline Hand in the article 'Government Corruption and Exploitation of Indigenous peoples. It was noted that around 30 tribes in the US for example own roughly one third of the surface accessible coal in West of Mississipi as well as 15% of all the coal reserves, 40% of all uranium ore and 4% of all oil found in the country.[604] These holdings along with mining and timber holdings are managed by Bureau of Indian Affair (BIA), and the agency's incompetence and corruption of the process has led to perhaps the world largest trust litigation.[605] This citation represents only the tip of the iceberg of the litigation that has continued for years. The government's records are so bad that it does not know how many individual accounts are charged with administering funds for Indian beneficiaries. The Interior Departments system contains over 300,000 accounts covering

---

600 Ibid 376

601 Anna Grear, Evadne Grant (eds.), *Thought, Law, Rights and Action in the Age of Environmental Crisis* 133-134 (Edward Elger Publishing, UK, 2015)

602 AIR 1982 SC 149

603 1987 3, SCC 304

604 Miavan Clech Lam, *At the Edge of the Stat: Indigenous peoples and Self-Determination* 19 (Transnational Publication, Inc. New York, 2000)

605 Cobell vs Norton, 240 F.3d 1081 (D.C.Cir. 2001)

approximately 11 million acres, but it acknowledges that this number is not well supported. The plaintiff asserts that the actual number is nearer to 500,000. In addition to lacking knowledge of the number of accounts, the government has no clear idea of their value. This case represents an almost unimaginable mix of corruption and incompetence going back to 19th Century.[606]

Instances of courts role in settlement of disputes between tribes and non tribal peoples are not new. There are many instances of the role played by the courts in settling long standing disputes. An important American case was the dispute that led to The Gila River Indian Community Water Rights Settlement. Establishing tribal water rights is a crucial step in building the economic and other capacity of tribes including building their homes. The water rights of tribes are protected along with much-needed resources for tribes to develop and use those rights through these settlements. Some of the instances of successful settlements are as follows:

Case 1: General Adjudication of All Rights of Water Use in the Little Colorado River System and Source (Ariz.)

The Zuni Indian Tribe, Arizona and non Indian communities in the Little Colorado basin entered into a settlement regarding the water right claims in the Little Colorado Basin. The settlement was an outcome of long standing dispute over water rights which the tribals could not afford to leave. The said settlement was later approved by the Congress and the court issued the final judgement approving the settlement in 2006. It shall be relevant to state that the majority of judgements in the US are guided by the principal that the laws of the tribes in tribal areas are excluded from laws outside their territory as the tribes enjoy their own sovereignty in those areas. It must further be noted that it is only when the Congress pass an order surpassing the rule, the tribals fail to exercise jurisdiction.

Case 2: United States v. Washington Department of Ecology (Lummi) (W.D. Wash.)

This case involved the tribes of the Lumni Nation in the State of Washington. The dispute relates to underground water rights of the Lumni Reservation. The settlement was a success as it resolved the long standing dispute between the Tribes and the private water users in furtherance of a lawsuit.

Case 3: In Re Warm Springs Tribe Water Negotiations (D. Ore.)

A settlement was entered into successfully after a long standing lawsuit of 15 years on water rights of the Confederated Tribes of the Warm Springs Reservation. The settlement was recorded and a large scale confrontation was avoided.

Case 4: In Re Snake River Basin Adjudication (Idaho)

The Nez Perce Tribe and the State of Idaho, and water users crafted an historic settlement of the Tribes' water rights claim. Congress ratified this settlement in the Snake River Water Rights Act. In 2007, the Idaho courts approved the entry of the settlement.

5.3. TRIBAL COURTS AND JUSTICE SYSTEM

Tribal courts have played a very significant role in dealing with the law and order system of the tribals for a considerable period of time. The tribal courts have a limitation in its jurisdictional aspect as it was

---

606 Ibid

limited to tribals only. Later this jurisdiction was changed to incorporate the non tribals as well. Some of the important features of the Tribal Courts are as follows:

1. In suits or proceedings in the tribal courts, the Code of Civil Procedure or the Code of Criminal Procedure does not apply.
2. The tribal courts does not have jurisdiction to try serious criminal matters like murder, rape etc. For these heinous offences the tribals are treated at par with the non tribals under special laws.
3. It was however the Governor who may even extend jurisdiction on such matters to the tribal courts conferring such power under CPC or Cr.PC.
4. In the year 1969 certain amendments to the Sixth Schedule to the Constitution of India was made. The primary objective of the said amendment was to enable the Tribal Courts to function more or less like Nyaya Panchayats as to the rest of the country and to make provisions for appeals from these courts to regular courts. The main aspects of the said amendment are provided herein below:
    a. Extending the jurisdiction of the tribal courts to the non tribals
    b. Taking away the appellate jurisdiction of the Regional Council and the District Council.
    c. Curtailing the power of the Governor to confer the power to the trial courts under CPC or CrPC.

A 2011 report by National Crime Records Bureau (NCRB) shows that Jharkhand, with a population of 3.29 crore, has reported only 35,838 cases under the Indian Penal Code whereas states, like Kerala[607], Haryana[608] and Assam[609], with similar or less population, have recorded more than double the number crimes commenced. This establishes the faith of tribal peoples in traditional dispute redress system like Panchayats and kangaroo courts. The development comes at a time when the state police are making every effort to reach out to the common man. This reduction in the recording of cases comes even when in the past 12 years, 95 police stations have come up in different districts of Jharkhand, which is one of the worst Maoist-affected states in the country and ranks 27th in NCRB's national crime index. At present, there are 426 police stations in the state. These statistics shows the faith of tribal peoples upon their customary dispute settlement mechanism and also their apprehensive towards modern justice system. T N Sahu, lecturer at the department of tribal and regional languages, Ranchi University, said tribal peoples prefer panchayats to police. The primary reason behind this practice is that, he quoted,

> *"It is part of their culture. If we have a look at the cultural shift, we will find that only those tribals who live in towns and cities go to police. People living in villages still prefer panchayats to solve their problems,"*[610]

In tribal-dominated areas, like Simdega, Khunti, East Singhbhum, West Singhbhum, Gumla and Lohardaga, panchyats play a crucial role in solving local problems. Human rights activist Shashi Bhushan Pathak said kangaroo courts are organized mostly in Maoist-hit regions. *According to him,*

> *"People fear police and CRPF and avoid going to police stations."*[611]

Former Jharkhand DGP B D Ram agreed that presence of kangaroo courts and powerful tribal tradition are behind such poor reporting of criminal cases in the rural pockets.[612]

---

607 Kerala, with a population of 3.3 crore, has reported 1.72 lakh cases

608 Haryana (2.5 crore) 60,000 cases

609 Assam (3 crore) 66,000 cases

610 Alok K N Mishra 'Tribal courts prevail over cops' TNN | Mar 2, 2013, 02.16 AM IST

611 Ibid

612 Ibid

5.4. THE JUDICIAL AWAKENING

The Human Rights jurisprudence relating to the protection of tribal rights flourished in India with the aid and influence of the judgments of the Supreme Court and the High Court of different states. Some of the remarkable decisions relating to the protection of rights and recognition of certain rights within the ambit of Constitutional Rights have helped the tribals to a great extent to retaliate in the Courts through a series of legal battles leading to further declaration of rights for the tribals. The most influencing aspect of these judgments is the right to use Article 32 and Article 226 to retaliate against the state administration. The case of Olga Telis[613] needs special reference in this regard as the apex court declared that right to livelihood is an integral part of the right to life as has been enshrined in Article 21 of the Indian Constitution. The Apex court declared "It would be great injustice to exclude the right to livelihood from the context of the right to life."[614]

Another landmark judgment came in the case of NCERT vs. State of Arunachal Pradesh[615]where the Supreme Court ordered the rehabilitation of displaced tribals. Again the Supreme Court in N.D.Jayal vs. Union of India stated that rehabilitation of the tribals displaced is within the right of life under Article 21 of the Indian Constitution.[616]

The Gujarat High Court made a commendable effort in the protection of the right of the tribes in Bipinchandra Diwan v. State of Gujarat.[617] This case is commonly known as the Gujarat earth quake case where a number of eminent members of the society have put forward their disappointment in the governmental approach towards the utilisation of the funds and resources given for the relief of the quake affected victims. The PIL was taken up by the court to provide the necessary steps that have to be taken in this regard and what rights the state has towards their subjects and more importantly the vulnerable classes.

The doctrine of *parens patriae*[618] creates the obligation and the duty of the state to help and support the victims. This obligation may arise out of the Constitutional provisions, statutes, contract or quasi contractual obligations arising out of torts. This obligation which does not fall in the said categories has been described by Salmond on Jurisprudence, 12th Edition by PJ Fitzgerald at Pp 127 as "In nominate Obligations". This obligation is explained as recognition of final and residuary laws having comprehensive and distinctive title. The state has the inherent power and authority to provide protection to the person and property of persons *non sui juris*, such as minor, insane and incompetent persons. The indigenous and tribal peoples also to a considerable extent fall within this category of *non sui juris* enabling them to create the duty and obligation of the state in furtherance of *parens patriae*[619]. The Constitution makes it imperative for the State to secure to its citizens rights guaranteed by the Constitution and where the citizens are not in a position to assert and claim their rights, the state can be activated and approached to effectively come over the scene and protect the Human Rights of the victims.[620] The Supreme Court has held that the Preamble of the Constitution

---

613 Olga Telis Vs Bombay Municipal Corporation AIR 1996 SC 180

614 Ibid

615 NCERT v. State of Arunachal Pradesh 1996 (1) SCC 742

616 N.D.Jayal v. Union of India (2004) 9 SCC 362 at p 394

617 Bipinchandra Diwan v. State of Gujarat AIR 2002 GUJ 99 at p 103

618 Literally means father of the country

619 In other words to protect those who have no rightful protector

620 Bipinchandra Diwan v. State of Gujarat AIR 2002 GUJ 99

read with Articles 38, 39 and 39A of Directive Principles of State Policy, enjoins the state to take up this responsibility.[621] It is the protective measure to which the social welfare state is committed.[622]

There have been some famous cases both national and foreign that uplifted the tribal rights and acknowledging the state inefficacy towards providing justice to these communities. One of the interesting decisions came in the famous case of Mabo,[623] given by the Australian High Court. It was with the background that Native title was not part of the common law; the application in Mabo v The State of Queensland was heard. The Court's decision was handed down on 2nd June 1992. It is one of the most significant decisions the High Court has ever delivered. The case was heard by a Full Bench of the High Court comprising seven Justices namely Mason C J, Brennan J, Deane J, Toohey J, Gaudron J, McHugh J, and Dawson J. Only Dawson J dissented from the decision to acknowledge the existence of native title. As is the case in many decisions of the Australian High Court although six judges supported the concept of communal native title the majority differed in their reasoning. A useful summary of the ratio decidendi of the case is found in the short judgement of Mason CJ and McHugh J where they state: 'In the result, six members of the Court (Dawson J, dissenting) are in agreement that (1) the common law of this country recognises a form of native title which, (2) in the cases where it has not been extinguished, (3) reflects the entitlement of the indigenous inhabitants, in accordance with their laws or customs, to their traditional lands and that, (4) subject to the effect of some particular Crown leases, the land entitlement of the Murray Islanders in accordance with their laws or customs is preserved, as native title, under the law of Queensland'. Australia was one of the last western countries to acknowledge native title. For many years native title has been acknowledged in New Zealand; the USA and Canada by Native Title Act 1993. As a response to the Mabo decision, just before Christmas 1993, the Federal Government passed the Native Title Act 1993. Legislation reflecting the model provided by the Commonwealth legislation has since been passed in all other states to regulate the acts of State governments whose activities often impact on native title. Main Objects of Native Title Act Section 3 sets out the four main objectives of the legislation. These objectives are: 1. Provision for the recognition and protection of native title; 2. Provision for the validation of past acts potentially invalidated because of the existence of native title i.e. where government has granted interests in land that impacted upon native title and did not pay compensation; 3. Establishment of a mechanism for determining claims to native title and; 4. Establishment of how future dealings effecting native title may proceed and setting standards for those dealings.[624]

Later to the Mabo decision Croker Island Case the question as to native title applies to the sea bed? If native title can extend to the sea bed what are the extent of the rights enjoyed? Can native titleholders stop ordinary marine transport or control commercial or recreational fishing? Certainly most people thought that native title could exist over the sea bed and it was contemplated in the definition of Native Title Act S 223. These issues were discussed in 2001 in The Commonwealth of Australia v Yarmirr (the Croker Island case) The case is significant for its further general discussion of the nature of native title and its elucidation of the applicability of native title to the sea. The facts involved an application for native title by a number of clans of aborigines to an area of the seabed surrounding Croker Island in the Northern Territory. The application incorporated a claim for exclusive possession of the area. If granted this would presumably mean that native titleholders could regulate or control fishing and navigation in the native title area. The Trial judge confirmed in accordance with the Native Title Act that native title is capable of being recognized in relation to the sea. He found the native title fights included the right to fish, hunt and

---

621 Ibid

622 Ibid

623 Mabo and Another v. The State of Queensland and Another (1989) 166 CLR 186 F.C. 88/062

624 Weir, Michael, "The story of native title," Vol. 8: Iss. 1, The National Legal Eagle 8 (2002)

gather for personal and non-commercial needs and right of access for travel and to protect places of cultural or spiritual significance. He said the evidence did not support the view the right was exclusive and could not exist because of the public rights of navigation and fishing at common law and Australia's obligations under international treaties. The Commonwealth argued that as the common law did not extend to the sea native title could not be recognized by the common law. The High Court of seven judges provided a joint judgement of Gleeson CJ, Gaudron Gummow and Hayne and separate judgments of McHugh; Callinan and Kirby. The court supported the native title claim subject to the public fights of navigation and fishing at common law and Australia's obligations under international treaties. This meant that the native title fights enjoyed did not extend to exclusive use of the area claimed.[625]

Later the famous Indian case of Samatha[626] gave rights to the tribal in furtherance to their forest land. Samatha was a triumph for the tribals struggling to protect their Constitutional rights to life and livelihood. Legislative intervention must also be needed to provide adequate relief to these communities who have suffered unilaterally and consistently for centuries.

In September 1997 the Supreme Court passed a landmark judgement in the Samatha case that established that government lands, tribal lands, and forestlands in the scheduled Areas cannot be leased out to non-tribals or to private companies for mining or industrial operations. Consequently, all mining leases granted by the State governments in V Schedule Areas therefore became illegal, null and void and the State Government was asked to stop all industries from mining operations mining activity should be taken up only by the State Mineral Development Corporation or a tribal co-operative if they are in compliance with the Forest Conservation Act and the Environment Protection Act at least 20% of the net profits should be set aside as a permanent fund as part of business activity for establishment and provision of basic facilities in areas of health, education, roads and other public amenities after the 73rd Amendment and the Panchayat (Extension to Scheduled Areas) Act, under the Gram Sabha are competent to preserve and safeguard community resources and reiterated the right of self-governance of Adivasis. In cases where similar Acts in other States do not totally prohibit grant of mining leases of the lands in the Scheduled Area, similar committee of Secretaries and State Cabinet Sub-Committees should be constituted and decision taken thereafter. Before granting leases, it would be obligatory for the State government to obtain concurrence of the Central Government which would, for this purpose, constitute a Sub-Committee consisting of the Prime Minister of India, Union Minister for Welfare, Union Minister for Environment so that the State's policy would be consistent with the policy of the nation as a whole.[627] It would also be open to the appropriate legislature, preferably after a thorough debate/conference of all the Chief Ministers, Ministers concerned, to take a policy decision so as to bring about a suitable enactment in the light of the guidelines laid down above so that there would emerge a consistent scheme throughout the country, in respect of the tribal lands under which national wealth in the form of minerals, is located.

Subsequent appeals by the Andhra Pradesh Government, and Union Government were, dismissed by the Supreme Court. Unbridled commercial interests and plunder by private and global capital has thus been legally kept out of the Scheduled Areas. However, with globalisation and liberalisation, private corporations and MNCs have put pressure and the secret note from the Ministry of Mines of 10 July 2000 (No.16/48/97-M.VI) is the result. The note clearly puts the interests of "foreign corporate bodies" to be superior to the interests of the people belonging to the scheduled tribes at that, and suggests that the SC

625 Ibid at p.10

626 Samatha v. State of Andhra Pradesh.AIR 1997 SC 3297

627 Samatha v. State Of Andhra Pradesh And Ors on 11 July, 1997 available at, http://indiankanoon.org/doc/1969682/ (Accessed on December 4, 2015)

judgement can be effectively be subverted by effecting "the necessary amendments so as to overcome the said SC judgement by removing the legal basis of the said judgement". This is now sought to be accomplished by making an amendment to Article 244, clause 5(2) removing the prohibition and restrictions on the transfer of and by Adivasis to non-Adivasis for undertaking any non-agricultural operations including prospecting and mining.[628]

This famous Samatha judgement raised several substantial questions of law as to the interpretation of the Constitution, which may be summed up as follows:

(i) The Constitutional Provisions (Fifth Schedule and Article 244) empower the Governor of a State to regulate and make regulations for Scheduled areas and for Scheduled Tribes so that what rightfully belongs to the tribals cannot be taken away by any means. The majority decision in the Samatha Case has held that the granting of mining lease to non-tribals in Scheduled Area is volatile of the Fifth Schedule. However, it is felt that Fifth Schedule and Article 244 cannot purport to take away the sovereign right of the government to transfer its land in any manner. Justice Pattanaik in his dissenting view has observed that "A combined reading of Article 244 and Fifth Schedule of the Constitution would indicate that there is no Constitutional obligation on the Governor to make regulations prohibiting transfer of Government land in favour of a non-tribal within the Scheduled Area".

(ii) The majority decision has directed for all States where similar Acts do not totally prohibit grant of mining leases to non-tribals in Scheduled Area, mining leases in such areas can be granted by the State Government only after formation of Committee etc, (para 129, 130). Such a direction raises fundamental interpretation issue relating to the Constitution on the applicability of a Central Act Mines and Mineral (Development & Regulation) Act, 1957 - (MMDR Act) which was enacted under the Constitutional Provisions of the Seventh Schedule of the Constitution (Entry 54 - List 1). The MMDR Act, 1957, which extends to the whole of India, empowers the State governments to grant mining leases and the Fifth Schedule to the Constitution does not fetter the operation of the Parliamentary Law.[629] Further, the Fifth Schedule empowers the Governor to make regulations, which he may not exercise, while the majority judgement at para 50 states that the Fifth Schedule 'enjoins' the Governor to make necessary regulation in furtherance of the benefit of the deprived tribals[630]

(iii) The decision in the Samatha case that the 1959 Regulations are retrospective in intent is a conclusion diametrically opposed to a binding decision (of September 1995) of a Bench of three Judges of the Supreme Court - Dy. Collector vs. S. Venkataramaniah 1995 (6) SCC 545.[631]

(iv) The 1959 Regulations were made by the governor under Paragraph 5(2) of the Fifth Schedule to regulate transfer of land in the Scheduled Areas specifically mentioned in the Regulation.[632] In the making of this Regulation, the Governor obviously did not intend to specifically affect any of the provisions of the MMDR Act, 1957 in the Scheduled Areas in the State, much less to add to repeal or amend any of its provisions.[633] The MMDR Act 1957, which extended to the whole of India, continued to apply to Scheduled Areas in the State of Andhra Pradesh in so far as they related to mining leases and prospecting licenses granted by the State Government under the provisions of the MMDR Act, 1957.[634] In making the 1959 Regulations

628 Attempts to subvert 'Samatha' judgement, available at http://www.pucl.org/reports/National/2001/samatha.htm (Accessed on December 4, 2015)

629 Ibid

630 Ibid

631 Ibid

632 Ibid

633 Ibid

634 Ibid

the Governor has not purported to add, to repeal or amend any part of the word "persons" in Clause 3 of the 1959 Regulations could not possibly have meant the State Government (as the authority empowered under the MMDR Act, 1957, to grant mining leases/prospecting licenses) as this would otherwise involve an amendment of the provisions of the MMDR Act, 1957, as applicable to the Scheduled Areas.[635]

It may be noted that Justice J.Pattanaik recorded in the minority Judgement in the Samatha Case that

"in my considered opinion the expression 'person' used in Section 3(1)(a) of the Regulation should have its natural meaning throughout the Section to mean a 'natural person' and it does not include the State".[636]

He further continued,

"Mabo and Samatha are two remarkable judgments of the 20th Century on the rights of tribals. On 3rd June 1992, the High Court of Australia decided to declare that all land, which belongs to the aboriginals, had been wrongly misappropriated by the settlers and had to be returned to the aboriginals. Two centuries of colonial history was reversed. The colonial assumption of res nullius was nullified."[637]

However, as mentioned earlier in this regard there has been very little implementation of these orders. The judicial decisions have been disrespected by the government in a series of cases. As Vidhya Das in an article quoted,

"...Why otherwise would the Orissa Government consider amending the PESA Act, and force consent on a gram Sabha through the district collector, why otherwise should the Supreme Court judgment on Samatha case be declared null and void in this state? And it is not Orissa where such steps are being taken. A Supreme Court ruling restraining the government from regularizing encroachments on forest lands has led to a circular from the Ministry of Environments and Forests for the eviction of encroachers through a time bound action plan."[638]

The administration has offered deaf ears to the legitimate demand of the tribals. There are innumerable instances of violation of fundamental rights of tribals in every form in the past 100 years. The poor and the uneducated of the modern civilization have been brutally humiliated day in and day out by the rich and the famous. The simplicity of tribal communities are used to exploit them and to rebut them with the armor of state machinery in case of tribal usurp. Unfortunate but true various analysis of laws for the welfare of the tribes are made by various legal experts, anthropologists, economists, politicians and judges, but the outcome is massively disturbing when it comes to the implementation of those legal provisions. The very basis of the rights as provided by the Constitution is unknown to these millions of people. Modern education is far away from them. Among the few thing that they know about is the law of nature, the law of responsibility and reasonability. This legal philosophy was acknowledged by Professor Hart in his work which led to the revival of the natural law theory in the 20th Century. The need of reason as the basis of law has been appreciated in all modern societies and India should not lag behind to protect that segment of the society who lives a life of poverty and oppression just because they are non-commercial in their approach. The progress of a country must not only be judged by its economic progress but also the rights

---

635 Ibid

636 Ibid

637 Dr.Rajeev Dhavan, "Mabo and Samatha", 10.The Hindu, March 9, 2001.

638 Ibid

the citizens enjoys in their motherland.[639] The author carried on and cited the example of the Coca Cola factory as quoted….

> "this link between the government and the corporate is becoming increasingly clear today, and it is not just in the tribal regions. Everybody knows of the struggle of the local people against the Coco Cola factory which has polluted ground water and surface water reserves in Plachimada, Kerala. Here, people has been waging a peaceful struggle for more than two years, but the Kerala government has chosen to arrest more than 300 local people including the leaders of the movement, rather than look at issues of pollution, and the way people livelihood has been affected. If the Orissa government is talking of amending the panchayati raj act, the Gujarat government is thinking to introduce a new mining policy that would enable mining in parks and reserve forests. While it has ordered eviction of tribal communities from these areas following the MoEF circular to this effect."[640]

Perhaps, it is too late today to bring the tribes back to the land and the environment they used to enjoy for hundreds of years. One of such effort was made in Kerala in furtherance of the Constitution.

Schedule V of the Article 244 of the Constitution of India make the State to ensure suitable legislation, total prohibition of transfer of tribal land to the non tribals. The Debar Commission appointed under Article 399 of the Indian Constitution, recommended that all tribal land alienated since 1950 should be returned to the tribals. But the Government of Kerala miserably failed to pass the necessary laws to protect tribal land. It passed the legislation in the year 1975.[641] But the rules needed to make it effective and operational was not passed. It took approximately 10 years to pass the Kerala Scheduled Tribes Restriction on Transfer of Lands and Restoration of Alienated Lands Act in 1986 providing the relevant provisions for restoration of tribal lands to the tribals who have been alienated from their land and forest dwellings. However, there has been no implementation of the act for a long span of time. This futile effort on the part of the executive and the legislation is yet another proof of tribal human rights violation. Even the right to speak for tribals may be a case of going against the nation.[642] The court must play its part to provide justice to the tribals and also those who speak for them.

In a recent judgment the Honorable Supreme Court has uplifted the right of land. The apex court stated that the tribes have right to maintain relationship with land which is their most important asset. In this famous judgment passed by Honorable Justice Aftab Alam, on April 2013, stated that it is the land on which the tribal life is sustained. It further stated that, the social status, economy, and social equality, permanent place of abode, work and living depends upon the land. Consequently, tribes have great emotional attachment to their lands. The apex court bench also reflected that the Scheduled Tribes and other Traditional Forest Dweller residing in the Scheduled Area have a right to maintain their distinctive spiritual relationship with

639 Shambhu Prasad Chakrabarty & Rathin Bandhopadhyay, "Alienation of Tribals from land and Forest vis-à-vis Rehabilitation in India: An analysis through the lens of Human Rights Jurisprudence", 2012 KJLS, 1:1, Vol 2, No. 1.

640 Vidhya Das, 'Democratic Governance in Tribal Regions, A Distant Dream', EPW, October 18, 4432 (2003)

641 While piloting the Bill in the House, Sir Baby John observed: "In a state which claims to be progressive, it is for us to think whether there is real progress or whether the so called progress is a fallacy. When one such segment of the population is suffering from and is in slavery, what is the point in boasting that we are progressing! It is on realization of all these facts that the said bill is introduced intending to prevent assignment of such land and to scrutinize and assignments already affected."

642 In a recent case the government of India justified the decision to stop Greenpeace activist Priya Pillai on January 11th 2015 from travelling to London for a meeting of the British all party parliamentary group. A matter was raised before the Delhi High Court, that the act of the Government (Intelligence Bureau) was simultaneous violation of the right to free speech, right to freedom of association and personal liberty of movement. Justice Rajiv Shakdher has reserved the order till date.

their traditionally owned or occupied and used lands. The court also referred to the Forest Rights Act and stated that the law intends to protect customs, usage, forms, practices and ceremonies which are appropriate to the traditional practices of forest dwellers. [643] In the judgment, the apex court stated that "The Legislature also has addressed the long standing and genuine felt need of granting a secure and inalienable right to those communities whose right to life depends on forests and thereby strengthening the entire conservation regime by giving a permanent stake to the STs dwelling in the forests for generations in symbolic relationship with the entire ecosystem."[644]

A brief study of certain eminent cases in India certainly provides a ray of hope to the poor and deprived tribals in India. The court has acknowledged the rights of the tribals and adivasis in relating to their right over land and forest resources. In Fatesang Gimba Vasava v. the State of Gujarat, the Gujarat High Court ruled that the forest department's action to prevent the transport of bamboo for sale to tribals at concessional rates was unwarranted.[645] Therefore, bamboo being a tree would certainly fall within Cl. (b) of the definition of 'forest produce', but toplas, supdas, and palas made out of bamboo chips would not fall within the definition of forest produce.[646]

The court ruled that once there is a conversion of bamboo to any other form due to human labour and skills, it no longer remains under the provision of the Indian Forest Act, 1927.[647] The court stated that,

> *"We may also state that according to us the view taken by the Gujarat High Court in Fatesang's case is correct, because though bamboo as a whole is forest produce, if a product, commercially new and distinct, known to the business community as totally different is brought into existence by human labour, such an article and product would cease to be a forest-produce. The definition of this expression leaves nothing to doubt that it would not take within its fold an article or thing which is totally different from, forest-produce, having a distinct character. May it be stated that where a word or an expression is defined by the legislature, courts have to look to that definition; the general understanding of it cannot be determinative. So, what has been stated in Strouds' Judicial Dictionary regarding a "produce" cannot be decisive. Therefore, where a product from bamboo is commercially different from it and in common parlance taken as a distinct product, the same would not be encompassed within the expression "forest-produce" as defined in section 2 (4) of the Act, despite it being inclusive in nature that bamboo mat is taken as a product distinct from bamboo in the commercial world, has not been disputed before us and rightly.*
>
> *In view of all the above, we hold that bamboo mat is not a forest-produce in the eye of the Act, and so, allow the appeal, set aside the impugned judgment[648] of the High Court and state that the order of confiscation passed by the Conservator of Forest was not in accordance with law."[649]*

---

643 Case on mining in Niyamgiri Hills of Orissa

644 Ibid

645 Fatesang Gimba Vasava and Ors vs State of Gujarat and Ors, AIR, 1987, Gujarat, 9

646 Ibid

647 P Leelakrishnan, *Environmental Law in India*, 20-21(Lexisnexis, Gurgaon, 3rd ed., 2005)

648 Suresh Lohiya vs State Of Maharashtra And Another on 23 August, 1996, available at http://indiankanoon.org/doc/155648/ (Accessed on December 4, 2015)

649 Suresh Lohiya vs State Of Maharashtra And Another (1996) 10 SCC 397 (By the Bench of Justice G N Ray and Justice B L Hansaria)

A study of the aforesaid judgement clarifies that a bamboo mat prepared from bamboo is not a forest produce under Section 2(4) of the Indian Forest Act 1927. It is held that the expression 'forest produce' does not take within its fold an article or thing which is totally different from forest produce, having a distinct character. In the case of Suresh Lohiya v. State of Maharashtra, 1996 A.I.R., SCW, 4111, the Apex court was considering as to whether bamboo mat is a forest produce or not and the court has held that bamboo mat is not a forest produce in the eye of law.[650] In this case it was decided that bamboo carpet is not a forest produce under the definition of the term under section 2(4) of the impugned Act. Mere change in the state of the forest produce does not make an article outside the scope of The Forest Act, 1927. Even factory made kattha, which is catechu, is a forest produce within the meaning of the definition of the word 'forest produce' as defined under Section 2(4) of the Indian Forest Act.[651] Thus it may be noted that it is the tribal art and knowledge that converts a forest produce and not the intervention of mechanical process. This is a way tribal livelihood has been honoured and protected by judicial decisions and activism.

In another case that reached the apex court was Sanjay Lodha vs State of Jharkhand and Ors.[652] This case was to determine whether 'Chiraunji' or 'gond' which is commonly used by the tribal and adivasi population in Jharkhand falls within the purview of the definition of forest produce. In deciding the matter, the court came to the conclusion that, "On bare perusal of clauses (b) and (c) of sub-Section (4) to Section 2, it will be evident that if the trees, leaves, flowers, fruits and all other parts are produce when found in or brought from a forest then only it is included within the definition of 'forest produce'. In the instant case there being nothing on the record to suggest that the Chiraunji or Gond, in question, seized from the premises of petitioners were found in or brought from a forest, even as per clauses (b) and (c) of sub-Section 4 to Section 2 of the Indian Forest Act 1927, seized materials cannot in any way under the said facts and conditions of the case be held to be 'forest produce'.[653]This elaborates the sad state of condition that was prevailing amongst the tribes in this part of the country. The forest produce has always been a subject of dispute. Apart from protecting the right of forest produce within the reach of tribals, the courts in India has played a dominant role in protecting the land rights of these people. One of the leading cases in this regard is Sri Machegowda v. State of Karnataka.[654]

In this case, the petitioners are purchasers of lands which had been originally granted by the State to persons belonging to Scheduled Caste or Scheduled Tribes. Such lands had already been transferred to the members belonging to and Scheduled Tribes under the provisions of Law or on the basis of rules or regulations governing such grant. After the passing of the Karnataka Scheduled Castes and Scheduled Tribes (Prohibition of Transfer of Certain Lands Act), 1978, notices have been issued by the appropriate authority to the transferees of such lands to show cause as to why the lands transferred to them should not be resumed in any way for being restored to the original grantees or their legal heirs or for distribution otherwise to the members of Scheduled Castes and Scheduled Tribes in accordance with the provisions of the Statute, as the transfers in their favour are in view of the provisions of the Act now null and void. The appellants, who were aggrieved by the said notices, challenged the *vires* of the Act. According to them, Sections 4 & 5 of the Act violated the provisions of Articles 14, 19 (1) (f), 31 and 31A of the Constitution. The High Court for reasons recorded in the Judgment upheld the validity of the Act and dismissed the

---

650 Mahadeo and Ors v. State of Maharashtra and Ors, A.I.R. 2001, Bombay, 434

651 M/S. Indian Wood Products Co. Ltd. vs State of U.P. and Another, AIR 1999, Allahabad, 222

652 A.I.R. 2003, Jharkhand, 64

653 Ibid

654 1984 AIR 1151,

petitions. However, the High Court granted certificates under Articles.132 & 133 of the Constitution and hence the appeals.

It was contended by the court in this case that,

> "Granted lands were intended for the benefit and enjoyment of the original grantees who happen to belong to the Scheduled Castes and Scheduled Tribes. At the time of the grant a condition had been imposed for protecting the interests of the original grantees in the granted lands by restricting the transfer of the same. The condition regarding the prohibition on transfer of such granted lands for a specified period, was imposed by virtue of the specific term in the grant itself or by reason of any law, rule or regulation governing such grant. It was undoubtedly open to the grantor at the time of granting lands to the original grantees to stipulate such a condition the condition being a term of the grant itself, and the condition was imposed in the interests of the grantee. Except on the basis of such a condition the grantor might not have made any such grant at all. The condition imposed against the transfer for a particular period of such granted lands which were granted essentially for the benefit of the grantees cannot be said to constitute any unreasonable restriction. The granted lands were not in the nature of properties acquired and held by the grantees in the sense of acquisition, or holding of property within the meaning of Art.19 (1)(f) of the Constitution. It was a case of a grant by the owner of the land to the grantee for the possession and enjoyment of the granted lands by the grantees and the prohibition on transfer of such granted lands for the specified period was an essential term or condition on the basis of which the grant was made. It has to be pointed out that the prohibition on transfer was not for an indefinite period or perpetual. It was only for a particular period, the object being that the grantees should enjoy the granted lands themselves at least for the period during which the prohibition was to remain operative. Experience had shown that persons belonging to scheduled castes and scheduled tribes to whom the lands were granted were, because of their poverty, lack of education and general backwardness, exploited by various persons who could and would take advantage of the sad plight of these poor persons for depriving them of their lands. The imposition of the condition of prohibition on transfer for a particular period could not, therefore, be considered to constitute any unreasonable restriction on the right of the grantees to dispose of the granted lands. The imposition of such a condition on prohibition in the very nature of the grant was perfectly valid and legal."

Eventually, the Supreme Court by dismissing the appeal ruled in favour of the adivasis and nullified the purchase of such land by private purchasers.

Another case that uplifted the rights of the tribal peoples in regard to their land is the case of P. Rami Reddy v The State of Andhra Pradesh[655]. Section 3(1) of the Andhra Pradesh Scheduled Areas Land Transfer Regulation 1959 (Regulation I of 1959) prohibited transfer of immovable properties situated in the scheduled areas from a member of scheduled tribe to non-tribals without previous sanction of the State Government. In order to facilitate effective enforcement of the said 1959 regulations, the Andhra Pradesh Scheduled Areas Land Transfer (Amendment) Regulation, 1970 was introduced. Regulation 1970 inter alia brought the following changes namely (i) transfers of land in scheduled areas in favour of 'non-tribals' were wholly prohibited in future and (ii) non-tribals holding lands in the scheduled areas were prohibited from transferring their lands in favour of persons other than tribals. The appellants who owned lands in the scheduled areas having acquired them from tribals and 'non-tribals' were affected by this amending Regulation of 1970. They filed writ petitions in the High Court challenging this regulation being unconstitutional. The High Court dismissed the writ petitions which lead to appeal under Article 133(1) (a) of the Constitution. The main contention of the appellants was that the impugned provisions

---

655 (1988) 3 SCC

were unConstitutional as being violative of Article 19(1)(f) of the Constitution as it obtained at the material time till it was repealed by the Constitution (Forty-fourth) Amendment in 1979 because they imposed unreasonable restrictions on the non-tribal holders of properties in the scheduled areas. Dismissing the appeals and while tracing a short history of the legislation, this Court.[656] While delivering judgement in the said case, the Supreme Court was flawless in delivering justice to the tribals. Apart from showing the legal paradigm based on exploitative history, the court provided justice for which it is famous for.

The apex court observed,

> *"As a matter of fact it would be unreasonable and unfair to hold that the impugned provisions are unreasonable on this account. Surely it is not unreasonable to restore up to the 'tribals' what originally belonged to them out of which they were deprived as a result of exploitative invasion on the part of 'non-tribals'. In the first place should lessons not be drawn from past experience to plug the loop-holes and prevent future recourse to devices to flout the law? The community cannot shut its eyes to the fact that the competition between the 'tribals' and the 'non-tribals' partakes of the character of a race between a handicapped one-legged person and an able bodied two legged person.[657] True, transfer by 'non-tribals' to 'non-tribal would not diminish the pool.[658] It would maintain status quo.[659] But is it sufficient or fair enough to freeze the exploitative deprivation of the 'tribals' and thereby legalize and perpetuate the past-wrong instead of effacing the same?[660] As a matter of fact it would be unjust, unfair and highly unreasonable merely to freeze the situation instead of reversing the injustice and restoring the status-quo-ante.[661] The provisions merely command that if a land holder voluntarily and on his own volition is desirous of alienating the land, he may do so only in a favour of a 'tribal'.[662] It would be adding insult to injury to impose such a disability only on the tribals (the victims of oppression and exploitation themselves) and discriminate against them in this regard whilst leaving the 'non-tribals' to thrive on the fruits of their exploitation at the cost of 'tribals'.[663] The 'non-tribal' economic exploiters cannot be installed on the pedestal of immunity and accorded a privileged treatment by permitting, them to transfer the lands and structures, if any, raised on such lands, to 'non-tribals' and make profits at the cost of the tribals.[664] It would not only be tantamount to perpetuating the exploitation and injustice, it would tantamount to placing premium on the exploitation and injustice perpetrated by the non-tribals.[665] Thus it would be the height of unreasonableness to impose the disability only on the tribals whilst leaving out the 'non-tribals.[666] It would also be counterproductive to do so. It must also be emphasized that to freeze the pool of lands available to the 'tribals' at the present level is virtually to diminish the pool. There is no escape*

---

656 Ibid at Headnote

657 P.Rami Reddy & Ors Etc v. State of Andhra Pradesh & Another on 14th July, 1988 available at, http://indiankanoon.org/doc/101893/?type=print (Accessed on December 4, 2015)

658 Ibid

659 Ibid

660 Ibid

661 Ibid

662 Ibid

663 Ibid

664 Ibid

665 Ibid

666 Ibid

from this outcome because the realities of life being what they are with the population increase amongst the tribals remaining unfrozen, increase in their population will automatically diminish the size of their pool if the same is frozen. No unreasonableness therefore is involved in making the prohibition against transfer to 'non- tribals' applicable to both the 'tribal' as also to the non- tribal' owners in the scheduled area. As a matter of fact it would have been unreasonable to do otherwise. In the absence of protection, the economically stronger 'non-tribals' would in course of time devour all the available lands and wipe out the very identity of the tribals who cannot survive in the absence of the only source of livelihood they presently have. It is precisely for this reason that the Architects of the Constitution have with far sight and foresight provided in paragraph 5(2) of Fifth Schedule that the Governor may make regulations inter alia "prohibiting or restricting the transfer of land in the scheduled areas notwithstanding any provision embodied in the Constitution elsewhere". And as has emerged from the foregoing discussion, it is unreasonable to restrict the prohibition against transfer to 'tribals'. It has to be made comprehensive enough to embrace the 'non-tribals' as well. With the improvement in the economic conditions of the 'tribals', there would not be much difficulty in finding 'tribal' purchasers. Besides, Section 3(1) (c) thoughtfully provides even for the contingency of not being able to find a 'tribal' willing or prepared to purchase the property. This provision obliges the State Government to acquire the property on payment of compensation as provided therein. One can envisage that some hardship would be occasioned to the owners to lands located in the scheduled areas. But such hardship would operate equally on the 'tribals' as well as the 'non-tribals'. Such hardship notwithstanding keeping in mind the larger perspective of the interest of the community in its entirety in the light of the foregoing discussion, the restrictions cannot be condemned as unreasonable. More so if the factor that the original acquisition by 'non-tribals' from 'tribals' was polluted by the sins of exploitation committed by the non-tribals' is not ignored."[667]

This amazing judicial outlook, coupled with the dismissal of the said petition was a boon upon the tribal masses of India.

A revolutionary judgement that changed the outlook of the entire country was the famous case involving the rape of a tribal girl. Famously known as the Mathura Rape case[668], this case led to the amendment the criminal law in force in India. Mathura Rape Case (1972) led to the large scale protest amongst common Indians and virtually forced the alteration of rape laws in India. Mathura, a young tribal woman, was raped by two constables within the premises of the Desai Ganj Police Station in Chandrapur district of Maharashtra.[669] The Sessions court judge found the accused not guilty. The reasoning behind this was (believe it or not) that Mathura was habituated to sexual intercourse.[670] This, according to the judge, clearly implied that the sexual act in the police station was consensual. [671]The amendments to the law that were forced by the protests got one thing right - submission does not mean consent.[672]

Another significant case relating to tribals is Nandini Sundar & Ors. v. State of Chhattisgarh[673]. In this case there has been large scale violation of human rights in the state of Chhattisgarh, more specifically in three

---

667 Ibid at p 433

668 Tuka Ram And Another vs State Of Maharashtra on 15 September, 1978

669 10 Most Interesting Indian Court Cases Everyone Needs To Know About, available at, http://www.scoopwhoop.com/ inothernews/indian-court-cases/ Accessed on Jan 10, 2016

670 Ibid

671 Ibid

672 Ibid

673 Writ Petition (CIVIL) NO. 250 of 2007

villages in the district of Dantewada. There has been large scale Maoist insurgency with anti insurgency movements and the area virtually became a battlefield. The situation was such that, about 350000 Tribals were forced to displace from their land. There have been cases and incidents of armed and strategic attacks which caused large scale mass killings. This affected adversely to say the least to the tribal population by state and state aided counter insurgencies. Instances of large scale law lessness coupled with attacks on innocent tribal women and children leading to large numbers of rapes by militia and security forces.

This situation was subsequently alleviated by the State policy of appointing local tribals in the temporary posts of Police with Rs.3000 as honorarium and armed them with firearms. This act was subsequently declared by the Supreme Court as violation of Article 14, 21 and other provisions of law. This case further declared the notion of calling the human right activists as Maoist as bad in law. In this case the Supreme Court gave appropriate directions including the transfer of investigation to CBI and provided relief to the tribals.

Amongst these encouraging judgements attention must be given to some decisions of the courts which were less sensitive to the rights of the tribal peoples. One of such case came up in the year 1997, the same year when the famous Samata judgement was pronounced.

In this case the Supreme Court extended the Forest Conservation Act, 1980 to include all lands yet to be finally notified under the Indian Forest Act, 1927 and the court totally banned the removal of dead, diseased, dying or wind fallen trees, dwarf wood and grass etc, from the National Parks and Wild Life Sanctuaries. It also banned collecting and selling of all non timber forest produce by all, including tribal peoples and adivasis. As an effect of this judgement, three to four million people living inside protected areas were deprived to access to non timber produces of the forest which is critical source of survival for them.[674]

In yet another disappointing case famously known as Dahanu Taluka Environment Protection Group v. Bombay Suburban Electric Supply Ltd, the Supreme Court okayed a project of constructing a power plant in an ecologically fragile area, including adivasis in them. Even when the Environment Appraisal Committee gave a report to the Hon'ble Supreme Court, it was ignored.[675] At least, the Supreme Court should have called for a review of the project. Time and again questions have been raised about the manner in which environmental impact assessments have been done but the courts have largely refrained from taking action unless an external funding agency has raised questions as in the case of the Morse Committee report for the Narmada.[676]

On the question of the right to inherit ancestral property by tribal women, the High Court of Himachal Pradesh in a very famous case concerning rights of tribals settled this dispute in clear terms. The position of women as to their rights over ancestral property has been the subject matter of dispute and debate as there had been many instances where they have been deprived from their right of inheritance. On 18th January, 2012, in the case of Rameshbhai Dabhai Naika v. State of Gujarat & Ors [Civil Appeal No.654 of 2012] the question was settled by the Hon'ble court. The question that arose before the Court was what would be the status of a person, one of whose parents belongs to the scheduled castes/scheduled tribes and the other

---

674 Rathin Bandyopadhyay, Dhiraj Subedi, "Developmental Invasion in Endangering 'Right to Life' of Forest Dwellers in India-Can the Contemporary Forest Conservation Law Prevent it?" 37 & 38, *The Banaras Law Journal*, 20. (Jan 2008-Dec 2009)

675 Upadhyay 2000: 3790

676 IJOART, "Tribes & Environmental Conservation" 3 *International Journal of Advancements in Research & Technology*, 71 (2014)

comes from the upper castes, or more precisely does not come from scheduled castes/ scheduled tribes and what would be the entitlement of a person from such parents to the benefits of affirmative action sanctioned by the Constitution.[677] The Bench held that "in an inter-caste marriage or a marriage between a tribal and a non-tribal the determination of the caste of the offspring is essentially a question of fact to be decided on the basis of the facts adduced in each case."[678] "In an inter-caste marriage or a marriage between a tribal and a non-tribal there may be a presumption that the child has the caste of the father.[679] This presumption may be stronger in the case where in the inter-caste marriage or a marriage between a tribal and a non-tribal the husband belongs to a forward caste.[680] But by no means the presumption is conclusive or irrebuttable and it is open to the child of such marriage to lead evidence to show that he/she was brought up by the mother who belonged to the scheduled caste/scheduled tribe."[681]

In another interesting case relating to tribals, the Supreme Court gave the benefit of customary beliefs to spare a rather dangerous act which took the life of one tribal lady and injures two ors. [682] In this case the facts go on like this, one Ram Bahadur Thapa was the servant of J.B. Chatterjee of a firm called Chatterjee Bros. Located in Calcutta. They had come to Rasogovindpur, a village in Balasore district in Orissa to purchase aeroscrap from an abandoned aerodrome outside the village.[683] Because it was abandoned, the locals believed it was haunted.[684] This piqued the curiosity of Chatterjee who wanted to "see the ghosts".[685] At night, as they were making their way to the aerodrome they saw a flickering light within the premises which, due to the strong wind, seemed to move.[686] They thought it was will-o'-the-wisp .[687] Thapa jumped into action as he unleashed his *khukri* to attack the "ghosts" which turns out to be local adivasi women with a hurricane lantern who had gathered under a *mohua*tree to collect some flowers.[688] Thapa's indiscriminate hacking caused the death of one Gelhi Majhiani and injured two other women.[689] The Sessions court judge however, acquitted Thapa declaring that his actions were the result of a stern belief in ghosts and that in the moment; Thapa believed that they were lawfully justified.[690]

677 Arun Sharma, 'Tribal women gets rights in ancestor's property, breaks age old practice', available at http://indianexpress.com/article/india/india-ors/tribal-women-gets-rights-in-ancestors-property-breaks-age-old-practice/ accessed on Jan 10, 2016

678 Ibid

679 Ibid

680 Ibid

681 Ibid

682 State of Orissa v. Ram Bahadur Thapa (1959)

683 Supra note 110

684 Ibid

685 Ibid

686 Ibid

687 Ibid

688 Ibid

689 Ibid

690 Ibid

5.5. THE WAY AHEAD

The need to protect the indignity of the indigenous and tribal peoples have been felt and acknowledged by the world community and have been advocated by many belonging to this community and beyond. The problems of assimilation, self governance and preventing the continuing menace over this vulnerable class has been plenty. The English doctrines, the religious dictates and the economic exploitation has been the hindrances to the protection of the tribals in most of the countries including the commonwealth. The judiciary has rightly identified them and had been providing relief to these people from such violation of human rights. State must ensure that these rights are not infringed by any of the state machinery and also such rights be not abused by any other people. Thus a comprehensive machinery is needed to be set up in furtherance of updated international standards to protect the rights of the people and to ensure justice in its comprehensive sense to all belonging to these communities and prevent the growing sense of intolerance and retaliation of these poor and deprived lot in the name of development, construction of dams etc. The way ahead is a way filled with struggle for these people but the struggle must continue in every possible way with the fruitful contribution of the judiciary.

However, in some cases the tribals have taken the extreme steps to prevent continued exploitation and violation of their human rights.

There have been terrible instances of 'tribal-state' and 'tribal–non-tribal' conflicts due to the continuous exploitation of the tribals by the State as well as the non-tribals with Government showing blind eyes to the legitimate pleas of the tribals.

The police firing on adivasis at Muthanga in Wayanad District of Kerela lead to the death of adivasis and policemen, and with hundreds of adivasis including women and children getting injured. The incident occurred when over 2000 adivasis occupied the protected forest land and were there in temporary huts and tents for 45 days with the demand which the then Chief Minister has made to them two years ago in Trivandrum. When the police came to evict them, the activists captured one policeman and one forest guard and keep them in custody. A massive police force was subsequently diploid which unleashed a brutal attack on the innocent adivasis and opened fire resulting in the death of two adivasis.[691]

Another incident happened in Madhya Pradesh in the district of Dewas, where the police opened fire on tribals in the village of Mehndi Kheda and has shot and killed four persons. The police had leashed a reign of terror and thousand of adivasis had fled their villages and were hiding in the forest while the police and administration ransacked their village. This state supported repression on groups' unarmed and unprepared shows the true nature of the state towards the tribes in India.[692]

In yet another incident there was retaliation by the tribes, in Orissa, in 1998, thousand of tribal prisoners demolished the jail, killed two under trial prisoners and then burnt both of them in front of the police station. In fact one of them was alive and had tried to run away from the fire but was quickly chased, killed and again thrown into the fire.[693]Thus is this struggle between the tribals and the non-tribals, which may be compared to a race between a disabled one legged person and an able bodied two legged person. Parallel,

---

691 Mathew Aerthayil, 'Muthanga Police Firing in Kerala: Tribal Reaction to Exploitation and Alienation of their Land', Mainstream, July 19, 2003 at p 28.

692 Srilata Swaminathan, 'A Tale of Continued Oppression: Government Atrocities on Tribals in Dewas', Economic and Political Weekly, May 5, 2001 pp 1510-1512 at p 1511

693 Lalit Das. 'Tribal Policing- A Nightmare, The Indian Police Journal, July-September 2001 at p 39

the two branches of the State, the Legislature and the Judiciary are in constant tussle relating to the various issues of tribals in the arena of both property right as well as the amending powers of the Constitution and more recently, on human rights violation.

A SUM UP

The above discussion includes a handful amongst the plethora of Indian and foreign cases (including a host of cases involving tribal courts in India), ideally reflects the changing condition of the tribal and indigenous peoples towards a more prominent position in the society. The chapter highlights the insensitive approach of the non tribals and the state governments towards the adivasi and tribal communities. Instances of developmental projects, leading to large scale displacement of forest dwellers and adivasis of the hills has been witnessed by the country. There have been instances of land grabbing by non tribal as well as governmental machinery in connivance with the capitalist class. Instances of large scale corruption in noticed in both Indian and American scenarios. The most positive aspect that has been notices in the last few decades is the contribution of the court towards the protection of the tribals and indigenous peoples all across the globe. The sensitive feeling towards the tribal deprivation has to a great extent provided them the much needed encouragement. In the absence of educated tribals to move to the court for redressal has permitted other social organisations and social workers to file cases on behalf of these vulnerable sections through PIL has been a welcome step in the protection of the rights of these people.

Another aspect that must be noted is that mere legislation will not suffice to protect the tribals against the market forces which are based on tribal exploitation and deprivation and more explicitly on the colonial structure and philosophy. Only laws implemented in conjunction with social activists, and raising tribal consciousness, can checkmate this process.[694] Such activism should come from the judiciary both including the judges and the prominent advocates who devote their life and profession for humanity and to abjure violence.

---

694 The Problem, Marginal Tribals, Seminar 412 December 1992 at p 14.available at, http://www.du.ac.in/du/uploads/Faculty%20Profiles/2015/Anthropology/July2015_Anthro_Vinay.pdf (Accessed on December 4, 2015)

CHAPTER 6

CONCLUSION AND SUGGESTIONS

The political will is directed toward greater good and for the greatest number of people. Hence, the tribals now only in marginalized number of the land where they were once the majority shall be inevitably deprived. Thus a comprehensive legal framework to protect the minority tribes for the future is the need of the day. Irrespective of their geographic locations, the tribals face hardships as their basic rights are violated. They are refrained from exploiting their natural resources or to seek justice within their own traditional and customary laws. Poor financial condition of the Government has been one of the many reasons for the socio economic degradation of tribes in India. Because of the scarcity of land with rich resource base, the state has moved towards =commercialization of various natural resources of the country which are mostly situated in the tribe populated areas. Commercialization and industrialization has led to the altered framework of forests from the natural way.

There have been plenty of instances of tribal right violation in the last century and the trend has continued in this century as well. Starting from land alienation to depriving them from forest lands and resources, the government whether central or state has done enough to vitiate the basic rights of the tribals which every human being is entitled to enjoy just by being humans. There has been massive annihilation and uprooting of tribal communities due to developmental projects leading to gross violation of human rights. The tribals have been indebted with the gradual erosion of their traditional rights to land and forests and a large scale intrusion of their culture. The judicial decisions, the legislations and the government notifications for the protection of tribal rights have been disrespected by the State in a series of cases. Today the settlements where these communities live in are in dire state as the promises made towards their welfare ended up in smoke. On the contrary the legislative efforts made on their behalf remained only in papers or ended up as colorable legislations. Grave instances of tribal-nontribal disputes followed. In the absence of any effort by the State various non-governmental organizations have come in their rescue but could do very little for the poor tribal communities apart from winning a few legal battles or formulating some tribal organizations.

It is the advent of globalization that ultimately brought a ray of hope to the tribal community. The light that establishes scientifically the methods used by the tribes are sustainable and the way of their life progressive. The approach of theirs towards the environment is the way the world should move into to prevent further destruction to the planet. The rights must be at par with other human beings on earth. We need to understand and acknowledge that their religion is their right. Their forest is their homeland. Their medicines at times are better than allopath and those invented in laboratories.

The poor and the uneducated of the modern civilization have been brutally humiliated day in and day out by the rich and the famous. The simplicity of tribal communities are used to exploit them and to rebut them with the armor of state machinery in case of tribal usurp. Unfortunate but true various analysis of laws for the welfare of the tribes are made by various legal experts, anthropologists, economists, politicians and judges, but the outcome is massively disturbing when it comes to the implementation of those legal provisions. The very basis of the rights as provided by the Constitution is unknown to these millions of people. Modern education is far away from them. Among the few thing that they know about is the law of nature, the law of responsibility and reasonability. The need of reason as the basis of law has been appreciated in all modern societies and India should not lag behind to protect that segment of the society who lives a life of poverty and oppression just because they are non-commercial in their approach. The progress of a country must not only be judged by its economic progress but also the rights the citizens enjoys in their motherland.

The whole legal framework reflects the dream that the forefathers of our Constitution has seen. But unfortunately most promises were never respected. The dreams of a world where the tribes can be what they were still remain a reverie. The continuation of the broken heart, the conspiracy to favor the business communities has ultimately raised the issue of the division of the integrity of our country. Various efforts are made by the tribals with the help of various extremist groups to avenge the deceit that the country did to them. The demand of separate tribal land[695] is the outcome of the erosion of faith on the broken promises of the administration and various politicians. The simple forest dwellers and food gatherers have now in various cases joined hands with the extremist movements today, inviting more bloodshed and gross violation of human rights.

The basic reason for not setting up a comprehensive framework for the tribes in India is the lack of proper acknowledgement to the problem of tribes not only in the regional level but also in the national and international level for a long period of time. However, over the last few decades the international movement of Indigenous and tribal peoples has grown extraordinary. The outcome of this long standing struggle has been the emergence of indigenous peoples as a distinct category in the arena of international human rights.

In the light of the said development a comprehensive research and study must take place to identify the problems and to study the level of the problem the different tribal groups of India are in. A research team must be framed under the guidance and supervision of a Standing Committee to assess the damage and distress the tribes have gone through and the modes by which they may be redressed and rehabilitated. The basic things that should be surveyed comprehensibly are inter alia the landholding system amongst the tribes which shall include the landholding pattern amongst different tribes, the extent and nature of dependence on land and land based resources, the legal perspective, taking in view the customary rights of tribals on land based resources, the effect of surveys and settlement operations already conducted, the role of regulatory Institutions, the changes in control and access of tribal peoples to land and land based resources due to developmental activities, Administrative measures, Legislative measures and proper and adequate Secretarial and Technical Assistance.

Apart from the aforesaid study a separate team must be framed to study the massive annihilation and uprooting of tribal communities due to developmental projects.

Study must be made to analyze to what extent the tribals are dependent on forest land and forest resources. What has led the tribes to the various movements as against the government and the non-tribal community?

Research must be conducted to bring the concept of sustainable development to bring back the natural way of exploitation of forests. This would automatically be a pro-tribe approach as they are themselves experts in it.

The government should implement the High Court and Supreme Court decisions relating to protection of land and forest rights of the tribals. Occupation of tribal lands through deceit or use of force should be made an offence. There should also be a ban on any transfer by a tribal to a non-tribal like that by way of lease, mortgage gift etc.

It has to be kept in mind that only short term poverty alleviation program or crisis management policies that are immediately needed, but broader structural development program are also needed, involving the tribals themselves as participants in the developmental process.

So is the story of the tribals or the indigenous communities all across the world. The tale that depicts the annihilation of the human wealth and human habitat by unlawful means. The tale of pain and agony. The tale of tears and suffering. The time has come to do justice. Justice to those, whose right to life has been denied for ulterior ends.

---

695 The first such state is Jharkhand.

If law is the means to achieve the end-called justice, then it is the time to make laws and amend the existing inadequate laws to protect these marginalized groups and communities, taking into consideration the human right issues to protect the social, economic and cultural heritage of these deprived classes.

In the era of industrialization and globalization where we live in, the biggest question is how long and how far and how much planet earth can tolerate the exploitation of mankind. Death is inevitable to all human being just like any other living being on this planet. Now the question is when that time would come for the entire human race. The world and its order are changing and the rate is really very fast. Apart from environmental issues another interesting factor is the human nature by itself, viz., greed, intolerance, corruption. Can we change this? If we can, would it be possible to protect this planet for human inhabitance? The issues are clear, not the process to address them. With the failure of Copenhagen the chances are few and far reached to have any unified effort in the near future to have a joint effort to protect us from slow poisoning. The Paris meet according to some is a mere fraud.

The next generation must be cautious of the facts and should take all possible steps to save themselves from annihilation. The technological boon perhaps have become insignificant in the era of mass economic downfall and the only way perhaps is to look at the pages of the past to take the lessons of sustainability to supplement and complement the modern interpretation of the term. The significance of the term rose to great height during the Stockholm Declaration. It also entered the Indian Legal arena to play a pivotal role in the famous MC Mehta V. Union of India case as pointing out the need of protection and conservation, Justice P N Bhagwati (Chief Justice, as he was then) used the term in an eloquent fashion.

The various dimensions of human being have been vividly simplified by tribal approach towards life. The need of the hour is to learn from past experiences as Friedrich Karl von Savigny approached the process of law making and apply them in a very systematic way acceptable to our modern society. The State must play a significant role in the formation of a comprehensive plan with the help of tribal literature, studies and even volunteers from these communities.

People today dream a life with purposeful existence. It is a boon on the continuous discrimination and corruptive practice of the members of the sovereign and their malicious motive that leads to the revolution of social change. It provides the paralyzed system an opportunity to move, a space to breath and an eye to see the way humans did for thousands of years.

A set of suggestions are available to explore the benefits that the seventh generation may achieve out of indigenous practice. Both short term and long term measures are needed to be taken for our own benefit and future. Some of the said measures are stated hereunder.

Incorporating indigenous knowledge in primary education including its physical applications, as far as possible should be the need of the hour so that every new member of our community would be aware of the nature around them.

The state must endeavor to conduct research for incorporating indigenous way *inter alia*, the protection of land and forest in the policy to protect land, forest and wildlife.

To acknowledge that indigenous knowledge is scientific and effective as has been accepted by many countries across the world.

State must protect and provide aid to the aged tribal peoples who are the storehouse of indigenous knowledge. It must be understood that these people are the last generation to carry indigenous practice and knowledge as most people of this generation has left their ancestral profession and joined modern professions for economic sustenance.

Another important thing that the government should do is to treat tribal movements more humanely and effectively to prevent further violation of human rights and Constitutional rights of the tribals. More participation of tribals in policy formulation system relating to their affairs on land, forest etc, would definitely ward off violent confrontation the country has witnessed so far to a considerable extent. This would also help to some extent in solving political turmoil prevailing in many tribal parts of our country.

There must be efforts on the part of the Government to implement the Supreme Court and High Court Judgments in protecting tribal rights. The Supreme Court specifically in the case of Samatha categorically formulated the procedural and substantive laws to deal with tribals in certain situations. This must be implemented by the state for better state tribal relationship.

Research shall also be conducted for incorporating indigenous ways of protecting the forest land and implement them in the policy formation system to protect the endangered species. There has been enough evidence of tribals and indigenous peoples being responsible towards protecting various endangered species and plants with medicinal values across the planet.

New laws solely with the objective of protecting various rights of the tribals should be made in consultation with experts from both India and abroad.

The state shall also acknowledge the mistake committed by the government by undergoing so many so called developmental projects and to make a comprehensive report on the number of tribals displaces from their motherland. In furtherance of the said research, proper efforts must be made to protect them from further suffering. Certain rehabilitation program must also be made for the displaced adivasis.

Another important aspect that has to be taken into consideration is the tribal way of healing. The State must also make necessary rules so that their knowledge may be protected from being economically exploited. Experts on medicine and law must work hand in hand with these people to identify the intellectual property involved and the viability of protecting them legally. This would also help them to have certain economic benefits for their intellectual rights.

Sustainability is one of the main features of every tribal and indigenous society. There are certain aspects that deserve systematic protection to preserve indigenous life and livelihood:
1. Tribals and indigenous peoples have a broad knowledge of how to live sustainably and this can be a source of guidelines for the future generations.
2. The formal education system has done more bad than good to these people as it disrupted the practical everyday life aspects of indigenous knowledge and ways of learning, replacing them with abstract knowledge and academic ways of learning. There has been a loss and destruction of mass knowledge base to live a sustainable way of life, available to the tribals because of this. It must be understood that modern education with traditional educational system must be the order of the day.
3. The indigenous knowledge may be integrated into education and thereby promote sustainable lifestyle. Various means must be identified as to how this gap may be bridged with the help of experts.

4. One of the immediate benefit that be achieved by this is to identify various ways to protect the environment.

In order to understand the concept of sustainability, it is important to understand the mechanism upon which it works. There are certain factors that could be identified after consultation with various research work done in this regard by various other scholars and philosophers.

- Spiritual tie with the Earth
- Natural Remedies and Medicines
- Sustainable Resource Management
- Sustainable Social Relationships

It must be understood that all these factors makes them what they are and what they aspire to be in their own ancestral land. It must be understood that the tribals bear the lamp for the future and this has been accepted by many social scientists and other philosophers equivocally.

The following are *sine que none* to the sustainable functioning of tribal and indigenous life. They are otherwise not present in other non tribal communities. Some of these notable aspects are:

1. Conservation
2. Appropriate Development
3. Democratic Participation
4. Social Equity and Peace

The man who works as a labour in the construction industry, the thousands of them involved in the big dream home projects and sky creepers, who work in the construction of big flyovers, bridges are those who have been either forced to leave their motherland or fled from the group which has lost its sustainability.

The handicraft industry in most tribal areas are dying a slow death as most of the current generation are not keen to carry on with the profession or trade of their ancestors as they are hoping to survive the onslaught the current economic situation is providing them with.

The raw materials involved in the business and the skill needed are no longer easily available and the chance to work on them to explore the skill and practice is reducing at an alarming rate. The greener pastures of the urban and semi urban developments are attracting and alluring the younger generations to a more modern life whether or not they are better is another question to answer.

Development of the current generation is in tune with the thoughts of the west which has more often than not been in direct confrontation with the nature and natural legal thoughts. The law that these people endeavour is tacitly different from the colonial British philosophy based upon the pillars of utilitarianism and positive law theory.

There are many instances which suggest that the social, environmental, cultural and legal system of the tribes all across the globe where the British hegemony has been successful to flourish their business and trade and later their administration, has been detrimental to the system both in short term and long term.

The system of the adivasis or the tribes has been emphatically abused and annihilated to introduce the western thought at the expense of balance that the world had by itself. The term tribe actually implicates the backwardness, geographical isolation, simple technology. However, this has been the subject matter of criticism in recent years as it has been established through historical evidence that there have been cultural and business contacts between castes and tribes.

Tribals in India may be classified into two broad categories for the purpose of this study into:
1. Those displaced and
2. Those who carry on their livelihood on their ancestral land.

A separate set of suggestions may be framed for those who have been subjected to large scale displacement caused by various reasons including various developmental projects. For them the primary objective of the state should be to formulate a comprehensive procedure to rehabilitate them to the best possible alternative. If the reasons for which they have been dispossessed have been in fructuous due to various reasons, efforts must be made to resettle them in their very own land. If resettlement is not possible under the said situation, and the people dispossessed are living a secluded life like that of subalterns, efforts must be made to immediately provide them with the necessary reliefs including that of essential medicines and temporary shelters.

There should be sufficient expertise as to how rehabilitation process can be carried on. In the absence of adequate knowledge to assess the reasonable and rational outcome of the steps taken, experts' advice should be taken at the earliest from the national and international forum. Adequate knowledge and training on human rights must be imparted upon those involved in the process of rehabilitation.

Apart from returning them to a proper accommodation, there should be sufficient aid for their reconstruction of social and economic establishments. Tribals should be provided with financial assistance at all levels during and after the rehabilitation process in concluded. Periodic review of the development of the tribals must be recorded for future reference and research. The system, if successful may be used for other cases of rehabilitation.

In case of rehabilitation to any new place, the tribals must be adequately informed with the necessary technical and expertise committee frame in this regard by the State Government and inform the tribals about the various viabilities of the said land. Continuous assistance should be provided to the tribals till they are self sustained in their economic and social conditions. There shall be adequate water, sanitation and health support for the newly inhabited mass in the relocated zones. It must be mentioned in this regard that the tribals must be allowed to visit the place from where they have been displaced because of various reasons. In case of any place of special interest, such places must be preserved by the State Government for continued cultural and spiritual attachments.

Both financial and technical assistance must be provided to the tribals for systematic and undisrupted rehabilitation. It has been recorded in many cases of rehabilitation, that the tribals do not accept the new areas easily. In order to overcome this challenge, the government must provide sufficient assistance to the displaced tribals in this regard. Efforts must also be made to understand the root cause of not accepting the allocated rehabilitation zones and proper steps must be taken at the earliest to overcome the same.

Talking about the un-displaced set of tribals, the challenges of the state to provide them with proper infrastructural development is even more difficult. Because of inadequate and misleading objectives, the tribals have been subjected to various kinds of atrocities at length for a number of decades. The state must identify the right chord between the traditional and the modern situations that pose the greatest challenge to their reconstruction and development in the true sense of the term. The lack of proper education amongst the tribals has made the situation worse for the state mechanism to communicate as the first problem that comes up is that of the medium of communication. Even when this hindrance may be overcome by an interpreter, the language of understanding for the tribals becomes the most difficult problem to address. Because of lack of modern education amongst the tribal communities in India, the communication becomes a bar to transfer intellectual information from either side. There should be a set of experts appointed by the concerned state government to mitigate and resolve these differences and help in the objective of such communication apart from primary education, the state shall endeavour to provide education in technical subjects like health and law amongst ors to help bridging the gap between what they are and what they want to be.

It must be understood that their invaluable cultural and technical knowhow must be protected at the earliest as we have already lost a lot of such information because of various adverse reasons discussed in various areas of this book.

Special committee must be made to identify the traditional knowhow and record them for assessment in national and international level. The information identified must be published for further interest creation and research. This knowhow may also be used by the non tribals under the supervision of tribals for betterment of the forest and environment amongst other areas.

The tribals must be provided with modern education with their traditional education based on practical applications. This blend of the two must be done in the best possible manner for the actual development of the tribals. There shall be efforts to provide the gram Sabha with adequate modern knowledge and education so that they can understand what is best for them than to apply some directions straightaway.

It must be understood that the tribals are the aboriginals of where they are staying for ages or from centuries. They must be protected in all regard and should be equipped with the modern as well as their traditional knowledge. The state must take adequate care to provide training to the tribals in the field of health, primary education and other relevant technical education through the aid and advice of the expert committee created by the concerned state government and the Gram Sabha.

Other aspects of development must be made in the areas so that they can actively participate in their own ways and be free to choose the profession they wanted to practice. Proper training must be provided to these people as they confront various environmental and social situations that the new world poses for them. They must be able to be in a position to choose what's best for them and not act out of compulsion created by various situations. Training programs and creation of market for the goods the tribals create must be made by the state agencies and other NGOs and SHGs working in and around these people.

Some of the suggestions are as follows:

- **Land**

Land is at the heart of tribal life. More than a thing of value, land to him is mother earth, which satisfies both his material and spiritual needs. Hence depriving him of his land is to snap his continuation as a self respecting member of society. In fact, the root cause of all human right violations perpetuated on them can be traced to land alienation, since the tribals depend on land for their identity, existence, security and livelihood[696].

1. Samatha has played a very significant role in protecting the land rights of tribals in India, very similar to the Mabo judgement of Australia. However, in reality, Samatha has not been able to

---

696 Douglas Sanders- *'Indigenous peoples on the International Stage'*, Social Action Vol.43, Jan-March 1993, pp 1-7 at p 1

achieve and provide the much anticipated relief like its Australian counterpart. The primary reason behind this is the lack of political intent to provide relief to these people. The judgement must be enforced at the earliest specially in areas of tribal land acquisition for private industries.

2. The Forest Rights Act, 2006 has come as a relief to the tribals in India. To make tribal participation in decision making process, Gram Sabha has been vested with various powers. However for more effective application of this Act, consultation with the Gram Sabha should be held as 'Prior Informed Consent'.

3. Gram Sabha must be involved in cases of Joint Surveys and its accent to such reports must be made mandatory for upholding the correctness of the report.

4. A mandatory compensation system must be sorted out with active participation of the Gram Sabha and with the aid of independent agencies under the supervision of the Judiciary in cases of acquisition being the last resort. The said compensation package must incorporate monetary compensation with alternative relocations and also a dynamic implementation body of experts to carry on such rehabilitation process and provide periodic report to the state as well as the judiciary under whose supervision such acquisition process has started. The judiciary must also be empowered to increase the compensation package when necessary.

5. In case of agricultural lands, acquisition should not be allowed unless as the last resort. Land laws must be amended where tribal lands are transferred from agriculture to other uses like housing etc.

6. Special training must be given to officers of the government who are to carry on the acquisition process so that there is no violation of human rights including social and religious rights. Human rights training must be made mandatory to all the government departments.

7. Special care must be taken to protect the religious and spiritual sentiments of the people displaced. Enough scope must be created for them to carry on the practice even after acquisition. Research must be conducted to understand the underlining value of plants or minerals etc present in the area which may be protected by these tribals for ages. In case of need various other departments like health, research, and laws must be involved for active participation and advice in this regard. Various universities should be assisting and aiding the government in the process of acquisition and the viability of such acquisition.

8. Special care must be taken to protect these areas for future access of tribals and other interested people for conducting research and other relevant activities. The government should have complete access to such zones and special measures should be taken to understand the social and cultural aspects of the said tribal sentiments.

9. The industries vested with such acquired lands must spent a part of their profits in furtherance of Corporate Social Responsibility to those displaced and a periodic report must be given to the concerned department of tribal affairs as to how the money was spent on the rehabilitation and other aspects to improve the position of these displaced. Such reports must be made public after due audit for public inspection.

10. Consent of the Gram Sabha must be made a mandatory clause before such acquisition is made and also at the time of transferring such acquired land.

11. The process of acquisition must be made transparent. The process of survey, reports made must be made public on the basis of which the government concerned has allowed such acquisition of land. The government in the said process must also provide detailed rehabilitation program published before carrying out the acquisition procedure.

12. Gram Sabha must be provided with necessary infrastructure with modern technological devises to carry on its functioning more effectively.

13. Separate fund to be allocated from the Constituent Fund of the state for the Gram Sabha to aid and assist the economic and financial need and independence f the funsting of the Gram Sabha.

14. Certain adjudicating powers must be vested to the Gram Sabha which shall have effect similar to that of Civil Courts.

15. Gram Sabha must be provided with the opportunity to work hand in hand in developing their expertise with Indian and foreign universities and other international organizations which would help them to assess the sub soil conditions and other resources present in the soil.

16. Proper training must be provided to the Gram Sabha to make available to them the modern indigenous movements and development for effective functioning and their decision making more scientific, prudent and reasonable. Such training must be made compulsory for other relevant departments of the government.

17. Involvement of technology and e-governance must be made available for transparent functioning of the Land Department. Proper record of rights should be made available for all interested to know about the land concerned through concerned websites and also by creating an 'App' for mobile accessibility.

18. Management of tribal lands must be vested to the Gram Sabha which should include the right to settlement of land on annual basis on such terms and conditions as the state government thinks fit and proper in this regard.

19. No tribal land should be owned by any non tribal except for certain developmental activities of the tribals. In case of any such transfer of ownership being already taken place, all such transfer be declared void and such land to be returned to the concerned tribal or in is absence to his representative in interest in the way of reversioner in remainderman or in his absence to the tribal community collectively. The government should implement the High Court and Supreme Court decisions relating to protection of land and forest rights of the tribals. Occupation of tribal lands through deceit or use of force should be made an offence. There should also be a ban on any transfer by a tribal to a non-tribal like that by way of lease, mortgage gift etc.

20. Formation of fast track courts, tribunals are to be made involving two to five Panchayats to dispose of the matters before it within a mandatory period of one, from the date of notice.

21. Councillors must be made from the members or an ex member of the Gram Sabha to hear the matter after filing of the case and a report to be taken from him within a mandatory period of two months from the date of appointment. It must be the duty of the said councillor to settle the matter amicably.

22. The majority of land reform laws have lacked in its implementation level. Priority should be given in those areas where these laws are being practiced in tribal areas and effective mechanism should be setup in this regard.

23. New land reform measures are needed to be taken and implemented in line with sustainable environment. Genetically modified crops must be banned in India and more specifically in tribal areas as this contributes adversely to the PH balance of the soil as genetically modified crops consume around ten times the water needed for production of general crops. This virtually and practically reduces the fertility of the soil and makes it unusable after a span of time.

- **Forest**

The forest policies as laid down at different times did little for the conservation of the forest and the habitat living in the forest. The tribes are the worse affected in the struggle between protecting their customary rights and the administrative policies. They are not only forest dwellers but also, for centuries, they have evolved a way of life which, on the one hand, is woven round forest ecology and forest resources and, on the other, ensures that the forest is protected against depredation by man and nature.[697]

---

697 Government of India, Report of the Committee on Forest and Tribals in India, New Delhi: Ministry of Home Affairs, 1982, p.ii, 62.

Majority of tribes in India are Hill Tribes and primarily resides in the hills in different parts of India. The reasons for choosing such a habitat have been discussed in this book before more elaborately in Chapter 3. Primarily hills tribes became affected by the colonial conquests during the process of extraction of forest wealth of the country. The reduction of trees in a systematic fashion by the British policy led to the exposure of tribal land to the British. Even after the independence of our country, the atrocities and displacement of tribes continued with various developmental projects leading to large scale displacement of innocent tribals. Lack of rehabilitation policies and reconstruction of indigenous population has led to the loss of tribal identity which was primarily there in most of the areas. Tribals are mostly found in the hills and the forests as they need a natural and peaceful habitat to live in. That is their heritage and that is their world. Everything surrounding the tribes is their land. They are recognized by their land and believe to live there even after their death. The tribals believe to have a direct nexus with their ancestors. They live with them as they live with their children. This gives them the satisfaction that every human being wants. The tribes shall thieve best in their forest land, in their hills, in the streams of the jungle. Let us pledge together to do our part to help them to be what they are, how they are and further the balance of the ecosystem. But an effort should be made in this direction to protect the forest, the wildlife, the tribes, in furtherance of the health and prosperity of the country and on the whole the entire world.

- **Hills**

A number of factors are responsible for the degrading condition of tribals in the hills. A set of reformative measures are essential to be a part of this study to protection of the socio economic interests of these communities.

1. The tribals in the forests have been subjected to various false cases and a number of such cases have piled up in various courts. These false and frivolous cases must immediately be withdrawn to prevent ulterior gains of non tribals over tribals.
2. Proper legal education should be given to the tribals for they would be able to fight their own cases in the days to come and also would be in a proper position to deal with their representation in the international scenario.
3. Immediate measures should be taken to prevent the forest produce to be systematically be taken away from the forest. This would provide the forest dwellers with the basic resources they need for their sustainable life. These produce must be acknowledged to be their property and effective measures should be taken to protect them from being otherwise used.
4. The forest department should take note of the involvement of tribals in various forest related issues rather than giving the job to contractors. The involvement of tribals would definitely provide the needed protection the forests need today.

- **Others**

Some of the other basic suggestions are given below in seriatim:

1. Incorporating indigenous knowledge in primary education as far as possible.
2. To conduct research for incorporating indigenous way of protection of land and forest in the policy to protect forest and wildlife.
3. To acknowledge that indigenous knowledge is scientific and effective.
4. To protect and provide aid to the aged tribal peoples who are the storehouse of indigenous knowledge.
5. To treat tribal movements more humanely and effectively to prevent further violation of human rights and Constitutional rights of the tribals.
6. To implement the Supreme Court and High Court Judgments in protecting tribal rights.

7. To conduct research for incorporating indigenous ways of protecting the forest land and implement them in the policy formation system to protect the endangered species.

8. To make new laws solely with the objective of protecting various rights of the tribals.

9. To acknowledge the mistake committed by the government by undergoing so many so called developmental projects and to make a comprehensive report on the number of tribals displaces from their motherland. In furtherance of the said research, to make prospective efforts to protect them from further suffering.

10. The tribal way of healing must be looked into as it is both safe and effective with minimum side effects.

Apart from the aforesaid recommendations, it is also suggested that separate team must be framed to study the massive annihilation and uprooting of tribal communities due to developmental projects.

Study must be made to analyze to what extent the tribals are dependent on forest land and forest resources. What has led the tribes to the various movements as against the government and the non-tribal community?

Research must be conducted to bring the concept of sustainable development to bring back the natural way of exploitation of forests. This would automatically be a pro-tribe approach as they are themselves experts in it.

It has to be kept in mind that only short term poverty alleviation program or crisis management policies that are immediately needed, but broader structural development program are also needed, involving the tribals themselves as participants in the developmental process.

In the words of Arundhuti Roy,

> *"On the one hand, it is seen as a war between modern, rational, progressive forces of 'Development' versus a sort of neo-Luddite impulse - an irrational, emotional 'Anti-Development' resistance, fuelled by an arcadian, pre-industrial dream."*[698]

> Thus, while carrying on the task of rehabilitation and reconstruction of tribal affairs in various fronts, a balance should be maintained between the modern and traditional interpretation of development.

The world is falling apart. People are forgetting their basic values. Morality and law has parted ways, since some time now. But it was not long when humanity reigned supreme. The world decided to change and the change came at a price. The irretrievable socio economic conditions of the original and aboriginal people of the planet, which grew with the planet itself, had to pay the ultimate price. The systematic annihilation of the third world countries and their resources by the first world has left them only to die the death that follows hunger and starvation. They have been waiting for death. But their spirit and courage and their motivation to survive has led to come out of debris to generate and build great international movements which forced the world to accept the fact that they are the deprived lot and the subjects of violation. World today has a different light to show, the light which leads the way to the new world. The modern civilization and the new world need these people to be part of the whole and not someone different in the struggle to survive the ordeal the future has stored for the human civilization.-

---

698 Arundhuti Roy, *'God of Small Things'*, available at, 103.55.108.22:8080/get/pdf/2146 accessed on Jan 11, 2016

Printed in the United States
By Bookmasters